D1247735

THE RABBI

Glimpses into the Life and Works of

RABBI DR. BENJAMIN W. HELFGOTT

THE RABBI

Glimpses into the Life and Works of

RABBI DR. BENJAMIN W. HELFGOTT

compiled and edited by

JOSEPH NEUMARK

THE JEWISH CENTER OF WAKEFIELD AND EDENWALD

Table of Contents

Section One: The Rabbi

Section Two: Selected High Holiday Sermons

Introduction

*T*he life and works of Rabbi Dr. Benjamin W.
Helfgott cannot truly be confined within the
boundaries of book covers. The dedication and
commitment of the Rabbi to the Jewish Center of
Wakefield and Edenwald, its members and friends cannot be
recounted in just a limited number of chapters. The love and
devotion that our "Super Zaida" showed his family cannot be
expressed with words alone. Thus, this work represents only
a glimpse of what was the reality of Rabbi Dr. Benjamin W.
Helfgott.

To prepare this work, it was felt that immediate family and
the circle of closest friends would not alone be able to provide
sufficient insight into the totality of the Rabbi's life.
Accordingly, we solicited letters from many friends and relatives, seeking anecdotes, recollections and incidents describing the Rabbi's impact on their lives. The outpouring of

response was overwhelming. The stories and reports contained in these letters described a dedication and selflessness of the Rabbi far beyond our own awareness. It gave us the realization that we alone were not the only mourners, but whoever came into contact with the Rabbi, whoever received his guidance and advice, whoever enjoyed his inspirational sermons, whoever listened to him at family gatherings, or simply sat in awe of his strength and vibrancy, all mourn the loss of the Rabbi.

Describing the Rabbi's life also necessitated describing the life of the Jewish Center of Wakefield and Edenwald until its dissolution. The Rabbi and the Jewish Center began their careers together, and they also closed their doors together. Accordingly, this work describes not only the Rabbi but also his involvement with and dedication to the Jewish Center.

While we have tried to utilize as much information as practical from the submitted letters, it was impossible to incorporate everyone's comments and stories. However, we thank all those who responded, since all the material was instrumental in forming the overall impressions contained within this work. All the letters and cards will, of course, be saved and cherished by the family. We also thank the many congregants who, over the years, gave of their time and funds to support the Jewish Center and to cooperate with the Rabbi in his activities. We are especially appreciative of the cooperation of Irving Lubin, Meyer Stein and Nathan Eisler, who stoically arranged for the sale of the Jewish Center and cautiously supervised the transfer of sacred articles and responsibilities to other religious organizations.

We appreciate the work of our editor, Joseph Neumark, who not only analyzed the material for this work and wrote its text, but also patiently bore the unwillingness of the bereaved family to accept the reality of their loss. We also thank Deenee Cohen for her creative contribution to the aesthetic aspects of this work. Special thanks to Mary Sepe for her coordination and cooperation in the successful completion of this work.

We trust that this work will serve as a remembrance to those families and friends who knew the Rabbi. We are confident that it will also be an inspiration to the students who are taking the Halachah Lemaaseh courses at the Rabbinic School of Yeshiva University, where these courses have been endowed in the name of Rabbi Dr. Benjamin W. Helfgott.

As the Rabbi preached in a sermon entitled "Life after Death" on Yom Kippur, 1984: "By setting up our loved ones as our constant mentors and advisors, by acting in harmony with their ways of life and wishes, we make them actually guide us from the grave as they did while on earth. They are no longer dead; and they continue to live in our lives and in our constant communion with their souls."

We hope that all those generations that knew the Rabbi personally, as well as new readers of this work, will follow the way of life described by the Rabbi as "work hard and love everyone."

Hannah Helfgott
Feiga Burnstein
Shim Helfgott

Section One:
The Rabbi

Prologue

*O*n June 3, 1996, as on almost every other day for over six decades, Rabbi Dr. Benjamin W. Helfgott rose with the dawn in his third-floor, walk-up apartment on East 236th Street in the Bronx. The night before he had made his usual telephone calls to the few Jews who lived in the neighborhood and some of the young men who traveled long distances to help the Rabbi maintain the *minyan*. He had not gone to sleep until he was assured there would be a *minyan* in the morning in the Jewish Center of Wakefield and Edenwald. Now, as he dressed in the early morning light, he looked forward to the new day with eager anticipation. There was much to be accomplished.

By the record of the calendar, Rabbi Helfgott was eighty-eight years old, but his appearance belied his age. Both in his physical appearance and by the boundless energy he exuded, he gave the impression of a vigorous sixty-year-old man in the prime of his life. And in his spirit and outlook, he was eternally young.

It was a typical start to a typical day for the Rabbi. For sixty-five years, in fair weather or foul, the Rabbi had picked up congregants from all over the neighborhood and driven them to the *minyan* in his own car. This day, however, he was still recovering from a recent illness, and the doctors had advised him not to drive until he was fully recuperated. But if his mobility was temporarily impaired, his determination was as powerful as ever. And thus, on this Monday morning, June 3, 1996, as he left his apartment at 6:00 A.M., he had the satisfaction of knowing he had once again arranged for a weekday *minyan* in the synagogue.

Hands thrust into his pockets, the Rabbi marched down the three double flights of stairs to the street without touching the banisters. The sky glowed red behind the apartment houses to the east as he stepped into the street, but the neighborhood still slumbered in the early morning breeze. He got into the car that awaited him at curbside and immediately launched into a discussion of the latest developments in Israel with the driver and the other passengers in the car. His own car remained parked in front of his home, waiting for the day he would drive it once again.

The car drew up in front of the Jewish Center of Wakefield and Edenwald at 641 East 233rd Street. The Rabbi quickly got out of the car and entered the familiar brick building nestled among storefronts and apartment houses. In the distance, a subway train clattered across the El on its way north to Mount Vernon.

After sixty-five years of close association, the Rabbi and the Jewish Center of Wakefield and Edenwald had fused into one identity. The Rabbi had been instrumental in the acquisition of this building for the fledgling congregation, and for sixty-five years, he had presided over it with inspired rabbinic leadership. The Jewish Center was the Rabbi's entire life, his *raison d'etre*, and in turn, the Rabbi was the heart and soul of the Jewish Center, its very lifeblood. One could not exist without the other.

On this day, the Rabbi prayed in his beloved synagogue with his *minyan*. He kissed the Torah after it was taken out of the Holy Ark, then he himself stepped up to the *bimah* to read that day's Torah portion in his strong, resonant voice. He was also called for an *aliyah*, and he had the privilege of pronouncing the blessings over the Torah.

After the services on that Monday morning in June, 1996, while wrapping his *tefillin* and folding his *tallit*, the Rabbi considered his busy schedule for the rest of the day—the preparation of the Center's Weekly Bulletin announcing upcoming meetings and events; return calls to make and letters to write; a review of the weekly Torah portion and a sermon to be prepared; plans to be finalized for the annual breakfast for the Helfgott Scholarship Fund at Yeshiva University. It promised to be a full and hectic day—as usual.

As the Rabbi rose to leave, he felt satisfaction that a *minyan* had prayed in his synagogue on that day, that there had been *tefillah betzibur*, that there had been a Torah Reading, that the Kaddish had been recited. His commitment to the members of the community had been fulfilled for yet another day in that exceedingly lengthy chain of days he himself had fashioned with his own hands.

The Rabbi was a man of great vision, a man with a clear understanding of the bigger picture, but he was also a man who believed in small victories. He never lost sight of the myriad little elements that went into the bigger picture. He never underestimated the importance of the tiniest step forward taken by his congregants, and he was always forthcoming with lavish praise and encouragement—even when he knew they still had miles to go. This was one of the secrets of his success. He treasured every little bit of good he was able to accomplish, and over the years, he accumulated a veritable mountain.

This day, too, he was gratified that he had been successful

in organizing that day's *minyan*, although he knew that the next day would be a struggle all over again. In this way, the little victories had accumulated, and the Jewish Center continued to serve the Jewish community in this corner of the North Bronx long after everyone had expected its doors to close. The Rabbi simply did not accept defeat. There were still people to serve, projects to complete, activities to plan, Bulletins to send out, and sermons to prepare for the upcoming High Holidays, just a few short months away.

After services, the men left the synagogue. Although still an active synagogue, the Center was no longer the bustling hub of previous decades with flourishing activities that filled the building with vibrant sounds day and night. In those days, the halls of the synagogue had reverberated with the boisterous shouts and laughter of the thousands of Jewish children who had begun their life's journeys in this building under the guidance of its revered spiritual leader. The walls still glowed with the warm voices of old friends and congregants, many of whom had since moved away or passed on. The exalted melodies of sixty-five successive Kol Nidres, and the impassioned sermons of the Rabbi reaching out to infuse each precious Jewish heart with his own love for God and Judaism, lingered in the corridors of the building. Many of the people who had shaped its colorful history over this long period had moved to other areas, but the synagogue continued to serve those still residing in that corner of the Bronx and the many who came back from time to time to refresh their connection to its ageless, tireless Rabbi who led his congregation with undiminished drive and energy.

Later that afternoon, the Rabbi sat down to write receipts for the contributions that came in to the synagogue. These contributions—mostly from congregants who had long since left the neighborhood but maintained their membership out of respect and gratitude to the Rabbi—covered the basic operating expenses of the synagogue.

The Rabbi himself filled out the receipt for each contribution, no matter how small. As was his custom for many years, he also wrote a personal note to accompany each receipt, either on the back of the receipt itself or on a separate sheet of stationery. He wrote about the latest news in the synagogue, about himself and his family, about shared memories, and he inquired about the welfare of the former congregant and that of the members of his family, each of whom he mentioned by name. These beautiful little notes nurtured the closeness that existed between him and the congregants. Over the years, people collected and cherished these messages of love from the Rabbi. And so, as the afternoon sunlight slanted in through the windows of his apartment, the Rabbi sat with his pile of receipts and wrote. And wrote. And wrote.

In the evening, the Rabbi took incoming calls and returned calls to people who had called earlier. It was a typically busy night, with no letup from the demands on his time and wisdom. Only the night before, the Rabbi had savored the pleasure of a visit by his granddaughter Dr. Penina Teitelbaum, her husband Robert and their newborn son. The Rabbi sat down to learn with Robert, as they did regularly each week. They had shown him a family picture and he had exclaimed, "This is my joy, my greatest *nachas!*" These were the twin passions of his life—his synagogue and his family.

A little after midnight, Rabbi Helfgott awoke with terrible chest pains. Accompanied by his wife, and his grandson Dr. Avi Saperstein, he was rushed to Our Lady of Mercy Hospital (previously known as Misericordia Hospital). The doors of the emergency room were closed, and no one was allowed to enter.

A short while later the doors opened, and the emergency room doctor informed Mrs. Helfgott that the patient had passed away. Minutes later, his son Shim Helfgott came running into the emergency room, followed almost immediately by his daughter Feiga Burnstein. The Rabbi had been strong, vigorous, ageless, active, an inexhaustible fount of vitality. He had been such an integral part of his family and the many thousands of people whose lives he had touched and influenced so deeply. Shocked and griefstricken, the family could not fathom that the Rabbi had succumbed.

The funeral took place the next day in the Rabbi's beloved Jewish Center. The word had spread quickly, and over four hundred people attended—rabbis, dignitaries, family members, friends, congregants and former congregants who lived close enough to come on such short notice.

In its final gesture of farewell to its illustrious Rabbi, the great sanctuary was packed to overflowing with the familiar faces of years gone by. Only this time, the faces were not wreathed in smiles but streaked with tears. And the speaker on the podium was not its warm and eloquent Rabbi. For so many years, the Rabbi had been the featured speaker for all the Center's occasions, always knowing the right and appropriate thing to say, but this time, the Rabbi's words and thoughts would not grace the podium. No, the Rabbi lay in his *tallit*-draped casket, and a long procession of other rabbis—including Rabbi Herbert Dobrinsky, Rabbi Zvi Flaum, Rabbi David Halpern and Rabbi Israel Miller from Yeshiva University, the Rabbi's alma mater—followed each other to the podium to pay their last respects to their esteemed colleague. Shim Helfgott and two grandsons also delivered emotional eulogies.

Dr. Bernard Potter, one of the Rabbi's congregants, also delivered a eulogy. "We live in a world," he said, "in which we are often confronted with the worst man has to offer. Rabbi Helfgott, in stark contrast, represented the finest of the human condition. He was saintly, kind, gentle, erudite, pious, humble, a man of keen intellect with no concern for the material. He was a man who cherished his family, loved his congregation, was true to his God, respected the Torah, was loyal to his people, held sacred Eretz Yisrael, and took kindly to mankind in general. And he in turn was held in the highest esteem by all those he touched and passed his way."

The eulogies, the intermittent sobbing, the stone-faced crowds that filled the synagogue to which the Rabbi had only yesterday come for the morning *minyan*—all these lent an air of unreality to the scene. Could this really have happened? Could it be that the Rabbi would never again stand on the podium in his synagogue, that he would never again offer kind words to his people, that he would never again kiss the heads of his young great-grandchildren, and the children and grandchildren of his congregants, and assure them that "this will make you smart"? Could it be that the heart of the huge extended family of the Jewish Center's congregants and lifelong members had stopped beating? Could it be that this rich and colorful chapter in the history of so many lives would finally reach a conclusion, that the vitality would drain away from the Jewish Center and it would close its doors forever? It couldn't be! The thoughts were too overwhelming, too sad to absorb.

After the services, the grieving people spilled out into the street, where over one hundred cars waited to carry them to the cemetery for the interment. Police were everywhere, directing traffic and keeping the crowds of curious onlookers in check.

Some of the older congregants were surely reminded of Rosh Hashanah in years gone by, when the Rabbi had led his people to Tashlich alongside the Bronx River, when special squads of police had kept a watchful eye on young mothers pushing strollers and holding toddlers by the hand, when the Rabbi had walked at the head of the group, his face aglow with pride, joy and love. But there was no joy on 233rd Street on that bleak Tuesday in 1996. This procession was saddened, subdued, somber beyond words. From now on, the Rabbi's glowing face would only appear in dreams and memories. For all the people who knew and loved him, life would never be the same again.

During the week of Shiva, literally thousands of people walked up the three double flights of stairs to the Helfgott apartment to offer condolences to the mourning family. The

Rabbi had been heard to say at the funerals of some of his dearest congregants, "I am one of the mourners." During that week of sorrow in the Bronx, practically everyone who crossed the threshold of the Helfgott home could say, "I am one of the mourners." Family, friends, congregants, all sat together in the modest apartment and spoke about the wonderful goodness of the Rabbi, the mutual love and respect they had always enjoyed, the profound loss they had suffered. They tried to help each other find consolation for their inconsolable hearts, but the loss was too great, the ache too deep, the pain too sharp to be so easily assuaged.

After the Rabbi passed away, the inevitable happened. The Jewish Center closed its doors, and the building was sold to Our Lady of Mercy Hospital, in whose emergency room the Rabbi had breathed his last; it will be used as a conference center for the medical staff of the hospital. The history of an entire Jewish neighborhood spanning nearly a century, an entire era, now comes to an end. The common thread that bound the thousands of people who had passed through this neighborhood had become unraveled with the passing of Rabbi Helfgott. But the strong values and teachings he implanted in the hearts and minds of so many people during his lifetime will continue to be passed on from generation to generation, so that his legacy will live on forever.

Who was this remarkable man? What had brought him to this part of the Bronx where he left his indelible mark? What were the values he represented and exemplified with his own life? What special personal qualities had engendered the deep devotion his congregants felt for him even decades after leaving the neighborhood?

To answer these questions, we must go back to the beginning . . .

Chapter One

The Making of a Rabbi

At the turn of the century, winds of change were sweeping through the Jewish communities of Eastern Europe. Millions of Jews were fleeing the harsh economic conditions and the persecutions of the imperial governments to seek a better future in America and other Western countries. More and more Jews were moving into the urban centers, where radical movements were capturing the imagination of the restless young. But in the small towns of Bessarabia, a heavily Jewish region on the border of Russia and Romania, Jewish life still clung to the old patterns.

During this turbulent time, Moshe and Chaitze Mirel Helfgott were married and embarked on the journey of life in the small Bessarabian city of Chotin, where Moshe earned his living by selling religious articles. He was a devout *chassid*, sporting a long flowing beard which had never been touched by a pair of scissors. Himself a descendant of the illustrious *chassidic rebbe* Rabbi Meir of Premyszlan, Moshe was an enthusiastic follower of the Czortkover branch of the Ruzhiner *chassidic* dynasty.

Moshe Helfgott was intelligent, strong-minded and dynamic, a very popular and personable young man. His young wife Chaitze Mirel, the daughter of a wealthy and learned Austrian Jewish merchant in Romania, had been reared in a more aristocratic environment than the homespun world of her husband. She had been taught to read music and sing beautifully. But she was completely devoted to her husband, and they enjoyed an idyllic existence in their quiet little corner of the world. In 1908, their first child was born, a little boy whom they named Binyamin Zev. Within the next few years, they were also blessed with two daughters, Sima and Yetta.

The outbreak of the First World War in 1914 quickly brought the peaceful existence of the Helfgott family to a shattering end. Chotin lay squarely in the path of the clashing armies of the Austro-Hungarian Empire and Czarist Russia. Bessarabia, which sporadically changed hands between Russia and the Austrian vassal kingdom of Romania, was now in Russian hands, and immediately after the declarations of war, the Russians forced all able-bodied men to serve in the army.

Knowing he would not be able to live as a Jew in the Russian Army, Moshe Helfgott decided to escape. After weeks of hopping rides on boxcars, he arrived on the coast of the Atlantic and managed to secure passage to America, expecting Chaitze Mirel and their children to follow soon after. Binyamin was six years old.

Instead of joining her husband in America, however, she and two of her relatives were forced to dig ditches for the Russian army. The three of them were killed. Binyamin learned of the death of his mother in a very brutal way. He was playing in the street when some men from the *shul* called him inside. He needed to say Kaddish, they told him, because his mother had been killed.

The three little Helfgott children lived for a short while with their mother's parents, who resided in a mansion. Soon, however, the Russians expropriated the mansion, and their grandfather sent them to live with their father's parents. During all this time, their father had been sending them money from America, but somehow, it never reached them.

Both grandfathers were learned and pious men, and they devoted much time to young Binyamin's upbringing in the absence of his father. Binyamin was an extremely intelligent young boy, and by the time he reached *bar-mitzvah* age, he already had a broad and profound grasp of the Talmud and the fundamental works of the Halachah. They also instilled in him a deep devotion to God and His Torah.

Meanwhile, Moshe Helfgott was building a life for his children in America. He agreed to marry a distant cousin named Mariam, whom he had never met, provided that she agreed to bring the children with her to America. In 1922, Mariam and the three children arrived in New York. Mariam also bore him a daughter, Rhoda, but the marriage lasted only a short time. In later years, Rabbi Helfgott would regularly carry envelopes containing his own scholarship money from *yeshivah* to Mariam and Rhoda.

During their ocean voyage, the Helfgott children had heard many stories about America and how life there was altogether different from anything they had known in the Old World. A priest pulled young Binyamin aside and assured him that in America there would be no need for *yarmulkes* or any of the other trappings of European Jewry. The children were very confused, but as soon as they were embraced by their father on the dock, all the nonsense they heard on the boat was instantly forgotten. "Your *yarmulke* stays on your head even in America," Reb Moshe declared. America had not daunted Moshe in the least. His beard was as flowing and untouched as ever. He had not compromised on his ideals and values. Instead, he had tramped out a firm path along which to lead his children in the spiritual wilds of America.

The newly reunited family settled on the Lower East Side. Young Binyamin, now Benjamin W. Helfgott, was immediately enrolled in the Rabbi Jacob Joseph School on Henry Street. Although he knew no English when he arrived, he adjusted quickly to his new environment. In 1924, he received a diploma for successfully completing the eighth grade. Furthermore, in a display of the dogged determination which would characterize his whole life, he used an English translation of the Bible to teach himself perfect English, and through sheer effort, he rid himself of any trace of a foreign accent.

In 1924, at the age of sixteen, he entered Yeshiva University, enrolling in the Rabbi Isaac Elchanan Theological Seminary. Here he had the benefit of studying under some of the leading lights of Talmudic scholarship and Jewish education, including the famous Maitcheter Ilui and Dr. Bernard Revel. In 1931, at the age of twenty-three, he received his *semichah* from Yeshiva University.

Three years earlier, in 1928, Benjamin Helfgott had already begun his lifelong association with the Jewish Center of Wakefield and Edenwald.

The neighborhood of Wakefield is situated in the northernmost extremity of the Bronx, a small notch protruding into Westchester County. Mount Vernon is eight blocks to the north of Wakefield, Yonkers five blocks to the west. In 1928, the area was still semi-rural, a summer resort district with private homes and clusters of stores interspersed among small farms. An elevated subway ran through the middle of the neighborhood. The area immediately to the east was known as Edenwald. The population of these neighborhoods was mostly of Italian extraction, but there were already a fair number of Jewish residents.

A group of men from the Wakefield neighborhood, who had been attending the Anshei Amas Congregation in a loft on White Plains Road and 226th Street, decided to organize their own congregation closer to home. They launched their new enterprise by holding High Holiday services in a storefront on 237th Street.

The neighborhood response was so enthusiastic that the group decided to organize the local Jewish community on a permanent basis. They rented an apartment over a store on White Plains Road for the purposes of establishing a synagogue and a school. They procured a charter for a religious institution, and with great pomp and ceremony they opened their doors. They also took one more crucial step which would shape the destiny of the fledgling congregation for the entire duration of its existence—they hired an unmarried twenty-year-old rabbinical student from Yeshiva University to teach the children and conduct Sabbath services. His name was Benjamin W. Helfgott.

In a letter dated September 1, 1995, Rabbi Helfgott wrote to Jay Goret about those early days: "Another year has passed by, and this Shabbat we will observe the *yahrzeit* of your grandfather, David Goretsky, who was my gracious host on Sabbaths and holidays in my early student days when I began serving the Jewish community in this area. He tried to make me feel comfortable. I recall that he put on a jacket and joined me in a cup of Shabbat tea prepared earlier by your grandmother. Occasionally, your uncle David Zaetz would come in to keep us company. They were all good, hard-working people. May their souls be blessed."

The hard work of the early organizers and their talented and dedicated young rabbi paid off. Before the end of the first year, the congregation moved into its own building at 4395 Byron Avenue. The rapidly growing congregation also absorbed a small group of families from the Edenwald section who had acquired property on Baychester Avenue and had begun their own synagogue building fund. The merger of these two groups brought into being the Jewish Center of Wakefield and Edenwald. Its doors would remain open for sixty-eight years, until the passing of Rabbi Helfgott in 1996.

The growth of the community was rapid and heady, but it needed leadership and direction. These were provided in ample measure by its young rabbi, who threw himself into the task of community building with inexhaustible vitality. The Center was constantly energized by new families that moved into the neighborhood and took an active role in the communal services and activities. The continuous absorption of these new families and their smooth integration into the dynamic new Center presented numerous situations which could easily have become problematic, but the young rabbi quickly developed a wisdom and sensitivity well beyond his years. His love for God and Judaism was contagious, and his love for each and every individual Jew—regardless of his level of observance and social station—was so obvious and genuine that the people could not help but respond. With consummate grace and diplomacy, he was a catalyst for all the highly active members and a leader who set rigorous spiritual and moral standards for his flock.

Over time, the Jewish Center became such an integral part of the Rabbi's life that his entire family was drawn into it as well. His father, now respectfully known as Reb Moshe, the gray-bearded and vigorous patriarch of the Helfgott family, moved into an apartment on Carpenter Avenue in the neighborhood with his two daughters, both of whom were eventually married in the Center. He opened a kosher butcher store. The patrons of the store were mostly non-Jews who bought the kosher meat because it was fresher than the meats available in other stores, and the business was quite successful. Reb Moshe stood in the store unabashedly wearing his *yarmulke*, his flowing beard wreathing his broad, smiling face. Every afternoon he closed the store for Minchah, regardless of how

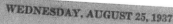

WEDNESDAY, AUGUST 25, 1937

Jewish Center of Wakefield, Edenwald Shows Rapid Progress Within Few Years

The Jewish Center of Wakefield and Edenwald, *(Daily Argus Staff Photos)* by the congregation in that district, under the leadership of a group of prominent North Bronxites. At right is Rabbi Benjamin W. Helfgott, spiritual director and instructor of Jewish Youth.

Religious Community Formed in 1928, with Charter Signed by 20 Organizers—300 Families Now Take Part in Religious, Social Activities

In the Fall of 1928, Jewish families of Wakefield and Edenwald assembled to form a local congregation to conduct services during the high holidays.

Prior to that time they attended high holiday services in Mount Vernon, Yonkers and the lower Bronx. Deciding to localize, a group headed by J. J. Grouf, the late M. A. Pollak, Samuel Mazer, Joseph Weiner and Harry Lesser instituted services in that district.

A store on East 218th Street was hired for the week of the high holidays. The large attendance encouraged the group to organize permanently as the Jewish Center of Wakefield and Edenwald. A charter was procured and signed by 20 members.

Rabbi Benjamin W. Helfgott, then a graduate student at the Rabbi Isaac Elchanan Theological Seminary, was invited to take charge. Meyer Simon was elected president of the nucleus already established. A Hebrew school was set up and temporary quarters secured at 4406 White Plains Avenue.

Rapid Growth Made

The rabbi was a bit dubious after a cursory examination, but closer inspection led him to believe that possibilities existed. Through a program of education and activities, the membership has expanded from the 20 signers of the charter to an affiliation with more than 300 Jewish families.

The problem at that time was to build a permanent home. A building committee headed by Abraham Schectman and Abraham Middleman gathered sufficient funds before the end of the year to buy two lots at 4305 Byron Avenue. Before the high holidays of 1929, members worshiped in their own building, erected at a cost of nearly $17,000.

By the time the Center building was erected on Byron Avenue, more than 50 neighborhood children were attending Sunday and daily classes of the Hebrew school.

Scroll Donated in 1930

The first scroll of the Torah was donated to the congregation in 1930 by Mr. and Mrs. Samuel Mazer. At this time a movement was started to organize the Jewish youth of the neighborhood for cultural and social activities. Adult classes for Jewish youth in elementary Hebrew, liturgy and Jewish history were conducted weekly.

Late Friday evening services were conducted regularly. Speakers including civic leaders and persons prominent in national Jewish life addressed the community from time to time.

Chanukah and Purim plays and concerts depicting the history and significance of the holidays have been presented annually by the children.

One of the largest groups at the Center, the Ladies' Auxiliary, was organized by Mrs. Esther Weiner.

Mrs. Weiner presided over that body for two years. In tribute to her endeavors, a tablet was erected in her honor in the Center building in 1932.

The Arlac Club, a junior branch of the Ladies' Auxiliary, was inaugurated in 1933.

200 In Men's Club

The following year the Jewish Club was organized, with a membership of more than 200. Boy and Girl Scout troops have since been organized.

The most recent acquisition was cemetery ground, near Peekskill, purchased and consecrated this year.

The Center associations have been instrumental in forming Zionist Organization District 21 of the Northeast Bronx.

The main hope now is to add another story to the Center building that will house educational, social and community activities. The plans are not far from realization, as a building fund established for this purpose has been growing steadily since 1932.

busy it was at the time. It was obvious to all from where Rabbi Helfgott had inherited his strongmindedness and high level of integrity!

In 1935, the Rabbi married Hannah Stern, and they rented an apartment on Brunner Avenue in the neighborhood. The shining young couple were the darlings of the congregation, who could not do enough to help them.

In a letter dated May 11, 1990, Rabbi Helfgott wrote to Joseph Shulman about the warm way in which they were treated: "Today is your mother's *yahrzeit,* and as I recited Kaddish in her memory I recalled your parents' devotion and help to us in the first few years of our marriage—fifty-five years ago. My weekly salary was then twenty-five dollars, and my rent on Brunner Avenue was thirty-two dollars. I believe your grocery supported us for some three dollars a week. Your parents refused to tell us the prices of each item. I do recall that the fish for Shabbat cost us thirty cents. They were not only good to us, they were simply *good* people."

From the very first days of their married life, Rabbi and Mrs. Helfgott established the patterns of devotion and commitment to family, a pattern that would become an ever stronger and deeper part of their lives. In later years, the Rabbi would tell one of his grandsons that, in his opinion, "the requirement of honoring parents was without limit." In 1937, the young couple moved to a larger apartment on 235th Street. Shortly afterwards, Reb Moshe Helfgott moved in with the young couple.

In 1936, a daughter was born to the Helfgotts; they named her Feiga. In 1939, a son was born; they named him Shimshon. At about this time, Reb Moshe moved out of their apartment and took up residence in Brooklyn.

Over the period of a decade, the Rabbi had developed a very powerful attachment to the Jewish Center, and his congregants in turn held him in the highest regard and esteem. The talented young rabbi and his burgeoning community were twin rising stars in the firmament of the Bronx, their futures seemingly inextricably intertwined.

In 1940, the Jewish Center experienced yet another surge in growth, and a group of members organized an unofficial fellowship for the purpose of acquiring a larger and more comfortable building for the Center. Just at that time, the most beautiful building in the neighborhood had become available for purchase—the Hopewell Masonic Temple on 233rd Street. It suited the needs of the Center perfectly, and the consensus was to go for it.

The building fund provided the down payment, and a large mortgage provided the rest. The Center moved into its new premises, with the understanding that there would be a concerted community campaign to pay off the mortgage as quickly as possible. But an unexpected complication arose. On December 7, 1941, a Japanese strike force attacked Pearl Harbor, and the United States was suddenly at war.

The effect on the Jewish community of Wakefield and Edenwald was electric. Many of the men from the Center were inducted into military service or joined the voluntary civilian defense system. The Red Cross set up a supply station inside the Center, and the Rabbi patrolled the street in an air-raid warden's helmet. It seemed as if the entire Jewish community was drawn into the war effort—at the expense of the newly acquired Center building. The burden fell squarely on the Rabbi's shoulders—or to be more accurate, the Rabbi, because of his overpowering sense of responsibility, lifted the burden onto his own shoulders.

The Rabbi threw himself into the task with all his formidable talents and energy. He was like a tornado dedicated to the furtherance of the Jewish Center. He was rabbi, secretary, custodian, fund-raiser and many other roles all wrapped in one. He organized Bingo games in the Center three nights a week, and disregarding his own dignity, he himself would conduct the games for the assortment of Jews and Gentiles

that came. He himself would hold up the winning numbers
and shout, "Bingo!" A lesser man would have long given up,
but Rabbi Helfgott did not know the meaning of giving up.
And thus, the mortgage was paid off, and the building was
secured.

But the effort took its toll. "I recall most vividly," writes
Jack Klug, "seeing Rabbi Helfgott wash the floors when no
help was available. I remember him calling the numbers at
Bingo games. I remember once, at services, hearing him call
out 'Bingo!' instead of 'Amen!'"

We chuckle at this amusing little anecdote, but the Rabbi's
dedication was being stretched to the very limit. His family
certainly did not find it amusing. His two little children at
home hardly ever saw him. Their mother would take them to
the window and when their father would pass in the street, he
would wave to them. He would also send his wife a questioning look, as if to ask, "Is everything okay?" She would nod,
and he would wave again and be on his way.

One of the early congregants recalls this period in the
Rabbi's life. "My association with Rabbi Helfgott," writes Abe
Schwartz, "goes back to the late Thirties, during which the
congregation of Wakefield and Edenwald was in its infancy
and had just moved into its quarters on 233rd Street. The
struggling Jewish community was laboring under a tremendous mortgage, and factions were beginning to stir. The challenge was getting the Hebrew school going so that the membership could be increased and maintained to cover the
expenses. The Rabbi played several roles in keeping peace
among the members: arbitrator, appeaser, teacher, superinten-
dent, janitor, handyman, spiritual leader, fund-raiser, confi-
dant and a host of other positions with duties very few religious leaders would assume. One of the projects that offered a
solution to the financial burden was running a Bingo game
three times a week . . . This proved to be a very successful activity, and it was instrumental in paying off the building debt."

The war effort also put pressure on the Rabbi from another direction. Many of the young men in the neighborhood had been inducted into the armed forces, and the Rabbi took it upon himself to maintain contact with them, to give them a sense of connection by keeping them involved in the day-to-day activities of the Center. This commitment foreshadowed the Rabbi's future commitment to former congregants, when he would maintain a warm relationship with literally thousands of them by corresponding on a regular basis. The war made the Rabbi a prodigious letter writer.

"When I was going into the service in 1942," Harry Warner recalls, "Rabbi Helfgott gave me a real heart-to-heart talk. He told me to be sure to come home safe and sound. I got bulletins from the Rabbi keeping me in touch with the *shul* and my friends who were also in the service. His interest in us was very heart-warming and sincere."

In 1943, Rabbi Helfgott was offered a position as Chief Rabbi of the Orthodox community of Youngstown, Ohio. He was to be responsible for all the Orthodox synagogues and for city-wide rabbinic functions such as *kashruth* supervision. It was a position of great prestige and honor which would draw on all his teaching, preaching and reaching talents. The position also came with very attractive compensations; instead of the thirty-five dollars per week he was receiving in the Bronx, he would receive eighty-five dollars per week and a large, rambling house with more rooms and porches and yards than the family could ever use.

Because of his devotion and loyalty to the Center, the Rabbi was reluctant to take the position, but his wife believed very strongly that the move would serve the best interests of the entire family. She and her children would have their husband and father back, they would all enjoy better living conditions, and the Rabbi would get the recognition he deserved.

The Rabbi bowed to the wishes of his gallant wife. He did not feel that by leaving for Ohio he was accepting defeat. On the contrary, he had accomplished the impossible. He had molded a beautiful congregation, and with the sweat of his own back he had provided them with a beautiful and spacious building which was the crown jewel of the neighborhood. He had fulfilled his responsibilities, and now, another rabbi would enjoy the fruits of his labor. And thus, after an association of fifteen years, the Rabbi and his family left the Bronx for the greener pastures of Youngstown, Ohio.

Rabbi Helfgott was an instant success in Youngstown. He brought a dynamism and charisma to the community which were much appreciated. There were many learned and highly educated laymen in Youngstown, and the Rabbi relished the challenge and satisfaction of delivering sophisticated lectures on a wide variety of subjects. He also enjoyed an excellent rapport with the Conservative and Reform congregations. He was universally recognized and respected as a man of integrity and sincere convictions, to the point that there was no resentment when he refused to preach in the Reform temple because an organ was used on Shabbat.

He also took advantage of a certain amount of free time available to him to attend classes at Western Reserve University, where he received a master's degree in the philosophy of religion in 1947.

Mrs. Helfgott and the children were also very happy in Youngstown. They loved the feeling of spaciousness indoors and outdoors—and the presence of the Rabbi at home on a regular basis. But the children were getting older, and the problem of providing them with a quality Jewish education began to loom ever larger in the Rabbi's mind. For the meantime, they attended public schools and private tutoring kept them on a fairly high level, but what would happen as they grew older in a city without *yeshivos*?

In 1947, when Faiga was eleven years old and Shim eight, the Helfgotts were visited by several rabbis who were starting the Telshe Yeshivah in nearby Cleveland, Ohio. They wanted

Shim to be one of the boys in their first class. Eventually, the Telshe Yeshivah became one of the finest *yeshivos* in the United States, if not the whole world, but at the time, it was only a dream and the Rabbi was not prepared to risk his son's religious future on a dream. He was becoming more and more convinced that he could not afford the luxury of remaining in Youngstown.

At about this time, a delegation arrived from the Jewish Center inviting him to return as their Rabbi. The position of rabbi in the Center had become a revolving door, with four different rabbis serving during the four years of his absence. It must have been a very disorienting process for the congregation, because one former congregant recalls "eight different rabbis during the four years Rabbi Helfgott was away." In fact, there were only four, but it must have seemed like eight!

The grandson of one of the early congregants recalls the stories he heard in his home: "The Ress family," writes Philip Ress, "goes back a great many years with the Rabbi in that my grandfather, Philip Ress, was a founder of the Jewish Center ... In the Forties, the Rabbi was offered an attractive position at a shul in Youngstown, Ohio. He chose to accept that very lucrative position and moved his family to Youngstown. The congregation filled his position but missed 'their' Rabbi terribly. After a year or so, the congregation decided to send a delegation to Youngstown to try to persuade Rabbi Helfgott to return. My father was selected and drove to Youngstown. The trip was obviously successful."

The trip was indeed successful, but for a number of reasons. The Rabbi was undoubtedly sympathetic to the pleas of his former congregation, his first love, the bride of his youth. But the delegation had also come at a time when the Rabbi was undergoing some serious soul-searching about the direction his professional future and the future of his family should take.

To resolve these questions, the Rabbi convened a family

meeting to be attended by himself, his wife and his two young children. The decision would be reached by democratic process. After much discussion, the matter was put to a vote. The Rabbi and his two children opted for returning to the Bronx. The family had returned to New York on a number of occasions to visit family, and the children were excited about the prospect of living there. Mrs. Helfgott cast the only dissenting vote, but she accepted defeat graciously. "What could I do?" she recalls with a gentle smile. "We took a vote, and the majority ruled. That's democracy, isn't it?"

The decision was made. The Helfgotts returned to the Jewish Center of Wakefield and Edenwald, where the Rabbi took a pay cut of about fifty percent. There were no apartments available for rent, and the large, wonderful house was exchanged for one room with "kitchen privileges" in a lady's apartment. But Feiga and Shim went to the finest *yeshivos*, where the private training they had received in Youngstown enabled them to start at the same level with other children their age. That was all that mattered.

The Helfgotts had come home.

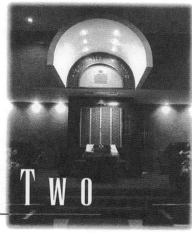

Chapter Two

The Days of Growth

he return of Rabbi Helfgott and his family could not have come at a more critical time for the Jewish Center. During the postwar years, the Bronx absorbed a large influx of Jewish immigrants, Holocaust survivors and refugees, as did many other parts of New York and other metropolitan areas. For the first ten years after the Rabbi's return, the neighborhoods of Wakefield and Edenwald experienced vigorous growth. Many Jewish families moved into the elegant co-op apartments that rose in the center of Wakefield. A short while later, a number of less affluent Jewish families settled in the new low-income projects that sprang up in Edenwald.

Under the energetic guidance of the Rabbi, the Hebrew school was expanded to meet the growing needs of the community. "The size of the Talmud Torah grew very much during my years there," Milton Erdfarb recalls. "I remember that one of the rows in the balcony upstairs had to be taken away in order to put in a sliding wall, creating two classrooms out of one. A new corridor was built to access the addition."

Besides all his other duties in the synagogue, the Rabbi singlehandedly fulfilled the functions of principal and executive director for the rapidly growing Hebrew school. He hired, trained and supervised the staff, and he managed and supervised the facilities and any construction deemed necessary. He took responsibility for finding the funds to cover the budget, and he kept the accounts. And in addition to everything, he handled a large share of the teaching duties, taking some classes himself and substituting when teachers were absent.

He approached the task of teaching young children with the same wise and innovative approach he applied to all his endeavors, large and small alike. "The Rabbi was our Hebrew reading teacher," Richard Kreisberg remembers, "and as we were just learning, he challenged us by giving each of us five pennies. The assignment was to read aloud a single sentence from our Siddur. For each mistake we had to give back one of the pennies. I got to keep the nickel."

In running the Hebrew school, however, the Rabbi had valuable personal resources upon which he did not hesitate to call—his family. For the good of the synagogue—and for the good of his family—the Rabbi drew them into his educational work, teaching them, preparing them, guiding them, infusing them with his own dedication and enthusiasm.

Rebbetzin Helfgott took upon herself the main responsibility for the younger ages and the supervision of the Junior Congregation. In later years, Feiga and Shim were also encouraged to take over a large share of the teaching—and were immensely popular with the children.

"I attended Junior Congregation, led by Rebbetzin Helfgott," remembers Milton Erdfarb. "I still use the melody for Mah Tovu which she taught me at the Shabbat morning Junior Congregation. My most influential teachers were my first, Rebbetzin Helfgott, and my second, whom everyone still lovingly calls Shim."

Paula Dicker Gold recalls: "Rabbi Helfgott told stories to the Sunday School students. I must have been about seven years old when he addressed the kids one morning. He told a story about a man who was complaining because he had no shoes, and then he met a man who had no feet. This mini-sermon and its delivery influenced me as a child and stayed with me into my adulthood. It was a heavy message for children, but I got it. I think often of the Rabbi's influence on my life . . . Later, my brother and I went to Hebrew school at the Jewish Center. Shim was one of my first teachers . . . and I also remember being in awe of Feiga, thinking she was like some kind of exotic princess."

The adults in the congregation also appreciated the quiet but important role Rebbetzin Helfgott played in the success of the Center. Dr. Julian Joseph recently discovered a notation he had written and shared with the Helfgotts, part of which reads as follows: "The Rabbi's wife humanizes our religion . . . She prides herself on her ability to conduct Junior Congregation services for the children up to the age of fourteen or fifteen.

"She once invited me to hear one of her sermons. She told about a man who could not decide whether to mount a donkey and lead his son or place the boy on the donkey, where he might topple off the beast. A crowd gathered to watch him try one way, then the other, cheering him on each way, on the donkey, off the donkey, on again, and so forth. The Rebbetzin's voice swelled in crescendos as she painted the man's dilemma, and then she let each child know that it is a fool who cannot decide his own mind but only follows the way of others.

"Her life is with the people of the congregation and especially their children. Her joy is teaching the young, ages six and seven, the knowledge of Hebrew history and language. She also attends congregation functions, dinners, board of trustees meetings, but there she prefers to listen quietly, to the point of self-denial."

Sylvia Adler remembers: "Our Rebbetzin was a kind and gentle person, always helpful to all who came in contact with her, and a great help to the Rabbi."

"Uncle Binyamin and Aunt Hannah made a great team," recalls Sipporah Binder. "Organized, efficient, loving."

For the children, the teaching of the Rabbi and Rebbetzin always held the warmest associations, even after moving to different neighborhoods. "I have very fond, warm memories of the Center, the Rabbi and his lovely wife," Shana Deitchman recalls. "My heart melts whenever I find myself in a car driving by the Jewish Center . . . I remember not liking my Hebrew school classes at the new Riverdale school nearly as much. It was a much more contemporary setting, but the look and feel of the Rabbi's Jewish Center had much more res-onance and depth and love."

The Rabbi did not limit his involvement with the youth of the Center to Hebrew school. In his inimitable dynamic fash-ion, he organized numerous social clubs and extracurricular activities in the framework of the Jewish Center to create a focal point in the neighborhood for young Jewish people. In addition to adult organizations such as the Ladies' Auxiliary, the Men's Club, the Cemetery Committee, the college-accred-ited Adult Education program and the PTA, the Rabbi also founded junior clubs such as Byron, Ariac, Caira, We Joys, Exodus, Granadas, Socialites and others, as well as Boy Scout and Girl Scout troops. But the most fondly remembered was the Club Maccabees.

"We socialized through our youth group Club Maccabees," Milton Erdfarb remembers. "We met on Saturday nights or Sundays for activities such as miniature golfing, bowling, movies, scavenger hunts or just getting together in the Mintz hall to talk, dance or do arts-and-crafts projects."

"He created a place in the *shul*," recalls Joan Unger Levy, "for all Jewish teenagers to come, meet one another and socialize, a club known as the Maccabees. It was a warm, safe atmosphere that drew hundreds of teenagers. It was a brilliant strategy on the part of the Rabbi to ensure that adolescents met other *Jewish* adolescents in a supervised atmosphere. It provided all the local Jewish teenagers with a place to go Saturday nights for many years."

In 1995, Joan Unger Levy voiced her feelings directly to the Rabbi in a warm letter: "It is truly to your great credit to have drawn in every Jewish family in the neighborhood and to have made us all part of the *shul* community. It was truly our home away from home. We all agree that we have not found a place as inviting, as *heimish*, as welcoming as was your *shul*. You have had a far greater effect on your congregants' lives than you can ever imagine. I speak for us all when I say you were truly our *rebbe*."

"The Jewish Center was the focus of my entire childhood and early teen years," writes Stephen Young, echoing the thoughts of countless others. "All the members of my family, including my grandmother, were constantly there for one activity or another. During my involvement there, a whole generation of good Jewish kids grew up together. The Rabbi was the spiritual guide and the mundane force that made the place function. His influence on people was of a nature to last a lifetime. Its profundity can scarcely be measured because it was so great."

Undoubtedly, the children were also drawn to the Rabbi because of his constant reassuring presence and his loving attention to even the smallest details of their needs and the needs of the Center in general, even replacing light bulbs and replenishing the toilet paper. Nancy Pincus remembers "the red office and the Rabbi typing out the Weekly Bulletin on the old typewriter. Lots of typos but from the heart! He was the Jewish Center. As a young child, I thought he lived at *shul*. He was always there." Milton Erdfarb remembers the Rabbi using

the "typewriter, special stencil and the very messy mimeo-
graph machine . . . taking the stencil out of the box, placing it
on the drum of the machine and meticulously applying the
correct amount of ink."

Despite his willingness to do menial chores, the Rabbi
was recognized by all as a brilliant intellectual with a wide
knowledge in both Jewish and secular fields of scholarship.
He was also recognized as a great advocate of the importance
of both kinds of education; it was one of his persistent themes.
In his sermons, he often reminded his congregants that "Jews
hold leading positions in commerce, law, medicine, accounting, communications, psychoanalysis and colleges faculties,"
declaring proudly that "ninety percent of American Jewish
boys and girls will receive a college education; we are both
admired and envied by other ethnic communities." At the
same time, he always insisted that "we need a united and concerted plan of action to intensify Jewish education," and he
spoke with great pleasure and satisfaction about the "system
of Jewish day schools reaching thousands of children who are
bringing home from their classes a new life and new hope for
the future."

These were the values he tried to instill in the children of
the Center—the importance of getting a first-rate secular education without sacrificing a first-rate Jewish education, the
development of the complete Jewish individual. These were
the values he instilled in his own children. These were the values by which he conducted his own life; he was an intensely
religious and learned rabbi who was also a highly educated
man of the world. And in this direction, he felt he still had
unfinished business. He had earned a master's degree in
Cleveland, and now he set his sights on a doctorate.

A few years after returning to New York, overburdened
as he was with synagogue responsibilities, he enrolled in a
doctoral program in Columbia University and managed to
attend classes regularly. Incredible as it seems, this was, in

fact, one of the Rabbi's most remarkable hallmarks. Because of his inexhaustible energy and strict management of time, he was always able to stretch his schedule, no matter how crowded, to fit in yet another unexpected activity. When he made up his mind to do something, he got it done.

"I remember his indefatigable energy," Stephen Young remembers. "Clearly, he loved his mission in life. I never saw him tired."

"He had an extraordinarily strong personality," writes grandson Avi Saperstein. "When he made up his mind, one would have to work very hard to get him to change it."

At Columbia University, the Rabbi studied under the celebrated Professor Salo Baron. The two men admired each other greatly and formed a friendship that would last for many years. The Rabbi would visit Professor Baron often and send him a case of wine before Passover, and Professor Baron would send the Rabbi a copy of every new book he published.

In 1952, the Rabbi earned a Ph.D. in the philosophy of religion. His doctoral dissertation, *The Doctrine of Election in Tannaitic Literature*, was a masterful scholarly examination of the conflict between the Rabbis of the Tannaitic period and the fledgling Apostolic Christian Church. It was published by Columbia University's King's Crown Press in 1954, and through the generous sponsorship of the Rabbi's good friend and congregant Meyer Stein, it was distributed to every university library in the country.

The Rabbi was a humble man who did not like to flaunt his brilliant scholarship, but flashes of it would nonetheless appear in his sermons and conversations. Nevertheless, the Rabbi's message was simple and straightforward, geared equally for the scholar and the simple person. He spoke with the power of intense conviction about the beauty of Judaism, about Jewish education, about ethical behavior, about filial devotion, about finding direction and meaning in life, and his message was universally effective. Moreover, the congregants knew that the Rabbi cared deeply about them, that he was dedicated to them body and soul, that he spoke for their own good, and they were predisposed to accept his advice and guidance.

The Rabbi had a special rapport with the younger people of the Center. He appreciated the idealism of youth and was uncannily attuned and sympathetic to the undercurrents of feelings experienced by young people during the stormy Sixties and Seventies. Instead of reproof, he advocated understanding and encouragement.

In a sermon delivered on Rosh Hashanah, 1971, he stated: "For years we have seen how our young men and women are disturbed by the irritating, irrational and international atrocities of our times. They have traveled to the South to fight for civil rights for the persecuted black people. They protest against the war in Vietnam. They are concerned about urban decay, the pollution of the environment and the depletion of our natural resources. They are disturbed by the poverty that darkens the lives of so many people in this rich and wonderful country where we live . . .

"We should be proud of our youth for their idealism. And we should also encourage them to direct some of this idealism toward their own people. They should not only protest against urban decay but also against the decay of the Jewish family. They should not only be concerned with the pollution of the environment but also the pollution of the Sabbath. They should not only worry about the depletion of our national natural resources but also the depletion of the spiritual resources of the Jewish home which the immigrants brought with them to these shores. We need the help of our idealistic youth. Let us ask for it."

Teenagers, in turn, responded very warmly to the Rabbi. Shana Deitchman remembers: "The Rabbi always had the air of the contemporary. Although obviously a much older adult, I never thought of him as old. He seemed quite tuned in to everyone, no matter what age, and I remember that I was very appreciative of that quality."

They also appreciated his wry sense of humor. "Along with his natural benevolence, dedication and ability to generate a soothing perspective, there was his humor," writes Ilene Gruenberg. "While driving my son Randy and Alan Smith to *yeshivah* one Friday, they stopped on Lydig Avenue for bagels. Alan asked for lox on his bagel. 'You have money?' asked the Rabbi. 'Twenty-five cents,' said Alan. The Rabbi chuckled and said, 'For twenty-five cents maybe the guy will let the bagel *smell* the lox.'"

The Rabbi exhibited phenomenal patience with his younger students, and it paid off. Sometimes, however, it took years to become apparent, as Dr. Roy Schoenfeld writes: "I was a desultory *cheder* student. Surely Rabbi Helfgott did not get much *nachas* from me. Indeed, I long suspected he regarded me as one of his failures (though he later denied this). Nevertheless, just as a pebble thrown into the sea does not know about all the ripples it makes, I was actually one of his long-range successes, for he left me with an awe for the rabbinate and laid the groundwork for a growing passion for Judaism that remains with me to this day."

For the most part, however, the effects of the Rabbi's tutelage were felt immediately. Larry Leff recalls that through his association with the Rabbi he "became attached. Attached to the Jewish Center, attached to Rabbi and Mrs. Helfgott, attached to Judaism itself. Without planning, without preparation and, for my parents, without warning, I made a commitment to Orthodox Judaism on December 6, 1963—Erev Shabbat of my *bar-mitzvah*. In large measure, I was influenced by Rabbi Helfgott."

The experience of receiving *bar-mitzvah* lessons from the Rabbi, in his warm and loving way, was indeed something truly out of the ordinary, a memory to be cherished for a lifetime. "My *bar-mitzvah* lessons were my first close relationship with Rabbi Helfgott," Mel Wasserman writes. "He used to move my pointer finger around the page to match the incantation of the *trop* and say to me that I was such a well-behaved child. He'd say he thought I was 'bathed in milk and honey.'"

The Rabbi was like a magician, able to succeed where lesser men would long have abandoned hope. "Our son Mark was a huge problem in Hebrew school," writes Rhoda Feldman. "He was constantly removed from the class by his teacher. But the Rabbi understood the problem and took Mark under his wing. He had developed a mutual love and bond with Mark and assured us he would be a young man of whom we would be proud.

"We were concerned about his education and *bar-mitzvah* lessons, especially when he broke his leg the summer of his lessons. We did not have a car, so the Rabbi picked Mark up and brought him home that whole summer. We weren't allowed to hear him practice, and on the day of his *bar-mitzvah* we couldn't believe the miracle the Rabbi had performed. If not for the Rabbi, I don't believe he would have made it, but Mark wouldn't disappoint the Rabbi. He sure did make us proud and happy with his accomplishment. We could never do enough to show our gratitude for all the Rabbi had done, but he assured us it was his pleasure."

"He had the power to bring out the best in everyone he touched," writes daughter-in-law Joyce Helfgott. "This is his greatness that will live on forever."

Recalls Nathan Eisler: "My impression of Rabbi Helfgott as kind yet firm, approachable yet proper, was formed at an early age and remained with me through my adulthood."

The relationships formed during these lessons were strong and lasting, because the Rabbi instilled values and maintained contact. For one thing, he organized the Tallit and Tefillin Club to accustom *bar-mitzvah* boys to attend daily prayers. "Upon my *bar-mitzvah*," Irwin Hamburger remembers, "I was convinced it was my obligation as a Jew to attend the daily *minyan*. The Rabbi was the tie that binds."

"I always felt a special bond and relationship with Rabbi Helfgott," writes Milton Erdfarb. "In preparation for my *bar-mitzvah*, Rabbi Helfgott felt I should also learn to lead the Shabbat morning Shacharit. We started getting together on a regular basis two months before, and he meticulously went through each paragraph of the Shabbat morning prayers, emphasizing all the special melodies. I still have the Siddur he marked with all the necessary diacritical notations indicating musical inflections.

"After my *bar-mitzvah* in June, I continued to attend the daily *minyan* through the summer, and when school resumed Rabbi Helfgott would pick me up at my home and take me to *shul* at 6:45 A.M. Afterwards, he got me something to eat and drove me directly to Olinville JHS 113. I can still smell his pipe, which he always smoked as he drove me to East 217th Street."

This sort of dedication characterized the Rabbi's entire relationship with the Center and its congregants. His people were his life. He cared about them as he cared about his own family, and he would go to unlimited lengths to ensure their spiritual, physical and emotional well-being.

Irving Lubin, a long-standing president, writes: "Our Rabbi's commitment and devotion were strongest when it came to the things he cared about most. His priorities were clear—the practice and preservation of the Jewish faith; his synagogue; the congregation membership; and his family. Concerning these, the Rabbi was intense and simply knew no limits or boundaries . . . The Rabbi's devotion to his membership was crystal clear—the congregation was his extended family, and in turn, we all considered the Rabbi a member of our families. He was available to celebrate good times, cope with tragedy and help, intervene and counsel as required. Thanks or gratitude were neither wanted nor expected. As a surrogate parent to all of us, he was surprisingly non-judgmental, as he tolerated much and forgave all."

"My most striking memory," writes Dr. Roy Schoenfeld, "was being told furtively by one of the elders that he had accidentally discovered the Rabbi secretly putting a portion of his meager salary back into the faltering synagogue's treasury to keep it out of default. I remember this so vividly because the Sages say that giving anonymously in this way is the biggest *mitzvah* of all."

The feeling of extended family was at the very root of the Center's great success during its heyday, and Rabbi Helfgott was its beloved patriarch.

"It was amazing," writes Mildred Dicker, as did many others, "how he remembered every single name of every single member of the congregation, and there were certainly many names to be remembered." Rita Guthartz also comments on the Rabbi's "phenomenal memory" and that "he carried in his head all the names of his congregants, their addresses, their families." But in actuality, the Rabbi's amazing recollection was as much an indication of his feeling towards his people as it was of his phenomenal memory. A father remembers the names of his children—no matter how many children he has.

The feeling of family and the Rabbi's benevolent disposition toward each of his people is aptly demonstrated by Philip Ress, who writes: "Back in the early Seventies, my wife, three-year-old son Michael and I attended High Holiday services at the Jewish Center. We had been away for some years and created a bit of a stir among old friends when we sat down. Rabbi Helfgott looked up and saw us from the pulpit. He broke into a big smile and welcomed us back. Then he realized that my son Michael was with us and asked us to hold him up for everyone to see. Michael was delighted to receive the attention and said rather boldly, 'I like that rabbi. He makes me feel like a big shot.' The congregation chuckled. Twenty-six years later, Michael still remembers that incident and fondly remembers Rabbi Helfgott for making him feel 'like a big shot.'"

In a more poignant recollection, Norma Levine writes: "As a Talmud Torah student and congregant of Rabbi Helfgott from 1950 to 1964, I had the opportunity to experience first-hand his commitment, warmth and total dedication to the people he served . . . About twenty years later, a few days after Yom Kippur in 1983, my grandfather passed away. My grandfather had always attended another *shul* in closer walking distance, but for whatever reason, my mother had asked Rabbi Helfgott to officiate . . . Upon seeing Rabbi Helfgott, who looked exactly as he did when I last saw him, to my amazement he remembered me and recited some of the worst incidents of my illustrious career as a Talmud Torah troublemaker . . . I really only had a chance to exchange but a few words with Rabbi Helfgott before I returned home . . . Several weeks later, I received a long handwritten letter from Rabbi Helfgott (which I have to this date) full of support and affirmation. In his letter he communicated to me as both a teacher and a friend, not judging me for what I was (or thought I was) but offering options for directions I might want to take in my life in the future . . . We had the opportunity to talk several times after that, and I treasure my memories of being able to continue the relationship."

That the Rabbi remembered her was certainly gratifying to Norma Levine, but the incident lodged itself in a place of honor in her memory because the Rabbi was so attuned to her, so responsive. She was important to him, and he listened to her, he truly listened, and heard what was in her heart. Only then could he offer her the balm of his advice and guidance. This was one of the Rabbi's outstanding qualities, the crucial but underrated ability to listen with total receptiveness, love and empathy. "Come to the Bronx," the Rabbi wrote to Joseph and Florence Shulman in a letter dated May 12, 1989.

"We have so much to tell you, and we are good listeners." This casual, offhand remark in a letter, certainly not intended as self-aggrandizement, reveals one of the secrets of the Rabbi's success, one of his keys to the hearts of his beloved congregants.

As with any father, the memories and recollections cover a wide range of sentiments and situations, sometimes in the same person. Mel Wasserman has vivid memories of being drawn into the circle of joy by the Rabbi. He remembers the Rabbi as "a serious man, although he had a sense of humor. But I remember the one day a year when he would allow himself to relax and maybe even have a little extra to drink—on Simchat Torah. I remember his singing and dancing and bringing everyone, young and old, into the circle."

And he also recalls the Rabbi's supportive presence in his time of need. "There are many times," he writes, "when a rabbi is called upon by individuals as they pass through the milestones of the life cycles, both religious and secular. When my father passed away after my eighteenth birthday, I was a college sophomore. Rabbi Helfgott made it possible for me to come to services and recite Kaddish each day. Each morning, he or Shim would wait for me in front of my house to be sure I got to *shul*. That summer it was necessary for me to attend summer school and to be in class at N.Y.U. at the other end of the Bronx by 8:00 A.M. I told the Rabbi I didn't think I would be at the *minyan* every day, because I had to be in school on time. Rabbi Helfgott responded that he would make sure I got to class on time. Each morning throughout that summer, either he or Shim drove across the Bronx just to get me to class. That was the year I formed my closest ties to Judaism and Torah."

Robert Goodman writes of similar memories: "I was all of fifteen when my father passed away at the early age of fifty-four. What was I to do? Where was my direction? With so much to sort out, my mind was going a million miles an hour trying to figure out what to do. For one entire year, Rabbi Helfgott picked me up at 6:10 A.M. so that I would be part of the *minyan* in order to say Kaddish. Do I remember the conversations? Not really, but I do know that the Rabbi gave me a sense of hope and optimism as I faced the rest of the day with my fellow students in high school."

Ilene Gruenberg recalls: "We all have profound memories of the Rabbi's special gifts of support and caring through our painful loss of Norman at age nineteen . . . I remember his words during the unveiling service, a time when the grief was overwhelming. He said, 'You can curse the God who has taken him from you, but better to bless the God who gave him to you.' These words came through my grief and have stayed with me through many difficult losses."

The Rabbi did not always have to draw on his great wisdom to bring joy and cheer into the lives of his congregants. A visit, a smile, a word or a kind gesture often did the trick.

"When I was hospitalized for a heart attack," recalls Harry Warner, "his visits and his good humor were always welcome. One day I met him while shopping. He didn't want me to walk the hill to the *shul* to 'sell the *chametz*.' So he said, 'Have tools, will travel.' He took me outside to his car, opened the trunk, and right then and there we went through the ritual of 'selling the *chametz*.' It was a most considerate gesture."

"When my mother became ill," writes Ruth Bergstein, "and could no longer attend services, the Rabbi would take the time to visit with her on the way to or from the Center. I still vividly recall the time, back in 1958, the Rabbi and Shim stopped by on the way home after the Yom Kippur services were concluded. I think Shim blew the *shofar* for her. My mother was thrilled, and I was so grateful."

"When I attended Ladies Auxiliary meetings my husband Joel would drive me," writes Evelyn Gleich. "While he waited, he kept the Rabbi company in his office—and loved it . . . When my husband passed away the Rabbi gave a speech I will never forget. He said he felt close to him as a friend, and that he had cherished my husband's company on the nights he had waited in the office."

The Rabbi was also instrumental in helping his congregants in very practical ways. Larry Leff is only one of many who benefited from the Rabbi's unending concern for the welfare of his people. "The Rabbi was pivotal in getting me my first job," writes Larry Leff. "This shaped my career and my whole life since. I remember telling him I had an offer of employment from the Transportation Authority in Philadelphia. He didn't want me to leave the Bronx so he asked Mr. Brandes to get me a better offer at the MTA—and he did!"

Barbara Friedberg Norton echoes the sentiments of many when she writes: "I was never able to find a rabbi who made me feel as comfortable and welcome as he did. When we moved, I tried to find another temple and rabbi, but no one was as wonderful as he was. I kind of lost my way after we moved. I did return to the temple when my son was of age to start Hebrew school and prepare for his *bar-mitzvah*. I only wish he could have done it where I grew up."

"The Rabbi once told me he loved my sons as much as his own children," recalls Betty Handberger. "My children would do anything for him, they loved him so much." In many ways, he probably did.

Louis Zarchan recalls the Rabbi as a "wonderful person, great leader and good friend" who struck terror into everyone's hearts when he asked for a pension at age sixty-five. Was the Rabbi considering retirement, Heaven forbid? Fortunately, the Rabbi was only concerned about some financial security in his advancing years. The thought of retirement was alien to him. Does a father retire from his position in the family at a certain age?

Or does a father take money from his children? Perhaps in this respect more than any other, his paternal love for his people was revealed. Many people commented on their amazement that the Rabbi refused payment for his services. Who had ever heard of a rabbi who did not accept pay? But Rabbi Helfgott refused to take anything beyond the basic and quite modest salary he received from the Center.

The following is representative of an oft-recurrent theme in the recollections of the congregants. Sidney Brandes writes: "My father-in-law, who lived with us, passed away, and I needed a rabbi to officiate at the funeral. I called Rabbi Helfgott, who at that time was a virtual stranger. Though I was a member of his congregation, I had had no personal contact with him. He conducted the service at the funeral and delivered a beautiful eulogy. He also conducted graveside services at the cemetery in New Jersey, an hour away. In the evening, he came to our apartment, with a *minyan*, to say evening prayers.

"After the Shiva period, I sent the Rabbi a check in an amount some friends advised me was the usual payment for such services. I think it was $150. The Rabbi returned the check with a note stating that he did not accept payment from members of the congregation. He added that he looked forward to performing his duties as rabbi at happier occasions such as the marriage ceremonies of my daughters, also without any compensation.

"This was a wonderful gesture, but it was unacceptable to me. In a note to the Rabbi, I advised him that I appreciate the return of my check, but that he had performed services for me in an outstanding manner and that I did not wish to feel under obligation to anyone. I enclosed a bank check to his order, which, I indicated, could not be returned. A few weeks later I received a letter from the U.J.A. that Rabbi Helfgott had donated my check for $150 in memory of my deceased father-in-law.

"This single act convinced me that the Rabbi was a unique moral man of principle and that it would be a privilege and an honor to be associated with him and get to know him better."

The Rabbi wove the Jewish Center of Wakefield and Edenwald into a fraternal community with his love, compassion, kindness and integrity, and he guided it with his wisdom and insight. "The Rabbi was generous with his time and advice," recalls Sol Greenberg. "He never intruded but was always available when and where he was needed. I remember attending a meeting of the Board where a question of some sort came to the table. The Rabbi could have solved the problem by telling the Board how it was to be done. Instead, he guided them around the problem until the Board members came to their conclusion. He was magnificent in his handling of the situation. He led by example."

It is not surprising, therefore, that people like Richard Kreisberg considered him the ideal rabbi. "To me, Rabbi Helfgott was the definition of rabbi," he writes. "He was kind and thoughtful." And he cannot help adding, "And what beautiful handwriting, in both English and Hebrew!"

"He was the most wonderful person I have ever known," writes Barbara Friedberg Norton. "How understanding and wise he was!"

"A rabbi's rabbi," declares Dr. Irwin Rifkin.

"My family respected no one more than the Rabbi," recalls Sol Greenberg. "As far as we were concerned, he sat at the right hand of God."

Chapter Three

The Thirty-Seventh Saint

ccording to an old Kabbalistic tradition, the continued existence of the world depends on the merit of thirty-six people of hidden but extraordinary saintliness who are alive at any given time. These people are called *lamedvavniks*, members of the "group of thirty-six." In Jewish folklore, they are mysterious figures, often misunderstood and unappreciated, a seemingly ignorant water carrier, for instance, who lives in seclusion and studies by candlelight in the stillness of the night. But in actuality, a great and famous man can also be one of these hidden saints—as long as people do not recognize the full extent of his righteousness.

Rabbi Helfgott's father, Reb Moshe, would often refer to his son affectionately as "my *lamedzayinik*," the thirty-seventh. In other words, he considered his son just one notch below the group of thirty-six, a very handsome compliment indeed.

Rabbi Helfgott's wife and children, however, are convinced he was one of the original thirty-six, that the scope of his righteousness was wide enough and deep enough to make him one of the pillars of the world, that whatever parts of his righteousness people actually were privileged to witness formed only the tip of the iceberg of the true essence of the man. The issue of thirty-sixth or thirty-seventh notwithstanding, however, there is no question that Rabbi Helfgott was a man of rare righteousness.

The common thread of righteousness that characterized the Rabbi's life was a remarkable selflessness and devotion to the welfare of others. He never considered his own pleasures or enjoyment. He was only interested in serving God and helping others. Everything else seemed trivial in his eyes, unworthy of his attention.

His attitude towards clothing gives us an immediate insight into his outlook on life. "My father never wanted any new clothes," writes his son Shim. "Although we bought him suits and hats for his birthdays, he always insisted on wearing the old suit and the same old hat. He claimed he had no need for them, that his old suit was still good, that he felt comfortable in his old hat and would not wear a fancy new hat. He was sure people would accept him for who he was and what he was, not for the clothes he wore. However, he always appeared dignified, neat and highly respectable. He was never unkempt or rumpled, but always properly dressed."

On his weekly visits to his children and grandchildren, he first went to the bakery and the delicatessen so that he would come in with his arms full of aromatic packages. He would play with the children and talk to them, but right after dinner, he was already signaling his wife that it was time to go. He didn't want to overstay his welcome and risk being a burden even for a few minutes. He had filled their needs, and it was time to go. In 1996, in honor of his grandson Yochanan

Burnstein's *aufruf*, he took the liberty of "imposing" on his daughter's family to stay for Shabbat. Right after Shabbat, however, he was at the door. "I'm going to lose my job if we don't get back right away," he explained. Hardly!

Even when he really needed help, he refused to accept it. "Rabbi Helfgott would honor any request but was very reluctant to have anyone do something for him," recalls Annabelle German. "He would always have some reason to refuse assistance. Some years ago, I asked Mrs. Helfgott who drove them home after Yom Kippur services. She said, 'No one. The Rabbi refuses any offers.' I asked several members why they didn't insist, and they said he always turned them down. It bothered me that he would walk home after fasting and standing all day. I did not ask Rabbi Helfgott but told him my husband would wait and drive him and Mrs. Helfgott. He gave me so many excuses why we shouldn't wait, but I wouldn't accept his refusal. We waited outside the entrance of the synagogue and drove Rabbi and Mrs. Helfgott home. The second and third years we did this the protests dwindled, and by the fourth year, he knew he had to accept the ride home. I never took no for an answer, and he knew it. It was an honor for us."

In spite of all his greatness and the powerful influence he exerted over the Jewish Center, it never crossed the Rabbi's mind to seek personal honors and privileges. Marianne Erdfarb remembers him as "a very humble man who always refused honor."

"The Rabbi," writes Sidney Brandes, "was the most honest, ethical, modest, dedicated and unassuming man I ever knew."

Robert Teitelbaum, a grandson-in-law, touches on an interesting point. He remembers the Rabbi as "a rare person who had both pride and modesty." And this made him all the greater.

This outlook is reflected in the Rabbi's own words, spoken

in a sermon on Yom Kippur in 1975: "Man is never so big as when he stoops to help a child. Man is never so wise as when he admits his lack of knowledge. Man is never so virtuous as when he acknowledges his shortcomings and admits his failings." This was the Rabbi's philosophy, and it was eloquently reflected in the way he lived his life.

The Rabbi's was not an abject humility, but a dignified humility manifested in his lack of pretentiousness and affectation, in his genuine warmth, his spontaneous friendliness, his open smile, full of joy and wisdom, that lit up his face.

When his daughter-in-law Joyce Helfgott met him for the first time, she was immediately captivated by the "blue eyes that danced and sparkled with warmth, bubbly friendliness, openness and enthusiasm. These qualities always came through no matter what he did, in bad times and good, to people he knew and to those he just met, when he was well or when he was sick." William Lacov remembers him as "very jovial, always with a smile."

Moreover, the warm smile, the compassionate word, the willingness to go to great lengths for others was not restricted to his family and congregation. His love for all people was so great that he made no differentiation. When he was called upon, he was always there—ready, willing and exceedingly able.

Speaking for many others, Roseanne Goldgell will never forget the Rabbi's kindness and consideration. She writes: "My dear father passed away on October 18, 1955, after suffering a lingering, painful death, and the rabbi of the synagogue which my father had attended for many years was immediately informed. He promised to officiate at the funeral the following day. The next morning, the well-known rabbi phoned to inform us he would not be able to attend, since he had to perform a marriage ceremony out on Long Island. Needless to say, we were not only devastated at our loss of a wonderful father but had no idea as to whom to call.

"We had attended one or two services at the Edenwald synagogue and were very impressed by Rabbi Helfgott. Hoping he could refer us to another rabbi, we contacted him. With a heavy heart, we spoke to Rabbi Helfgott, who reassured us he would be honored to attend the funeral. He dropped everything he had planned for the day, drove to the cemetery himself and gave a beautiful, sensitive memorial service, which touched us all.

"When we wanted to pay him for his time and service, he refused one penny, saying that it was his honor to do what he could for us. At that time, he hardly knew us, and his *mentchlichkeit* impressed us so much that it was the beginning of nearly a half century of a relationship that spanned time and distance.

"After we moved to Florida, we could no longer visit Sam's mother's grave. The Rabbi would write and tell us each time he went to her grave and recited prayers. We cannot express how touched we were by this kind and caring act."

In stark contrast to the rabbi who left the bereaved Goldgell family with no one to officiate at the funeral is the following recollection about Rabbi Helfgott: "My dad was ninety years old in 1975," writes Judy Engel. "He had three birthday parties to celebrate this event, to one of which I invited Rabbi and Mrs. Helfgott. That particular Sunday, the Rabbi had to officiate at a wedding in Queens. How did the Rabbi problem-solve that situation? In between the duties of the Rabbi at the wedding, both he and Mrs. Helfgott drove to the Bronx to attend my dad's celebration. Their presence made me the happiest daughter of a nonagenarian in the whole world."

Sheila Shapiro remembers the Rabbi's consideration for someone he had never even met: "When I became a teacher at P.S. 21 on East 225th Street, I had a student named Larry who was Jewish. He was a slow learner, and he told me he could not have a *bar-mitzvah* because his parents didn't have the money to attend the *shul* or make anything for him. He really wanted to have a *bar-mitzvah*. He could barely read in English, but I went to Rabbi Helfgott and explained the story. Guess what! The Rabbi taught Larry enough to have a *bar-mitzvah*, and he also provided a lovely *kiddush* for the family."

One of his nieces, Sipporah Binder, remembers the kindness shown to her by Rabbi and Mrs. Helfgott: "About fifty years ago," she writes, "my mother was hospitalized with a serious illness. My father worked long hours and couldn't take care of my brother and me, ages six and seven. Without hesitation, Uncle Binyamin and Aunt Hannah opened their home and hearts to us. We were treated as their own children. Although our uncle was needed in the synagogue eighteen hours a day, he made time for us. Daily he took us on picnics, outings, to amusement parks so that we shouldn't feel homesick. In ninety-five-degree weather, he took us to play baseball in Van Cortlandt Park, joining us in the activities with great expertise. Not only did Uncle Binyamin possess a keen intellect, he was also physically strong and a great ballplayer."

As much as he extended himself for his congregants and others, his sense of duty, responsibility and caring towards his father knew no bounds. Just a few short years after their marriage, the Rabbi and his young wife had invited Reb Moshe to share their small Bronx apartment while he ran his kosher butcher store nearby. Reb Moshe stayed with them for four years, until a heart attack forced him to sell the store. Afterwards, he lived for a while with his daughter Yetta. Finally, he moved into his own place in Williamsburg. He bought some houses in Williamsburg and lived modestly off the rents he collected himself.

In the Fifties, Reb Moshe was stricken with cancer of the colon. He underwent surgery to remove his colon and from then on he needed special care and attention. He had to be cleaned, washed and changed every day. A local man had been hired for this purpose, but the Rabbi would not hear of leaving the care of his father in strange hands. Every morning he would drive down from the Bronx, and with his own hands, he would tend to all his father's needs and make him comfortable. Moreover, every Purim he would drive down from the Bronx to read the Megillah for his father, who was unable to attend the synagogue. In his opinion, the obligation of honoring parents was "without limit." Nor did he view it as an unpleasant chore. He considered it an honor and a privilege. His reward for cleaning his father, he once told his sister Yetta Weg, was "the privilege of doing the same thing again the next day."

One summer, when Reb Moshe was staying with his daughter Yetta in the Catskill Mountains, he was stricken with intense abdominal pains on a Friday afternoon. He was taken by ambulance to Mount Sinai Hospital in Manhattan, where he had been treated for his earlier ailments; he was diagnosed with a twisted intestine and underwent surgery.

Right at the beginning of Shabbat, the Rabbi received an emergency call that his father had been taken to Mount Sinai. Immediately, he collected his father's medical records, which were in his possession, and left for the hospital on foot. Although he was technically permitted to ride to the hospital on Shabbat, since he was bringing his father's records, he refused to do so. Instead, he walked all the way from the North Bronx to Manhattan, passing through Harlem in the middle of the night. He stayed with his father all through the night until the next afternoon, consulting with the doctors and nurses, making sure his father was receiving the finest care. On Saturday afternoon he walked back to the Bronx so that he would not have to miss teaching his class in Pirkei Avoth in the Jewish Center.

Even in this life-threatening situation, he did not forget that a group of men would be deprived of their weekly encounter with the Torah if he was absent, and he found a way to fulfill all his obligations, where a lesser man would have accepted defeat. All it cost him was a long day of sleeplessness and tremendous effort, and the Rabbi was willing to pay the price. He was blessed with great strength and stamina, and he did not hesitate to draw on them for causes in which he believed.

Reb Moshe passed away in 1969. He had originally been a *chassid* of the Czortkover dynasty, but when the last Czortkover Rebbe passed away, he transferred his allegiance to the Vizhnitzer dynasty. Over the years, he gave large sums of money to the Vizhnitzer Yeshivah, and when he passed away, the Vizhnitzer Rebbe came to the Bronx during the Shivah with two burly attendants, who waited at the door while he paid his respects.

For years after Reb Moshe passed away, the Rabbi would visit his grave many times throughout the year, tenaciously keeping alive a tangible connection to his beloved father long after he was gone. In fact, he would even make a special trip to the cemetery on Purim and read the entire Megillah over his father's grave, just as he had become accustomed to doing during the last years of his father's life. In his mind and in his heart, he kept his father alive.

The same care and devotion he showed to his father he also lavished on his children, grandchildren and great-grandchildren. He made it his business to see each of them at least once a week, to take a real interest in what was going on in their lives, to show them his love.

He always tried to make each of them feel special, an endearing nickname, a "huppah" ride on his legs, a special smile, small things that made them all feel loved and cherished in their own right.

"I am a millionaire," he told one of his grandchildren, and indeed, he was. He had no interest in material riches, and he was abundantly wealthy in spiritual riches. The smiles on the faces of his grandchildren were all the reward he ever needed.

When we hear of a saintly or holy person, we involuntarily think of someone reciting Psalms in a corner far removed from the mundane world, but this is not so. Wiping away the tears of a child is a holy act. Helping a person in need altruistically, without any interest in reward or compensation, is a holy act. Bringing a person closer to God is a holy act. Making a person feel warm and esteemed and special is a holy act. These are the things the Rabbi did without measure, and in doing so, he was elevated to a higher level of existence, his whole being illuminated by the holiness he had achieved.

"Anyone who was fortunate enough to know Uncle Binyamin," declares niece Sipporah Binder, "was impressed by his vitality and couldn't help but sense the inner beauty that radiated from within."

The beauty which radiated from within reflected the holiness which characterized his whole life, a holiness which awed those who knew and loved him, who truly viewed him as the thirty-seventh saint or better.

"I have seen the face of holiness," writes Dr. Roy Schoenfeld, "and it belonged to Rabbi Benjamin W. Helfgott . . . I believe that Rabbi Helfgott was one of those very rare individuals who qualify for sainthood, not so much because he was a superior Jew but because he was a superior human being. It was my honor and pleasure to have known this man for sixty years, first as his *cheder* student and then as his doctor."

Adele Walkes Lambert saw him as "a gentle, warm intelligent man who lived his faith. He exuded love—love for God and his fellow man."

That sense of Godliness is beautifully expressed by Dr. Bernard Potter, who writes: "I felt protected in his presence. When I received an *aliyah* with him at my side on his *bimah* in his shul, I felt that this was as close as I can get to my God. I will always be grateful for having been counseled by him, more peaceful for having been comforted by him, blessed for having been touched by him and privileged for having known him."

Chapter Four
Teacher and Guide

One of the most accurate measures of a man is the willingness of others to accept his guidance. Rabbi Helfgott's congregants, family and all associated with him sought his guidance because they admired and respected his wisdom, knowledge and his complete devotion to his people. Everything he said was meant to inspire them, to encourage them to grow, to enrich their lives with the spiritual treasures of Judaism. Everything he said emanated from deep love, caring and sincerity and, as such, penetrated into their hearts and left a profound impression that would carry through for generations.

Rabbi Helfgott was the teacher who showed them the eternal truths of the Torah. He was the guide who pointed out the moral and ethical signposts on the journey of life and helped them find the route to true happiness and contentment.

The Rabbi brought formidable credentials to his role as
teacher and guide. He was a brilliant man with a vast knowledge of Jewish law, thought, history and lore; a respected doctor of philosophy with a scholarly understanding of many
intellectual fields; an incisive and insightful thinker; and a
man of the world with an extraordinary awareness of the
dynamics of society.

"Rabbi Helfgott was extremely dedicated, knowledgeable,
erudite, friendly and energetic," writes Dennis Young. "I recall
his familiarity with literature and scholarship . . . I also
remember with fondness the smell of his pipe, despite my
general antipathy towards tobacco . . . In my mind, the Rabbi
was a giant personality who stood out among men as a scholar, a spiritual and intellectual leader, and a person who put his
social responsibility far above personal gratification. He *was*
the Jewish Center in my mind."

"Rabbi Helfgott was our Jewish conscience," recalls
Stephen Young. "He found a way to find compatibility
between the American secular ethic and Orthodox Jewish life
. . . I regarded him as the archetypal sage—a man of enormous
scholarly depth and unimpeachable integrity . . . At the same
time, he was one of the friendliest people I ever encountered.
What most impressed me was his utter lack of pretentiousness. He was always completely approachable and interested
in everyone's welfare. He accorded the same respect to everyone, from prestigious professionals to janitors. I never saw
him make any distinctions. A person was a person—that was
all that mattered to him."

In addition to all his intellectual qualifications, the Rabbi
was an excellent and enthralling speaker. He exuded a powerful presence and charisma which captured the attention of
his audiences even before he opened his mouth. And when
he spoke, his passionate voice reached out to touch every one
of his listeners individually. His mobile face, his sparkling
blue eyes, his spontaneous gestures, his genuine warmth, his

skillful modulation of his voice and his message, his tasteful blend of humor and gravity, all these combined to transport the listener to an illuminated world of exciting ideas and emotions. The congregants of the Jewish Center were fortunate to enjoy this experience every Shabbat and holiday and on all special occasions and celebrations, but Rabbi Helfgott was also in great demand wherever he went. He always had an appropriate *dvar Torah* in his repertoire, and he never failed to captivate his audiences.

These talents and skills all came together in the Rabbi's masterful sermons. Standing on the podium, his presence dominating the Sanctuary, his voice drew his hushed audience into the hallowed pathways of the weekly *sidra*, opening for them new vistas of thought and challenging them to reach inside and find the greatness that lies in each of us. The Rabbi's sermons were taken on different levels by the different congregants, but all of them were profoundly affected.

"Rabbi Helfgott's sermons were traditional in thought," recalls Nathan Eisler, "always germane to the *sidra*, well-prepared, detailed, historical and profound. The messages he delivered were easy to incorporate into our own lives and became part of our values. He placed great importance on honoring parents, observance of the Sabbath, not speaking ill of our fellow man, honesty, Torah study and other basic precepts of Jewish law. He was an absolutely brilliant historian and could recite by date the occurrence of events in Palestine and the surrounding area beginning a millennium before the common era. But he never used his scholarship as showmanship. He was modest, and his teaching was always done in a matter-of-fact style . . .

"Rabbi Helfgott was my Judaism. He made me feel close to God. He also taught me that Judaism is a religion which, unlike others, requires tangible observance—prayer, certain dress, observance of *kashruth* and the like. He brought me great discipline, which I will always retain and value. He brought tremendous dignity to everything he did, from conducting our annual memorial breakfast for the Holocaust victims to our annual breakfast honoring the daily Minyannaires, to whom he would refer as the pillars of our congregation . . . I remember putting on my *kittel* while he put on his on Yom Kippur morning before I led the preliminary prayers. He would hand me a hanger and insist that I not throw my jacket down on a chair. He brought dignity to every little aspect of life."

The Rabbi also used his sermons as his basic vehicle for conveying general values of morality and ethical behavior. "I remember one of his sermons," recalls Stephen Young, "in which he told us about the time when he was still in Youngstown and Feiga was just a little girl. She came home from school saying, 'Kill the nigger! Kill the nigger!' The Rabbi asked her if she knew what the word meant. She did not, and the Rabbi explained to her the horror of what she had said. The Rabbi gave this sermon during the Fifties, well before the civil rights movement reached its zenith. To my recollection, there was no particular call for such a theme. It was simply natural for him to equate a real Jewish life with human decency and respect."

The effectiveness of the Rabbi's message was due in large measure to the widespread perception of him as a nonjudgmental person. Recalls Ilene Gruenberg: "He had a way of making everyone feel welcome and included" no matter who they were or their level of observance.

He always saw the good side of people, as he himself said in a sermon on Rosh Hashanah, 1975: "It is not my nature to find fault with people. And it is particularly difficult to find fault with a congregation of good men and women who have come to worship, to express good wishes to their friends and neighbors; it is embarrassing to tell such a congregation how wicked they had been all year and how they have to improve their way of life."

Mel Wasserman points out that "as learned and pious as the Rabbi was, he respected others for their accomplishments, large or small, and would always take note of a person's good deeds rather than dwell on the negative."

Marianne Erdfarb offers another instance of how the Rabbi chose to look at the good side: "One day, while I was president of the PTA, one of our women members came to a meeting wearing pants. I asked the Rabbi what he thought of pants. He replied, 'Pants are better than miniskirts.'"

Very often, this positive outlook led him to see hope where others could not. "When my husband Steve and I were married in June, 1962," recalls Sharon Wasserman Margulis, "Rabbi Helfgott, of course, performed the ceremony. A month later we moved to Minnesota and, since then, have lived in four other states. Although we have not moved back to New York City, we still think of the Jewish Center as an important link with our Bronx roots . . . When we were dating, Steve had told me he was an agnostic. I decided we should break up, since his lack of religiosity would be a strain on my family. My mother asked the Rabbi about the situation. He said, 'Tell her to go back with him—we'll change him!' Well, he was right. Among other religious activities, Steve now attends Sabbath services weekly."

What did the Rabbi expect of people? By what standards did he measure them? It was always by their own standards. He encouraged them to look at who they were and what they could be and try to reach their potential. Within these parameters, he was very demanding but not judgmental; he criticized but did not condemn.

In a sermon delivered on Rosh Hashanah, 1995, less than a year before he passed away, he made the point very succinctly: "Here we stand alone in prayer and examine ourselves. Behold, we tell ourselves, today is the anniversary of creation. I am a specimen of the highest creature of God's handiwork. As a human being, I have been endowed with an intellect to discern between good and evil. I have been given free will to choose what is good, just and useful. Have I lived up to my potential?

"My family claims descent from the *chassidic* dynasty of the nineteenth-century miracle worker Rabbi Meir'l of Premyszlan. One of the legends repeated in our family in his name is his confessed fear of judgment in the world to come. He remarked that when he would come before the High Tribunal and be asked why he was not as creative in the study of Torah as R. Akiva, he would answer that he lacked R. Akiva's high intellect. If he would be asked why he was not as charitable as R. Tarphon, he would answer that he did not have R. Tarphon's wealth. What he feared most was to be challenged as to why he was not 'a good Meir'l,' why he had not fulfilled his own potential.

"Within our own limitations, we have the ability to do so much good—and fail. As parents, did we fulfill our obligations in raising our children, or did we conveniently cop out? As children, have we properly carried out our responsibilities to our parents? Husband, wife, neighbor, we have benefited so much from these relationships but contributed so little."

This was what the Rabbi felt he could demand, that people fulfill their obligations, that they do as much good as they can within their own limitations. Nevertheless, although he condemned no one for lack of observance, it pained him to see people living less than fully Jewish lives. One time, on the eve of Yom Kippur, the Rabbi was saying Tefillat Zakah and crying.

"Why are you crying?" his son Shim asked.

"Because I think of all the marriages I perform, and it hurts me that many of them won't observe the marriage laws."

But for all his tolerance, there were times when he felt he had to stand on principle. "When I was twenty-one," writes Paula Dicker Gold, "I was to be married and the Rabbi was to officiate at the 'non-sectarian' chapel at Columbia University.

When he came to the chapel, he called me aside to say that he could not go through with the ceremony because there was a crucifix above the podium. He left. I was into the Yellow Pages looking for a rabbi with eighty people waiting for the wedding. The marriage lasted about five months. Rabbi Helfgott had married my parents and my brother and his wife. When I was ready to do it again—for real this time—the Rabbi came to my mother's house and performed the ceremony. That was ten years ago."

The Rabbi believed that as long as there was life there was hope, and consequently, as long as a person kept up some semblance of Jewishness, there was hope that at some point in the future he himself or his children would return to a full Jewish life. Assimilation through intermarriage and missionary activity, therefore, were his main fears, because there was such a finality to them.

In a sermon on Rosh Hashanah, 1972, he spoke about intermarriage with bitter humor: "The story is told of a Jewish girl who was missing from home for a week and then called her mother to tell her she had eloped and married.

"Ma: 'Can we come see you, dear? Where are you?'

"Daughter: 'No, we have no place for you to stay. My husband has no job.'

"Ma: 'Come home with your husband, then. We'll take care of both of you.'

"Daughter: 'I can't bring him home. He is not Jewish.'

"Ma: 'That's all right. Don't tell anyone, and no one will know he is not Jewish.'

"Daughter: 'But he is black, Mommy.'

"Ma: 'Bring him home, dear. You know we are a liberal-minded family.'

"Daughter: 'But we have only one bedroom, so where are we going to sleep?'

"Ma: 'I have it all figured out. You two will sleep in the bedroom, and Papa will sleep on the couch in the living room.'

"Daughter: 'And where will you sleep, Mommy?'

"Ma: 'Don't worry about me, dear. As soon as you hang up the phone, I am jumping out the window.' "

In a sermon on Rosh Hashanah, 1973, he spoke with horror about the inroads of Jews for Jesus. "Our major defenses against the new missionary activity is *teshuvah*," he declared, "a return to joyous and meaningful Jewish living—a revamping of our homes and life styles to accommodate more and more Jewish habits, associations and experiences. *Yeshivot* are our strongest fortresses. Undergraduate courses in Jewish history and culture given on various campuses have also been helpful. The old example of the futility of fighting cancer with aspirin when major surgery is required is applicable. Our kids cannot combat the Christian missionaries with the memories of the childish lessons in the stories of Adam and Eve. They need Torah, our age-old stronghold, Torah in all its ramifications: practice, knowledge, appreciation."

This call to *teshuvah* was one of the Rabbi's principal recurrent themes. *Teshuvah*, he believed, was a gradual process of adjustment, as he explained in a sermon on Yom Kippur, 1984: "Regardless of how low a man may fall spiritually, socially, emotionally, he can always rise again and stand erect. We don't have to die in sin and be reformed again. A *baal teshuvah* is not a 'newborn' Jew in the same sense as we understand a 'born again' Christian. A *baal teshuvah* is adjusting his way of life." The sincerity and sophistication of his message transformed the lives of many of his secular congregants and made them into *baalei teshuvah*.

"I had little contact with the Center," writes Dr. Julian Joseph, "until 1961, when I began to attend religious services frequently and through this became active in the affairs of the synagogue. As a matter of fact, I became, through Rabbi Helfgott, a *baal teshuvah*, attending regularly with my family. My return to Judaism began with my chanting the Sabbath Haftorah, the first time I had done so since the time of my *bar-mitzvah*, an absence of some twenty years. Rabbi Helfgott found a way in his remarks from the pulpit to show that the first step one takes leads to a second and so forth . . . The most significant part of the synagogue for me was Shabbat morning service, and the high quality of Rabbi Helfgott's sermons. Listening to him, I felt I was in the presence of a giant."

Sidney Brandes recalls: "I think of myself as a secular Jew, devoted to Jewish causes but with little interest in formal religion. Though I was brought up in a kosher home, my father was not religious. He came to America as a fourteen-year-old boy. He knew no one and was on his own from the day he landed in this country. With his newfound liberty, he rebelled against the strict Orthodoxy imposed upon him in the *shtetl* where he had lived. When I was a young boy, I was not sent to a Hebrew school. Instead, I was sent to a Workmen's Circle school where I received some Bible instruction and was taught to read and write Yiddish. The ritual of the synagogue was extremely foreign to me . . .

"Hitler made me conscious of my Jewishness, and I was determined to do my part to insure the survival of the State of Israel. Jews were a small minority in the Edenwald area, where I lived, and principally to identify as a Jew, I joined the Jewish Center of Wakefield and Edenwald . . .

"When Harry Mintz, the president of the congregation died, Rabbi Helfgott asked me to take on the office. I was most reluctant to do so. I explained that I was a secular Jew who could not read Hebrew, was unfamiliar with ritual, did not observe the Sabbath or keep a kosher home and would not be a very good example for the rest of the congregation. He replied that, in fact, this was a description of the largest part of the congregation, that he would 'hold my hand' when it came to ritual, that ritual was actually his part of the job. He said he knew I would be a fine president, that the members admired my achievements and that he needed my help. I had great respect for the Rabbi. I still felt beholden to him, and thus could not say no.

"The Rabbi did, in fact, 'hold my hand.' Despite my shortcomings, I at length felt at ease with ritual. I was president for over ten years. They were good and fruitful years for me and the congregation."

Louis Zarchan had a similar experience. Born to an observant family, he drifted away. Still, he decided to send his sons to Hebrew school, and when he discovered that Shabbat attendance was required, he felt it would be hypocritical not to attend himself as well. With the passage of time, he became more and more involved, eventually serving as president. Today, retired and living in Florida, he still goes to *minyan* daily. And he still remembers his days in the Jewish Center as "a good part of my best years."

One senses a certain tone of pleasant surprise in the statements of these people that their years of close involvement in Judaism were some of the best of their lives. But it was no surprise to the Rabbi. He made this point to his congregation again and again. In a sermon delivered on Rosh Hashanah, 1961, he posed the question: "Is the American Jew happy as a Jew? No, he displays all the symptoms of bewilderment, suspense and uncertainty. We fill the offices of psychiatrists, practitioners and quacks. We are overanxious and overambitious, nervous and uneasy. Books with titles like *Peace of Mind* or *Peace of Soul* are found on every Jewish bookshelf. What's troubling us? What's disturbing us?

"I believe the American Jew lacks spiritual backbone. That fountain of strength which gives life its meaning and man his dignity has been sapped out of our veins. We have discarded the spiritual wealth we accumulated in the course of centuries. We threw away the Jewish manual of life—the Shulchan Aruch—and found no other spiritual discipline to replace it, leaving us in a vacuum of bewilderment."

In a sermon delivered on Rosh Hashanah, 1984, he

declared: "Our modern lives have become so complex, so obsessed, so challenging. Advanced technology adds to the complexities, drives, goals, failures and achievements. We cannot stop for a moment! Problems! Personal problems, family problems, education for our children, best colleges, paying bills, repairing the house, vacations, mortgages, doctors, operations, pills, drugs, dinners, theater, insurance, banquets, and more and more."

And where does all this lead? "Have you noticed how many psychiatrists have Jewish names?" the Rabbi said on Yom Kippur, 1973. "There are also numerous Jewish psychologists, practitioners and therapists. It has become a Jewish business. The majority of the customers are Jewish, and they can relate better to their own kind.

"Why have we become so afflicted with psychiatric problems? We suffer from fears, frustrations, guilt-complexes, psychoses, neuroses. These seem to be new Jewish ailments.

"Unfortunately, we lost the inherent Jewish therapy for these mental and emotional disturbances. The Jewish therapy has been *teshuvah*, a firm belief that we have been born good, children of a gracious God, in whose merciful care we trust. With wholesome faith in God's redeeming love, we fear no evil. In the closing verse of the popular hymn *Adon Olam*, we say: 'As long as my body and soul are united, I know that God is with me, and I shall have no fear.'"

On the High Holidays, the Rabbi had the opportunity to carry his message to a much broader audience. On these days, he shone with a special radiance, and his message rang out with special clarity. This was the high point of the year for all Jews and for the Jewish Center in particular. During this time, all the seats were occupied, and the Sanctuary was overflowing.

The atmosphere in the Jewish Center was electric, imbued with a transcendent holiness. In the Rabbi's own words on Yom Kippur, 1972, "A simple congregation of men and women gathered to hear Kol Nidre undergoes a metamorphosis from the mundane to the heavenly, from mortals to angels. A spiritual cleanliness permeates the synagogue."

This spirit was palpable because of the shining example of the Rabbi. "I recall a Yom Kippur," writes Dr. Julian Joseph, "when at a recess period in the service I felt Rabbi Helfgott was radiating beams of light as Moses returning from Sinai."

"He was highly inspirational," recalls Nathan Eisler, "particularly during the High Holidays, when the sight of him in his *kittel* and his heightened formality and more rigid manner leading the services brought a tremendous sense of divine presence to us all. His chanting of Kol Nidre was unique, and will never be the same for me."

Louis Zarchan remembers the spiritual and physical strength of the Rabbi with awe. The Rabbi did everything on Yom Kippur, leading the prayers, reading from the Torah, delivering sermons before Kol Nidre and Yizkor, making appeals for charitable causes, standing on his feet all day. "The people felt like angels, light-headed from hunger and light-pocketed from the appeals, but who could complain?"

In his sermons for the High Holidays, the Rabbi often took the bull by the horns, so to speak, speaking in a very direct and forthright manner, but no one was offended. Even the people who only put in an appearance on the High Holidays knew full well that the Rabbi spoke out of love and concern for their welfare, and they listened attentively and receptively.

"I am going to pose a rather impertinent question to you," he began his sermon on Rosh Hashanah, 1961. "Why did you come to the synagogue today? The question is addressed only to those who do not come to the synagogue all year. What brought you here today? I do not question your right to be here. The synagogue is open to everyone who desires to come . . . My question is, What motivated you to come today? Is it a desire to come and recite prayers? How is it that such a desire does not come to you on the other three hundred and sixty-four days in the year?

"You didn't come to listen to my sermons. They are not so attractive. I prepare sermons for every Sabbath throughout the year and preach to a half-empty synagogue. The seats you occupy today accumulate dust the whole year round.

"You did not come just because it is the nice thing to do, because your friends and neighbors will be there. No, you are not that naive.

"I'll tell you what I believe is the real strong, although unconscious, force that drove you to the synagogue today. Unhappiness! You are unhappy. American Jews are basically an unhappy lot. You are driven to the synagogue to find some inward contentment, a measure of happiness."

Speaking on the same theme on Rosh Hashanah, 1993, he said: "In our pursuit of what we call happiness and fulfillment, we stop at nothing. We rush, we run, we fly. From home to the shop, to the office, to the train. From work we rush home, from the television to the kitchen table, exhausted, we rush to sleep. We have no time, no patience to stop, to examine how far we have gone astray. Are we on the right path? What is our goal?

"On Rosh Hashanah, the shrieking blasts of the *shofar* call upon each of us to stop for a moment, to mentally withdraw from the hustle and bustle, from all the pressures and preoccupation, and listen to the *shofar* addressing our souls: Look at yourself, time is fleeting. You live for a higher purpose! What are you doing to fulfill it? Turn your heart and mind to your Father in Heaven, for only in His service will you find peace."

The Rabbi did not limit himself to generalities in his sermons. "Were I to rewrite the confessions of Yom Kippur," he declared in 1971, "I would change them to read as follows:

"*Al chet*—for the sin—we committed in the desecration of the Sabbath. For centuries, our people lived among Moslems and Christians who observed Friday or Sunday as their days of rest. But we steadfastly kept the Sabbath, thereby sanctifying ourselves and our way of life throughout the remainder of the week. We have destroyed our greatest heritage—the Sabbath.

"*Al chet*—for the sin—we committed in polluting our homes and bodies with *tarfus* and *chazerei*. The nations of the world respected our disciplined eating and drinking habits. We were known as the Chosen People for our selection of proper food. Our tables were altars, and our dining rooms were temples. Alas, what's happening today? I asked a boy if his father recited the Kiddush on Friday night. And his answer was, 'My father comes home too tired on Fridays. He throws off his hat and coat and goes for the grub.

"*Al chet*—for the sin—we committed in the neglect of synagogue attendance.

"*Al chet*—for the sin—we committed in the neglect of Torah study.

"*Al chet*—for the sin—we committed by denying our children a religious education.

"These are the sins for which we should repent and beg forgiveness."

Denying children a proper Jewish education, in the Rabbi's opinion, was one of the cardinal sins. For the education of his own children, he had sacrificed a prestigious and comfortable rabbinical position in Youngstown. He had given all his talents and energy to developing the Hebrew school for the children of his congregants. Education was the answer. "What we need," the Rabbi said on Rosh Hashanah, 1972, "is a united and concerted plan of action to intensify Jewish education and training. We must reevaluate our goals in American Jewish life in the light of changing conditions. Our federated charities that collect and spend millions to erect hospitals, orphanages, old age homes—some of which cater only to a small percent of Jewish patients—must recognize the greater needs of the community in the schools and colleges."

On the High Holidays, the Rabbi would stand on the podium and look out over the crowded Sanctuary, knowing full well that a large number of these people had only come to say Yizkor in honor of a deceased parent or other loved one. "It is most painful," he declared in 1977, "that the *mitzvah* of the respect for the dead has become the sole expression of religion for a large number of Jews. To them, the Torah is no longer a beacon of light for righteous living, but a means to respect the memories of their deceased relatives. In the place of the Sabbath, festivals, family purity and dietary regulations, they have substituted Shiva, Kaddish, Yahrzeit and Yizkor. The cemetery has replaced the synagogue."

And yet, the Rabbi was able to look at the positive side. "Kaddish and Yizkor," he pointed out in 1983, "have proved to be the strongest links in the chain of our tradition to hold our people tied together, even such as have been fully assimilated. It cannot be denied that today the word Kaddish has more direct emotional appeal for the Jew than the word Shema. The word Yizkor conveys more to him than the words Shemoneh Esrei, although no one with an understanding of our prayers would compare their religious values." With his singular blend of realism and high idealism, the Rabbi was able to call on all his congregants to embrace a full Jewish life while at the same time expressing appreciation for a seemingly minor religious observance such as Yizkor in maintaining a tenuous connection between even assimilated Jews and their heritage.

The poignant recollections of grandson Yochanan Burnstein give us a profound perspective on the Rabbi's role as teacher and guide: "He was not a simple man of faith. Nor was he a philosopher, an intellectual removed from the daily experiences of real life . . . He was the friend with whom I would walk down White Plains Road to *shul* arm in arm when I would visit on Shabbos . . . the person with whom I still talk at times in my dreams, but alas is not there when I awaken."

Touching on the same theme, Dr. Rick Deitchman writes: "As part of my being centered, in touch with myself, I will often get in touch with an inner guide, who came to me during guided meditation some years ago. This inner guide counsels me and helps me. I can tell you that this inner guide looks a great deal like the Rabbi."

Chapter Five

Keeping the Flame Alive

For fully a quarter of a century after Rabbi Helfgott's return from Youngstown, the Jewish Center of Wakefield and Edenwald enjoyed tremendous growth and vitality. There were seven hundred children in the Hebrew school, overflow services on the High Holidays, numerous clubs, programs and activities. But time and demographics affected the character of the Jewish Center. Congregants died, others moved to other parts of the country.

By the early Seventies, the complexion of the community changed. "I was the last official youth group leader," writes Milton Erdfarb, "because by the early Seventies we ran out of youth for whom to create programs."

It would have been easy to accept defeat in such a situation, to close the doors, look back at the accomplishments of the past and accept the inevitable future—as so many other synagogues in deteriorating metropolitan neighborhoods had done. But the Rabbi was made of stronger stuff. "Caring for the congregation in a depleted Jewish community," he wrote to Joseph and Florence Shulman in 1988, "(notwithstanding our relatively good health) is a challenge." And as he had done all his life, the Rabbi rose to the challenge with wisdom, determination and relentless tenacity.

Drawing on the loyalty and financial support of former congregants, he maintained the Jewish Center as one of the few viable outposts of Yiddishkeit in the Bronx. "Of course, we appreciate your generous and continuous support of the congregation," he wrote to Sidney Brandes in 1988. "From the income of the remnant Jewish population we could not meet our expenses. What I appreciate more is your kind and warm notes. It serves like balm on an aching wound. The diminishing population, and the aging of those who were formerly active and helpful, have laid the burden of maintenance heavily on me, particularly before the High Holidays."

Sometimes, the Rabbi himself was amazed at the changes that the passage of time had wrought. In a letter to the Shulmans in 1993, he wrote: "I have made a habit that when I have to recite Kaddish of a Yahrzeit on our memorial tablet, I announce the person to the *minyan* before we start to pray, and I ask who remembers the person. I was shocked that when I asked yesterday who remembered Eddie Rothman, no one responded. Then I mentioned the grocery on Pittman and Edson, and a Mr. Weiss, who still resides on Grace Avenue (a man in his early seventies), responded that he recalls the grocery but did not recall Jewish owners. Alas, how time and death play havoc with our past! I pointed to the Venetian blinds in the chapel room where we worship weekday mornings and told them that Eddie donated them when he was still single in 1941."

By nature, the Rabbi was progressive, optimistic and

extremely vigorous—the quintessential builder. And in many ways, the task of building a vibrant Jewish center in a "depleted Jewish community," as he called it, was more daunting than any he had ever undertaken in his life. "I simply cannot keep up with all I want to do!" he wrote to the Shulmans in 1987.

Recalls Irving Lubin: "Rabbi Helfgott, especially in the later years, was a one-man show, acting as everything from teacher to secretary to counselor to janitor. He was committed to maintaining the synagogue long after it was practical, and no task was too difficult, too great or too menial for him to undertake. The continuation of the synagogue was a struggle due to the aging of the congregation, the changes in the neighborhood and the tiny Jewish population that remained. But the Rabbi took these adverse conditions as a challenge and became more and more devoted to the synagogue. Over the years, the Rabbi witnessed the various teaching and social arms of the congregation disband due to lack of interest, but this did not discourage him. Instead, he took these negative factors and turned them into positives by devoting himself to the continuance of the core congregation and supporting his remaining members. All this was certainly not glamorous or easy, but during this period, Rabbi Helfgott showed us a more personal and softer side of his personality as he and his remaining congregants focused on the desire to maintain an outpost in our neighborhood for the practice of Judaism."

The first order of business, the Rabbi realized, was to maintain the role of the Jewish Center as a true house of prayer, not only on Shabbat and holidays but every single day of the week. To this end, he organized a group of dedicated men, known as the Minyannaires, who undertook to make every effort to come to the daily *minyan*. Between all of them, there were virtually always at least ten men for the minimum daily *minyan*. But it did not happen by itself. Every night the Rabbi and the Rebbetzin were on the phone, making sure that

at least ten men had committed themselves to coming the following morning. And there was also the problem of transportation. Some of these men needed to be driven to the synagogue, and the Rabbi took it upon himself to leave his house
at the crack of dawn and drive around the neighborhood pick-
ing up whoever needed a ride. The Rabbi also organized an
annual Minyannaires breakfast to acknowledge the dedication
of these men and encourage their continued participation in
the future.

Recalls Irving Lubin: "What impressed us most, as congregants, was his commitment to the daily practice of the
Jewish faith. He was dedicated to the administration of the
daily prayers, the observance and celebration of the Sabbath
and other festivals and the enforcement of Jewish laws and
practices. At the synagogue, he was stubborn and unyielding
in maintaining the morning *minyan*—and went to outrageous
lengths to preserve it! Waking up members from sleep, col-
lecting the men by driving in dangerous weather, organizing
attendance days in advance, these were all the norm for our
Rabbi. His goal was simple—maintain the *minyan*! The
achievement of this goal brought him satisfaction, and he
would proudly comment that his 'little synagogue' in a non-
Jewish neighborhood had one of the few daily services in the
area."

"We admired the way the Rabbi ran around in his car,"
writes Sol Greenberg, "to pick up the Minyannaires who
either lived too far away to walk or didn't have transportation
to get there. He was the youngest senior citizen I ever knew—
always running around doing for people. I could never figure
out where he got the strength to do what he did."

"On Sunday and during the week," writes Ruth Barth,
"Rabbi and Mrs. Helfgott made calls the night before to be
sure there would be enough men for a *minyan* the next day.
Those that needed it would be picked up by the Rabbi and a
few dedicated men. During the winter months, there were

many days when the weather was below freezing, but this did not stop the Rabbi. My husband Philip needed a ride, since he was in poor health, and during the conversation in the car, the Rabbi spoke about Mrs. Helfgott and how indispensable she was to him and how much he needed her."

"Today one might say that the tenth man makes the *minyan*," writes Larry Leff, "but back then, Rabbi Helfgott made the *minyan*, not by being the tenth man but by driving most of the *minyan* to *shul*. I was a frequent passenger, and each time there would be lively and stimulating discussions— from why God gave man free will to why the Rabbi carried an empty bottle in the back seat!"

Louis Zarchan recalls receiving a telephone call from the Rabbi, who had been hit by a car and was worried about the *minyan*. Who would pick up the people? The Rabbi asked Louis Zarchan to fill in until he could resume his regular routine. That Shabbat, the Rabbi, still bruised and battered, walked to *shul* with a herculean effort. The congregation needed him, and if it was at all humanly possible, he would be there.

The Rabbi allowed nothing to stand in the way of the *minyan*. Day in and day out, he carried the responsibility on his shoulders. "We are holding our own," he wrote to David and Esther Rosenberg in 1992. "With our regular visits to our children and grandchildren, plus congregational and communal duties, there is no time left to attend to our aging aches and pains. There is a good chance we will visit you in Bat Yam this summer. All we are waiting for is a promise from my people that they will maintain the daily morning *minyan* in my absence, since I pick up half a *minyan* each morning as I drive to the synagogue."

Three years earlier, in 1989, he had indeed canceled plans for an Israel trip, as he wrote to the Shulmans, "We were planning to go to Israel this summer, but had to cancel our plans. The daily morning *minyan* depends on my bringing along a couple of elderly gentlemen, and I don't want to challenge my depleted *minyan*, of which we are very proud."

Although attendance at the Center had become "depleted" over time, the Rabbi's broader constituency was greater than ever. Former congregants who had moved away remained loyal to the Center and their beloved Rabbi, and they kept up a steady stream of financial support for the Center. Many of them remained members and relied on the Rabbi for guidance and counsel on sad and happy occasions.

The Rabbi acknowledged each and every one of these contributions personally, sometimes with a few lines inscribed on the back of the receipt, sometimes with a separate handwritten letter. In these communications, the Rabbi would express his appreciation and gratitude, convey news about himself and the Center and ask about the welfare of the contributor. The notes—and there were literally thousands of them—were warm, thoughtful and full of poignant memories. They elicited similar responses from the former congregants and kept the relationships alive and faithful. "I am still answering mail from September and October," he wrote to the Shulmans in December of 1993. "As the years progress, the correspondence and responsibilities increase."

The responsibilities may have increased along with the Rabbi's age, but the Rabbi remained as youthful, strong and vigorous as ever. "I knew him for more than forty years," writes Richard Kreisberg, "and he always appeared the same. He didn't age much at all."

Nancy Pincus recalls: "Rabbi Helfgott changed little over all the years. He seemed an ageless wonder—always the same in looks and demeanor."

The Rabbi's seemingly inexhaustible vigor may have been due in part to the tremendous joy and *nachas* he derived from his growing family. During these years, his grandchildren grew into adulthood, married and presented him with many great-grandchildren.

"The Rabbi had no time or interest in personal activities or hobbies," writes Irving Lubin. "Any spare moment he did have was devoted to his son, daughter and their families. His commitment to them was fierce, and we all took pleasure in observing the joy he received from being the head of this large, great family. He took such pride in the accomplishments of his children and, later, his grandchildren, and he was always thrilled to announce yet another great-grandchild! Rabbi and Mrs. Helfgott took the job of grandparenting seriously, and we all gained from this, since it seemed as if the pleasure they received from the family gave them the energy to continue their difficult work at the synagogue well into what should have been their retirement years."

The Rabbi's own letters speak most eloquently about his life, his congregation and his family.

In February of 1987, he wrote to the Shulmans: "From your letters, it appears that you really have a taste of what I call the good life—and that is *nachas* and closeness with children and grandchildren. We are so thankful to Heaven for our share of these blessings. We see our children and grandchildren at least once a week. They are all in the metropolitan area, and we drive about five hundred miles a week to be with each of them. Feiga lives in Mill Basin (a Brooklyn outskirt). She and her husband (a non-practicing rabbi) teach school— literally night and day. Shim is a patent attorney (he was ordained and holds two doctorates—one in law, the other in Hebrew literature), and his wife is a social worker. Following a trend in modern Orthodoxy, our oldest four granddaughters are all in medicine. Feiga's oldest, Shira, and her husband are residents; her second daughter, Adena, and her husband are residents; her third daughter, Penina, is a second-year medical student at Columbia Presbyterian; and Shim's oldest daughter is in N.Y.U. Medical School—all *yeshivah* graduates and strict observers. The other four grandchildren are students in different *yeshivot*. We are already great-grandparents of a year-old bundle of happiness—Meira, who is taught to call us 'Super-Zaida' and 'Super-Bobee.' To the others, we are Zaida and Bobee. As for our health, we follow a system of pills and keep moving.

"I can appreciate your enjoyable retirement, but it is so hard to identify with such a lifestyle. We have always been continuously occupied and cannot even fathom the idea of retirement. In the last thirty years, we took five vacation periods to go to Israel for a month, and after the first week, we count the days and hours for our return. I am up daily at five. At six, I am on the street, driving around to pick up five or six 'elderly men' (I am only seventy-eight) to bring them to the daily *minyan*. I am home at eight, and by nine o'clock we are off—congregational work, communal work, visits to hospitals, mourners, etc. Actually, we have no time to *krechts* like other old people."

One year later, he wrote to them: "We have been blessed with a second great-granddaughter, Tehila. She is three weeks old and 'smiles.' I touched her little feet yesterday—and they are so *soft*. Heaven has been good to us."

In 1990, he wrote to them: "Hannah and I . . . are fortunate to see our children, grandchildren and four great-grandchildren regularly. We celebrate twenty-five birthdays and eight wedding anniversaries. On some birthdays, we all come together. Heaven has been very good to us. We are constantly occupied and find no time to complain of old-age disabilities. The congregation requires many hours of activity, and the rest of the time, we go riding (driving) all over the metropolitan area—from Riverdale to East Lawrence, and from Mill Basin to Boro Park—the family is scattered, yet within reach."

In 1993, he wrote to the Shulmans: "We have not taken a day's vacation in six years. It is difficult to detach ourselves from the little ones."

Later that year, in a letter to Sidney Brandes, he wrote: "As for us, we thank Heaven for His many kindnesses. Last

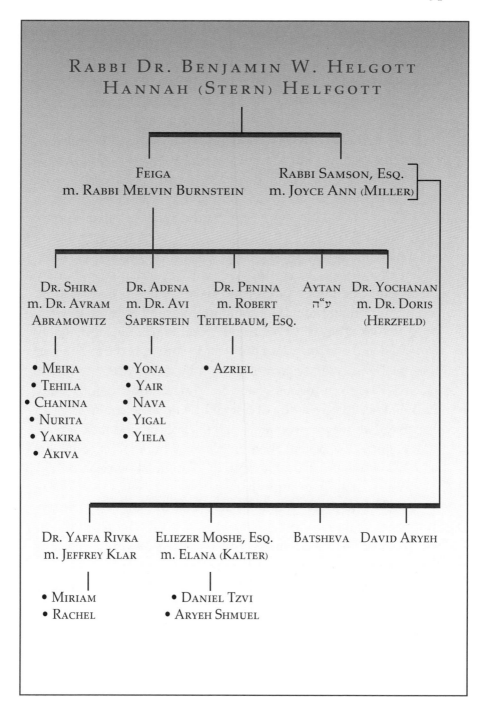

RABBI DR. BENJAMIN W. HELGOTT
HANNAH (STERN) HELFGOTT

FEIGA
m. RABBI MELVIN BURNSTEIN

RABBI SAMSON, ESQ.
m. JOYCE ANN (MILLER)

DR. SHIRA
m. DR. AVRAM
ABRAMOWITZ

DR. ADENA
m. DR. AVI
SAPERSTEIN

DR. PENINA
m. ROBERT
TEITELBAUM, ESQ.

AYTAN
ע״ה

DR. YOCHANAN
m. DR. DORIS
(HERZFELD)

- MEIRA
- TEHILA
- CHANINA
- NURITA
- YAKIRA
- AKIVA

- YONA
- YAIR
- NAVA
- YIGAL
- YIELA

- AZRIEL

DR. YAFFA RIVKA
m. JEFFREY KLAR

ELIEZER MOSHE, ESQ.
m. ELANA (KALTER)

BATSHEVA

DAVID ARYEH

- MIRIAM
- RACHEL

- DANIEL TZVI
- ARYEH SHMUEL

Sunday, Shim's daughter, a pediatrician, gave birth to our eighth great-grandchild. Hannah and I are constantly occupied—the congregation and our family."

In 1995, again writing to Sidney Brandes: "I hope you are adjusting yourself to an unexpected but unavoidable situation. Try and find comfort in beautiful memories of useful and productive years that you shared and in your children and grandchildren . . . Hannah wishes to be remembered. We enjoy the love of eleven great-grandchildren and look forward to the arrival of three more. The mothers are all physicians—busy doctors!"

The Rabbi's consummate love for his family is beautifully illustrated by a story told by his grandson Yochanan Burnstein. The Rabbi and the Rebbetzin used to visit each of their children, grandchildren and great-grandchildren at least once a week. They always brought food for dinner from a delicatessen and a bakery, and they made sure to leave as soon as the meal was over, so as not to be a burden. After the Rabbi passed away, one of his granddaughters stopped in a Boro Park bakery to buy a box of her child's favorite cookies.

"Say, I know who you are," said the lady behind the counter. "I recognize the order. There is a man who always comes in here and buys those cookies exactly. You must be related."

"Yes, that's my grandfather."

"Well, I must tell you, he is so proud of his grandchildren and great-grandchildren. He cannot stop talking about them. We call him the cookie man. You know, we haven't seen him for a while."

The Rabbi was so enthralled with his family he could not resist talking about them to perfect strangers!

The most precious gift, in the Rabbi's opinion, was *nachas*, and he enjoyed it in abundant measure. The word jumps out from his letters again and again—*nachas*! That was what he lived for, *nachas* from his family, *nachas* from his congregants.

In May of 1995, one year before he passed away, the Rabbi

wrote to the Shulmans: "We, too, had an interesting gathering. Since it was our sixtieth anniversary in January and Shim's thirtieth in February, Feiga and Shim arranged for a family Shabbat at the Orthodox Jackson Hotel in Long Beach. We all arrived late Friday afternoon on March 21. They allowed us a separate dining hall and a separate synagogue. We brought our own ark and a Torah. We had a *minyan* of our own. Yochanan, Feiga's youngest, an ophthalmology resident at Bronx Lebanon, has a golden voice. He is a Yeshiva University graduate and a cantor for the High Holidays. When he chanted the Mussaf service so melodically, and I looked around and saw our blessings, I literally broke down with *nachas*. It was very touching!"

The Rabbi had a special relationship with each of his grandchildren. When they were little, he called some of them his little buttercup or princess, and as they grew older, he took an active interest in their lives. He also instituted the very charming family custom of designating a special Shabbat for each of his grandchildren and great-grandchildren. As he explained at the *bar-mitzvah* of his grandson Dovid Helfgott: "Our oldest grandchild is named Shira. When the first Shabbat Shira came around, we sent Shira a gift for Shabbat Shira, 'her Shabbat,' and we have been continuing it until now; every Shabbat Shira we send a gift to Shira for Shabbat Shira. But then her sister was born, and the thought came: Are we going to ignore her? We won't have a special Shabbat for Adena? We looked for a Shabbat which has to do with Adena. We found it . . . And so we went on. For every single child, every one of our grandchildren and great-grandchildren, we have a special Shabbat."

On that special Shabbat, the child could expect to receive a beautiful letter in the mail, full of love and inspiration. And there was no age limit on the "child" receiving the letter. "Heaven has been good to us," he wrote to his oldest granddaughter Shira. "We have had the good fortune of your close companionship for years. And we succeeded in seeing you shine, not just in a new little dress, but in a wedding gown, in a physician's graduation gown and, best of all, in a maternity outfit. You have indeed fulfilled our fondest dreams and hopes."

Nor was any "child" too young to receive a letter. "Dearest Chanina," he wrote to Shira's son, "we know that you cannot read as yet, but you can smile, you can talk—eh,eh,oo—and you can gaze at things with questioning and intelligent eyes. You are a darling little boy!"

Tucked away inside these beautiful letters, there was always a twenty-dollar bill. The Rabbi was a very generous man, always ready to give large sums to his grandchildren or to charity without a second thought. For himself, however, he never wanted anything. "Why do I need this?" he would always say.

At that same *bar-mitzvah*, he revealed another charming personal custom born of his transcendent love for his grandchildren: "On Friday nights, since we can't have my children, grandchildren and great-grandchildren with us, and I want to bless them, I have made a certain habit for myself. I take time before Kiddush. I stand up and let each one pass by me in spirit, and I pray for each one in absentia. I pray for this one for what she needs, this one for what she needs, this one for what he needs, this one for what I believe he should have, and this one for what she should have. Before the candles, before Kiddush, I spend time and bless each one: 'Yevarechecha Hashem Veyishmerecha.'"

Speaking at the *bar-mitzvah* about his love for his grandchildren, the Rabbi suddenly turned pensive, facing the thought of his own mortality in front of the assembled guests.

"When Dovid was born thirteen years ago," he said softly, "I had already reached my three score plus ten, and my young wife was not much younger. Naturally, the immediate thought when we looked at that little infant was: Are we going to live to see his *bar-mitzvah*? When his older brother Eli became *bar-mitzvah*, we took Joyce, Shim and Eli to a *sofer* to buy *tefillin*. We examined the *tefillin*, and we also examined the *parshiot*. It was a sort of family gathering—buying *tefillin* for a grandson. The thought came to us: Are we going to live to buy Dovid a pair of *tefillin*? That was our greatest wish.

"But suppose we are not there. Suppose we can't make it. What then? So I bought an Israel Bond for $250, which at maturity would be worth the price of *tefillin* then, and I gave it to Dovid. He was only one year old. We lived to see another year, and we invested another $250 bond. Oh, God forbid in case we can't be there to buy *tefillin*! And so we did continuously for the thirteen years. When he was thirteen Shim said, 'When do we go buy *tefillin*?'

"It was the greatest pleasure that we lived to order *tefillin* from Eretz Yisrael, written by a most prominent *sofer*. It was really a fulfillment, and we didn't touch the bonds. Let the bonds stay there. We paid for it, we enjoyed paying for it. I'm thinking now perhaps . . . maybe . . . *hayad Hashem tiktzor* . . . we will start praying . . . and maybe God will help us live to see him under the *chupah*."

But it was not to be. His younger grandchildren and his great-grandchildren would not have the benefit of having the Rabbi stand beside them under the *chupah*. They would not hear his kind and gentle words encouraging them to treat each other as king and queen. They would not hear him pronounce the blessing in his strong, resonant yet tender voice. But they would always feel his presence in spirit, and the warm embrace of his undying love.

Just weeks after the Rabbi passed away, the Helfgott family celebrated the *pidyon haben* of the newborn son of Penina and Robert Teitelbaum at the Jewish Center. Although the Rabbi was not there in the flesh, his presence was very strongly felt throughout the ceremony. The night before the Rabbi passed away, they had visited him with the infant, and he had mentioned that he was already preparing a *dvar Torah* for the occasion. Unfortunately, it was never delivered. Instead, Shim Helfgott spoke about the legacy his saintly father had left for his grandchildren.

He told the story of a young traveler who came to a crossroads and found the signpost uprooted and lying on the ground. The young man was very distressed. How was he to know which direction to take for the continuation of his journey?

Standing nearby was an old man. "Do not be distressed, young man," he said.

"But how am I to find my way?"

"Do you know from where you have come?" asked the old man.

"Yes, I certainly do."

"Then set up the signpost in such a way that the arrow with your city's name on it is pointing in the right direction. Then you will know all the other directions as well."

Rabbi Helfgott's entire life had been a powerful beacon to his congregants and his family. He had stood for the highest ideals, for the clear separation of right from wrong, for closeness to God and His holy Torah. After his passing, he would no longer be there to give direction to all the people who had looked to him for guidance. But the signpost was still there. As long as they could look with assurance to the past, they would also know the road to the future. The Rabbi had passed away, but his teachings, his insight and his inspiration would live on forever.

Chapter Six

Forever in Our Hearts

he news of the Rabbi's passing struck the broader community of the Jewish Center's congregants and former congregants like a thunderbolt. Shock and disbelief were the most common reaction in the vast outpouring of sympathy and condolences to the bereaved family.

For one thing, the Rabbi gave the impression of having discovered the fountain of youth. "The Rabbi never seemed to age," recalls Sharon Wasserman Margulis. "He looked the same in our 1962 wedding album as he did when we last saw him at my mother's funeral in 1996." The Rabbi was strong, vigorous and bursting with energy and plans for the future. Judith Yuni Kirk echoes the thoughts of just about everyone who knew him when she writes, "We all thought he would live forever." And thus, his sudden passing was totally unexpected and thoroughly shocking.

But perhaps an even deeper reason for the shock was the Rabbi's role in the lives of his congregants. His wisdom, love and genuine devotion to each and every one of his people had earned him an honored place within the nucleus of every family. He was there to provide guidance and comfort in times of need and to share in the celebration in times of joy. No family occasion was complete without his participation. Even when long periods of time passed without contact, the mere knowledge that this wise and caring man was there, ready, willing and able to come at a moment's notice, was a profound stabilizing influence. And thus, when the people heard of the Rabbi's passing, their entire world trembled—for one of the pillars on which it rested was no longer there.

"Our lives changed when Rabbi Helfgott died," writes Yetta Rebacoff with simple eloquence.

"My mother felt an extreme sense of loss when the Rabbi passed away," writes Shana Deitchman. "As long as the Rabbi was alive, she felt a strong sense of comfort and safety in the world. She was just so hard hit when she learned of the Rabbi's passing—and still is. There is an indescribable void in her life because the Rabbi is no longer on this earth."

Even young people and others who did not have a long-standing relationship with the Rabbi felt disoriented by the sudden absence of the bulwark of the community. Judith Yuni Kirk writes: "When we learned that the Rabbi has passed away, the reaction of both our children was, 'Now what are we going to do?' Both had assumed the Rabbi would officiate at their weddings, as he had for their parents and grandparents."

"When I found out that the Rabbi had passed away, I was devastated," writes Sol Greenberg. "My wife Joyce, who had met him just once, about five years ago, said she was as sorry as if he had been a member of the family. That's how much she was impressed by just the one meeting . . . There have been very few sad times in my life, thankfully, but this occasion ranks with the passing of my parents and my sister. May his memory be blessed."

This was the special gift of the Rabbi in his relationship with his congregation. He was the bedrock upon which everything rested and flourished. He provided the guidance, the encouragement, the love, the devotion, the stability and the vision. He was the heart and soul of the congregation, the binding force that held it together, and with his passing, an entire era came to an end. The sacred articles were donated to other Jewish institutions, and the building was sold. Along with its great guide and mentor, the congregation of the Jewish Center of Wakefield and Edenwald closed it's doors.

"I know that with his death the glue holding the Jewish community is gone," writes Nancy Pincus. "In a way, it is fitting that the building be sold and not function as a synagogue. That was truly his life, his pulpit, his community."

"So sad," laments Sharon Wasserman Margulis, "so sad that it's all over."

The era of the Jewish Center of Wakefield and Edenwald had come to an end, but it had enjoyed many years of success. Thousands of people had passed through its doors and had been imbued with the strong sense of Jewishness and Jewish values fostered by the Rabbi. Thousands had enjoyed his wisdom and warmth, and had grown through their association with him. As Shana Deitchman writes so poignantly, "Oh, what a warm sadness overwhelmed me," a sadness colored by warm and sweet memories, a sadness deepened by loss and longing.

"The Rabbi was an integral part of our daily lives," Irving and Stella Lubin recall, "and we, as many others, miss him greatly. Of course, we miss our rabbi, but we also miss our dear friend. We miss the simple yet elegant man who was always there to help us, support us and just be with us. He

Disposition of Religious Articles of the Jewish Center of Wakefield and Edenwald

Cong. Anshe Shalom West Hempstead, NY Rabbi Yehudah Pearl	Rabbi Adelman 5 memorial tablets and all memorial plaques
Cong. Beth Emeth Synagogue Larchmont, NY Rabbi Hershel Portnoy	Benches, 1 memorial tablet, outside Menorah, inside wall Menorah, Bemas Lecturns
Chabad Lubavitch of Westchester Scarsdale, NY Rabbi Velvel Butman	1 standing Menorah, Talis holder, Torah, pointer and breast plate
Yeshiva Chofetz Chaim of Radin Monsey, NY Rabbi Zacks	1 standing Menorah, Torah, and pointer
Olympia Shul-Khal Zichron Erez Monsey, NY Rabbi Levitan	Torah and pointer
Cong. Sons of Israel Bronx,NY Rabbi Moshe Fuchs	Torah and pointer
Cong. Ahavas Achim Highland Park, NJ Rabbi Ronald 1. Schwarzberg	Torah, pointer and breast plate, metal lions on Ark
Young Israel of White Plains White Plains, NY Rabbi Greenberg	Torah Crown and Cemetery property
Young Israel of Smithtown Nesconsett, NY	Main Ark, small Ark

Siddurim and Chumashim were given to members of the congregation.
The Holocaust Plaque was returned to Sidney Brandes.
The front door Mezuzzah was given to Shim Helfgott.

cared about all of us unconditionally, just as parents care for their children. We were most fortunate to have had him as part of our lives for many, many years. We shall now honor his memory by never forgetting his commitment and devotion to all of us. We sincerely hope Rabbi Helfgott realized how loved and respected he was by his congregation, his extended family, since, as in most families, the feelings of love and gratitude were rarely expressed in words."

An amazing outpouring of letters, cards and other communications expressed a depth of feeling that overflows the boundaries of words. But there is also a parallel theme that runs through these communications, an appreciation for the Rabbi's values and teachings and a sense of responsibility in perpetuating them.

"When I lapse into the sadness I feel now that the Rabbi is no longer with us," writes Nathan Eisler, "I try to refocus on the values he instilled in me and the knowledge he passed on to me. This was his message to us about the observance of the memory of the dead."

"Rabbi Helfgott was a truly saintly man," writes Dr. Roy Schoenfeld, "and like all saints, he lives on forever through those whose lives he touched. Thus, while his physical body may have ceased to exist, his essence lives on and on. Did Moses ever die? I say a resounding 'No!'"

"His devotion, wisdom and spirit live on in the hearts of all," write Sam and Jean Kratz, echoing the sentiments of all who knew him.

The Rabbi himself developed this theme on many occasions. In 1984, before Yizkor, he told the congregation, "There is a form of immortality more easily understood than the spiritual existence in the hereafter. I believe that it is for this form of immortality that we pray in the Yizkor formula for our beloved: 'And bind their souls in the bundle of life.' That bundle of life is usually understood to refer to the universal spiritual divine repository of soul material. No, I believe that the reference is to us, the bundle of life into which the memory of our beloved have been deeply imbedded.

"The immortal souls of our beloved have remained implanted in our hearts, in our minds, in our actions, in our very lives. We the living constitute the continuity of the lives of our parents. As we recall the sweet memories of the love of a spouse, a child, parent, brother or sister, a tenderly loving grandparent, they remain tied eternally to our lives and cherished in our hearts. By setting up our loved ones as our constant mentors and advisors, by acting in harmony with their ways of life and wishes, we actually let them guide us from the grave as they did while on earth. They are no longer dead, and they continue to live in our lives and in our constant communion with their souls."

By implanting his values and outlook on life so deeply into the hearts of his family and congregation, the Rabbi had ensured his own immortality. Even as the inexorable passage of time moves us ever further away from the years the Rabbi walked upon this earth, his influence will never fade away. On the contrary, it will continue to grow ever stronger. Each individual who had the good fortune of associating with the Rabbi and of being nurtured by his wisdom and saintliness will carry his teachings and values forward to the next generation. In this way, his influence will pass on to all future generations, reaching countless thousands of people and bringing them closer to God and His Torah.

The passing of the Rabbi was a painful and tragic loss for his family and his congregation, and no amount of consolation can replace the sublime experience of being in the living presence of this remarkable man. And it is perhaps this unyielding sense of irreplaceable loss that stands as the most eloquent tribute to the life of a man of rare greatness.

"All of us here today," Dr. Bernard Potter remarked at the conclusion of his eulogy, "have gathered to pay tribute to this wonderful and saintly human being who has left us richer and wiser for having known him, but poorer and with a deep sense of loss on his passing. The demise of Rabbi Helfgott for me, as I am sure for all of us assembled here, represents the profound loss of a personal treasure."

Memories

The Jewish Center of
Wakefield and Edenwald

Left: Rabbi Helfgott awarding the UJA Scroll of Honor to the Lubins

Below: The 40th Anniversary Dinner

*The Rabbi officiates
at weddings.*

Top:
The Jewish Center's
Annual Minyonnaire
Breakfast

Below: Three
Generations

The Family Gathers

Enjoying the family.

May they grow like Ephraim and Menashe.

The 60th Wedding Anniversary

Section Two:
Selected High Holiday
Sermons

by Rabbi Dr. Benjamin W. Helfgott

Rabbi of The Jewish Center of Wakefield and Edenwald, Bronx, NY

Author of
THE DOCTRINE OF ELECTION IN TANNAITIC LITERATURE

The Secret of Happiness

Rosh Hashanah 5722 1961

My topic for the sermon today is "the Secret of Happiness." I am going to pose a rather impertinent question to you: Why did you come to the synagogue today? The question is addressed only to those who do not come to the synagogue all year. What brought you here today?

I do not question your right to be here. The synagogue is open to everyone who desires to come. Besides, you are either a member and therefore entitled to two seats, or you probably paid for the seat you occupy. My question is: What motivated you to come today? Is it a desire to come and recite prayers? How is it that such a desire does not come to you on the other three hundred and sixty-four days in the year?

You didn't come to listen to my sermons. They are not so attractive. I prepare sermons for every Sabbath throughout the year and preach to a half-empty synagogue. The seats you occupy today accumulate dust the whole year round.

You did not come just because it is the nice thing to do, because your friends and neighbors will be there. No, you are not that naive.

I'll tell you what I believe is the real strong, although

unconscious force that drove you to the synagogue today. Unhappiness! You are unhappy. American Jews are basically an unhappy lot. You are driven to the synagogue to find some inward contentment, a measure of happiness.

We begin the season with a massive exchange of New Year greeting cards. The cards read significantly "A Happy New Year," with the emphasis on the "happy." The greeting does not translate the traditional *Leshanah tovah teikateivu veteichateimu*—May your judgment be inscribed and sealed for a good year. That has reference to the old belief that every human being is judged by the Heavenly Court, presided over by the Supreme Judge of the world.

The mystic assumption was that in the celestial court there is a defender and an accuser. The accuser is synonymous with Satan. The judgment is allegedly inscribed on Rosh Hashanah and sealed on Yom Kippur, and a prayer is established for a good judgment. But that is not expressed in our conventional greeting. We wish for a happy New Year. Because that is what we are lacking—happiness.

Let us first examine the causes for this unhappiness and observe the symptoms.

The American Jewish community is the most fortunate in the long history of our people. The Jewish population in America is estimated at about five and one half million. At no time were there so many Jews in one country under one flag.

We fully enjoy the civil, economic, social and religious privileges without limitation. The Jewish population has risen to the highest levels of our society. We are adequately represented in industry, education, science, politics, military forces and government. Sons of Jewish immigrants hold important Cabinet posts. Jews fill university campuses in the faculties and student bodies. We raise millions annually for local and national Jewish enterprises. What more can a minority ethnic group hope for?

And yet, is the American Jew happy as a Jew? No, he

displays all the symptoms of bewilderment, suspense and uncertainty. We fill the offices of psychiatrists, practitioners and quacks. We are overanxious and overambitious, nervous and uneasy. Books with titles like "Peace of Mind" or "Peace of Soul" are found on every Jewish bookshelf.

What's troubling us?

What's disturbing us?

I believe the American Jew lacks spiritual backbone. That fountain of strength which gives life its meaning and man his dignity has been sapped out of our veins. We have discarded the spiritual wealth we accumulated in the course of centuries. We threw away the Jewish manual of life—the Shulchan Aruch—and found no other spiritual discipline to replace it, leaving us in a vacuum of bewilderment.

Let us take the loss of the Sabbath as an example.

On my way to the synagogue on Saturday morning, I see a young man walking aimlessly. He is one of the millions of other Americans who do not work on Saturday. His children are waiting on line in front of the movies. His wife is doing the week's shopping. The Sabbath has no meaning for the family. On Sunday, the family stays late in bed. They are ashamed to walk down the street and watch their neighbors prepare for church services. All our attempts to transfer the traditional Sabbath observances to Sunday have failed. Our Sunday *bar-mitzvah* celebrations have turned into burlesques. Our Sunday weddings have been removed from the sanctity of the synagogue into bars and restaurants. Even the Sunday funerals have changed from genuine mourning to bagel-and-lox parties. Golf, pinochle or mahjong cannot fill the spiritual vacuum left by the loss of the Sabbath.

There is a striking contrast between the American Jew and the Jew in Israel. The Jew in America, the prosperous graduate of a college or university, lives unhappily amidst wealth and security. The Jew in Israel, a recent graduate of Majdanek or Auschwitz, surrounded by enemies on sight at all borders, lives a happy and contented life without television, refrigerator or automobile.

We have been detecting an aura of arrogance among our Israeli visitors. We are mistaken. It is not arrogance. It is a feeling of self-importance, of dignity and stature. The secret of his happiness is the conquest and recapture of that ancient fountain of life—the Torah. People stemming from different countries, different color and race, speaking diverse languages, have become united in a common heritage, a spiritual heritage which gives meaning to their struggle for human dignity.

Is there room on the American scene for the full expression of the Jewish personality?

Yes, indeed, our prayers for happiness can be realized. The answer can be found in the words of God, "Behold I place before you this day the life and the good, the death and the evil. And you shall choose life."

Our Youth, Wake Up!

Rosh Hashanah 5732 1971

The Haftorah of the first day of Rosh Hashanah tells the story of the birth and commission of the prophet Samuel. The story is old—more than three thousand years old—and yet so beautiful and so vividly told in the opening chapters of I Samuel.

Let me outline for you today the main points of this story. A wealthy farmer named Elkanah, from the town of Ramataim in the hill country of Ephraim, made a habit of an annual pilgrimage to the Sanctuary at Shilo. Every year, after the harvest, he would take his family and go. Elkanah had two wives, Peninah and Hannah. Peninah was the proud mother of many children, while Hannah was childless but beloved by her husband.

One year, while in Shilo, Elkanah brought an offering at the Sanctuary and brought back the parts on which the family would feast. He distributed goodly portions to Peninah and her children and an especially good portion to the childless Hannah. Peninah, jealous of the attention Hannah was getting from her husband, tormented her rival and mocked her infertility. Hannah sat through the feast without eating, only weeping continuously. Elkanah attempted to cheer her up by assuring her he would bring her the comfort of as many as ten children. But Hannah refused to be comforted.

She repaired to the Sanctuary in the darkness; she stood alone crying, praying and mumbling, voicing her entreaty to God—that if He granted her a son she would offer him to the ministry of the Tabernacle.

Eli, the elderly high priest, was in the Sanctuary when he noticed a woman in the darkness moving her lips without a sound.

"You drunk," he scolded her. "Get out of here."

"I'm drunk indeed," was the reply. "Drunk with sorrow, since I am barren without a child."

"May the Lord of Israel accept your prayer," the elderly priest assured her.

With confidence and faith, she returned home and gave birth within a year. She called him Samuel, the gift of God.

Hannah did not join the family on its annual visit to Shilo until Samuel grew up. She remembered her pledge to transfer the boy to the ministry and honored her vow. When Samuel was of age, Hannah brought him to the Sanctuary and introduced him to Eli with the words: "This is the boy for whom I prayed." She prostrated herself in prayer and left the boy in the care of the old priest.

Those were turbulent times. The Philistines were molesting the Tribes of Israel on all borders. The Holy Ark was taken to the battlefront to inspire the armies of Israel, but it fell into the hands of the enemy. The service in the Sanctuary was corrupt. The two sons of Eli, Chofni and Phineas, were notorious for their criminal conduct. And in this atmosphere, Samuel began his youthful ministry.

One night, as the boy Samuel went to bed, he was disturbed by a call. He rushed to Eli and told him about it.

"It's nothing, son," the old man said. "Go back to sleep."

Again Samuel was awakened, his sleep disturbed. Again, the old priest Eli reassured him, "Go back to sleep."

But Samuel could not sleep. He rebelled, and later emerged as the prophet to unite the tribes of Israel under the Davidic Kingdom.

The obvious association of the Haftorah with the Scripture reading of the day is the barrenness of Sarah who was blessed with Isaac and the barrenness of Hannah who was blessed with Samuel. Moreover, according to tradition, both Isaac and Samuel were born on Rosh Hashanah.

But there is a stronger lesson in our Reading of this Haftorah. Before the sounding of the *shofar*, it is appropriate that we read the story of the divine call which Samuel heard and was determined to follow.

For years, we have seen how our young men and women are disturbed by the irritating irrational and international atrocities of our times. They have traveled to the South to fight for civil rights for the persecuted black people. They protest against the war in Vietnam. They are concerned about urban decay, the pollution of the environment and the depletion of our natural resources. They are disturbed by the poverty that darkens the lives of so many people in this rich and wonderful country where we live.

So what do we tell our rebellious youth? Like the old priest told Samuel, we say, "Go back to sleep. Don't worry about these things. Have faith in democracy to bring prosperity and educational equality to all people."

But our youth refuses to be lulled into false dreams. Our youth has heard the divine call, and the time has come to answer it, to stand up and say, *"Hineni!* Here I am!"

We should be proud of our youth for their idealism. And we should also encourage them to direct some of this idealism toward their own people. They should not only protest against urban decay but also against the decay of the Jewish family. They should not only be concerned with the pollution of the environment but also the pollution of the Sabbath. They should not only worry about the depletion of our national natural resources but also the depletion of the spiritual resources of the Jewish home which the immigrants brought with them to these shores.

We need the help of our idealistic youth. Let us ask for it.

May the haunting sound of the *shofar* fill our hearts with a desire to heed the divine call and the determination to dedicate ourselves to goodness, peace and happiness.

Hidden Jews

Yom 5732
Kippur 1971

For a long time, preachers have assumed that the Kol Nidre was inserted into the Yom Kippur ritual to accommodate Marranos visiting the synagogue during the infamous Spanish Inquisition of the fifteenth century. Recent scholarship, however, has discovered that Kol Nidre arose in Spain in the seventh century, before the Mohammedan conquest, when the Jews were grievously persecuted by the ruling Visigoths, who were newly converted to Catholicism. Threatened with torture and death at the stake, the Jews were forced to perjure their faith. But their persecutors knew how little reliance could be placed upon forced conversions of this kind, and they bound the Jews by the most solemn and fearful oaths nevermore to practice any Jewish observances. When the persecution abated and they were able to return openly to their ancestral faith, these Jews felt themselves perjured before God and man. Their consciences were troubled by the oaths they had taken, and it was in order to ease their consciences that this formula of Kol Nidre was instituted. (Rabinowitz, p. 199)

However, the introductory passage to Kol Nidre, recited by the cantor or rabbi holding the scrolls of the Torah, seems to have direct association with the Spanish *anusim*, the Marranos as they were called, victims of the Holy Inquisition. Outwardly living a Catholic life, wearing the crucifix, attending church masses, their children baptized, these secret Jews could not detach themselves completely from their people and religion. At the risk of losing their lives and their properties, these *anusim* made their way clandestinely through subterranean passages to be in synagogues during the recitation of Kol Nidre.

Each member of the congregation would cover his head with his *tallis* so as not to recognize these unfortunate penitents, who were in dead fear of the Inquisition's spies. In a veiled welcome to these penitent brothers, the holy scrolls were taken out of the Ark and held in the hands of the elders of the congregation as the rabbi intoned the apology: "In the presence of the Heavenly Court and the court of the congregation, with the permission of the Almighty and this holy congregation, we declare it now lawful to offer prayer with *avaryonim*."

Avaryonim! Transgressors! Every age has its share. Every country has its group, Jews who—by choice, force or coercion—give up their people and destiny, but cannot detach themselves fully. How tragic is their lot! How pitiful!

The Jerusalem *Post* of last week reported an interview with Professor Dan Meron, a member of an Israeli delegation which recently visited the Soviet Union. Here are the words of Professor Meron: "We visited a synagogue in Odessa and were nearly jumped upon by a *gabbai*, who quite clearly attempted to be around us all the time and keep other people from getting close to us. He did not let us talk with anyone. He gushed out stories of how great the Soviet Union is, and how Jewish religious needs—such as kosher slaughtering and *matzos*—are provided. And he kept on denouncing the hooligans who offended the Soviet Union. The whole impression was hard to bear. We saw before us a Jew who had—how do you say it?—a Jew who had sold out." A modern Marrano in the garb of a *gabbai* in a synagogue.

Professor Meron told of meeting by arrangement a Jewish factory worker who was holding feverishly and nervously a Yiddish newspaper—*Der Birobidzhaner Shtern*—to demonstrate the existence of a Jewish press. The poor fellow turned white when the professor noticed the newspaper was fully a year old.

My friend from the Soviet Union, a lawyer employed as a public defender, visited me two years ago and told me that in June 1967, when the Six-Day War began in Israel, Jews locked their doors, pulled down their window shades and listened to foreign broadcasts throughout the night. In the morning, the Jewish lawyers wished each other *mazal tov*, and then walked into court to condemn the Israeli aggressors. Poor *anusim*!

A visitor to Kiev reported some time ago the story told to him by a *mohel* who circumcises Jewish children in secret at the risk of his life.

In the darkness of the night, there was a knock at the door. The *mohel* opened the door and was faced by an officer of the secret police. The officer ordered the *mohel* to take his instruments and follow him. He blindfolded the *mohel*, and after a long drive in an automobile, he led him to an apartment. When be removed the blindfold, he faced a mother and an infant baby boy. "Our son," said the secret police officer. "We want you to circumcise him." After the circumcision, he blindfolded the *mohel* again and drove him home.

Is this not reminiscent of the Marranos who served as priests and bishops?

During the Russian occupation of Czechoslovakia, a Jewish physician who escaped to Vienna related the following experience: Traveling in his old car, he and his family rushed to reach Austria. As they came closer to the border, they found a Russian tank blocking their way. The tank commander asked them where they were headed, and the physician told him the truth—that he was trying to get to Vienna and from there to escape to Israel. He showed the officer a visa for his family to emigrate to Israel. The officer ordered the tank removed and the road opened. As the doctor and his family were about to depart, the Russian officer said to them in Yiddish, *"Ich bin a Yid. Fort gezunt erheit. Zeit matzliach un bet Gott far unz.* I am a Jew. Have a safe and healthy trip. Good luck, and pray to God for us."

Tonight, hundreds of thousands of Russian *anusim*, denied the privilege of expressing their Jewishness, hidden in their houses or milling around the remnant of a synagogue, are praying: "May the period from this Yom Kippur until the next Yom Kippur bring us relief that we may be reunited with our God, our people and our heritage."

Tonight, we must also express sympathy and compassion for the numerous *avaryonim* in our midst, hundreds of men and women who, for social or economic reasons, have become totally estranged from Jewish life. Others are blinded by pseudo-intellectual glamour to desert the destiny of their people and escape into total assimilation. These men and women hear the cry of Soviet Jewry, of the United Jewish Appeal, and they are not touched. They pass by synagogues with a feeling that they no longer belong to them. But when Yom Kippur comes, a strange magnetism draws them to listen to Kol Nidre or be present when Yizkor is recited.

Synagogues which are practically empty throughout the year fill up on Yom Kippur at Kol Nidre or Yizkor. In brotherly love and forgiveness, we pray with them: *"Selach na la'avon ha'am hazeh.* Pardon, we beseech, the iniquity of this people, according to the greatness of Your mercy."

We invoke the divine response from Scripture: *"Vayomer Hashem, 'Salachti kidevarecha.'* And God said: 'I have pardoned as you have asked.'"

Alas, not all our *avaryonim* return to the synagogue on Yom Kippur. Some have closed even this last gate of mercy.

And yet, there is a spark of Jewish life within them. I meet such *avaryonim* when they come to give their newborn children a Jewish name after a deceased relative. When I ask such a parent his own Jewish name, the answer is, "I don't know. Let me call my uncle, he may know."

I meet these *avaryonim* at weddings, when I ask the bridegroom if his father is a Kohein or a Levi, and his answer is, "My father is a plumber."

I meet these *avaryonim* at *bar-mitzvah* celebrations who, when called to the Torah, stand motionless, as if transported into a Chinese pagoda.

I meet these *avaryonim* at the graves of their parents, where their repetition of the Kaddish sounds like a comic opera of *"Ve-chee-rotcho-te-chee-ko-cho."*

Let us pray for these *avaryonim* as well. Let us pray they remember who they are and where they come from, and that, at least on this holy day of Yom Kippur, they come to join their people in the synagogue.

In the course of the Yom Kippur service, we repeat several times the Al Chet confession. We beat upon our breasts and confess to some forty-four crimes based upon a double alphabetic acrostic.

These confessions appear archaic, outdated, simplistic and innocent. We confess to unchastity, unclean lips, the folly of the mouth, lying, taking bribes, scoffing, slander, wanton eyes and haughty looks. What innocence! How unpractical for modern sophisticated society to beat upon our breasts for such minor behavioral transgressions!

Were I to rewrite these confessions, I would change them to read as follows:

ल *Al chet*—for the sin—we committed in the desecration of the Sabbath. For centuries, our people lived among Moslems and Christians who observed Friday or Sunday as their day of rest. But we steadfastly kept the Sabbath, thereby sanctifying ourselves and our way of life throughout the remainder of the week. We have destroyed our greatest heritage—the Sabbath.

∾ *Al chet*—for the sin—we committed in polluting our homes and bodies with *tarfus* and *chazerei*. The nations of the world respected our disciplined eating and drinking habits. We were known as the Chosen People for our selection of proper food. Our tables were altars, and our dining rooms were temples. Alas, what's happening today? I asked a boy if his father recited the Kiddush on Friday night. And his answer was, "My father comes home too tired on Fridays. He throws off his hat and coat and goes for the grub."

∾ *Al chet*—for the sin—we committed in the neglect of synagogue attendance.

∾ *Al chet*—for the sin—we committed in the neglect of Torah study.

∾ *Al chet*—for the sin—we committed by denying our children a religious education.

These are the sins for which we should repent and beg forgiveness.

As we stand on the threshold of a new year, we are witnessing a new awakening in Jewish American life. Thousands of young men and women are visiting the State of Israel and returning with a new vitality and inspiration to learn and develop in the rejuvenated Jewish culture. There is a new Jewish awakening on college campuses, where ninety percent of Jewish young men and women spend at least four years of their lives. It is encouraging to read of the large Hillel associations and the overcrowded classes in Jewish culture. Despite the vociferous self-hating Leftists, Jewish culture is flourishing on the college campus.

There are also encouraging developments in the education of our children. Because of the decay and decentralization of the urban public school systems throughout the United States, a system of Jewish day schools has sprung up. These schools are reaching thousands of children who are bringing home from their classes a new life and new hope for the future.

In our neighborhoods, the clamor for Jewish social status in suburbia is bringing back to the portals of the synagogue Jewish families who were lost for many years in the melting pots of the urban apartment buildings.

Indeed, we see so much evil and so much good. The Talmud (Kiddushin 40b) states that the world is equally divided between good and evil. We must look upon our surroundings as balancing equally on two scales. By our individual actions, we may tilt the scale either way—for salvation or damnation.

Let us resolve on this holiest of nights to bring out the noblest in the tradition of our people by our individual conduct and behavior. And may we all merit that our Father in Heaven grant us a year of life and peace.

The Outlook for the Future

Rosh Hashanah 5733 1972

*I*n an apparent play on the similarity of sound of the Hebrew verbs for "to end" and "to begin," the liturgist implores: *"Tichleh shanah vekileloseha, teichal shanah ubirchoseha*. Let the outgoing year end with its curses, and the new year come with its blessings."

Does this prayer reflect our natural habit of remembering only our difficulties of the past and ignoring our blessings? Would a true appraisal of American Jewry of the past year reveal only curses?

Each individual may have had his ups and downs in health, in business, in family relations. As a people, however, as an American Jewish people—call it ethnic, religious, national, racial or whatever—with a common interest and destiny, has the past year been a failure?

Let us also examine the prospects for the new year. The liturgy speaks hopefully of its blessings. How promising does the future look at the threshold of the new year?

The American Jewish Yearbook speaks of six million Jews in the Untied States. At no time in the long history of our people have six million Jews been gathered in one country under one flag enjoying the benefits of democracy available to all its citizens. At no time in the history of our people did six million of us enjoy such freedom of worship, freedom of speech and freedom of residence and movement. We know there are some Americans who do not like us. That's their sinister privilege. We don't like them either. And there it ends.

We constitute approximately three percent of the total population, a very small minority indeed, but our importance is far beyond our numbers. On a religious level, we are rated together with the dominant faiths of Catholics and Protestants; one speaks of Catholics, Protestants and Jews.

In literature, the arts, the theater, our influence, position and contribution are great. Books on Jewish theories are prominent on the best-seller lists throughout the country.

In industry, Jews hold leading positions in commerce, in the manufacture of soft goods, in the service professions of law, medicine, accounting, communications and psychoanalysis.

Colleges have numerous Jews on their faculties, in their administration and student bodies. It is predicted that within a decade ninety percent of American Jewish boys and girls will receive a college education.

Jewish cultural, social and religious life has intensively increased in the last year. From coast to coast, Jewish day schools and *yeshivot* are mushrooming, with thousands of boys and girls trained and reared in the best traditions of our people and American society. Jewish publications in Hebrew and English have flourished. More and costlier synagogues are erected in the new suburbs of the old Jewish establishments—each enjoying large membership rolls and huge mortgages. American Jews take pride in their synagogue membership and communal leadership.

In diplomatic and political participation, American Jews certainly have good reason to be satisfied. As we watch the presidential election campaign [of 1972], we get the impression that the dominant issue is how pro-Jewish each of the candidates promises to be. We deny the existence of a Jewish vote, but we proclaim our interest in America, in Israel and in helping save Soviet Jewry. With a sense of pride and apprehension, we regard the prominent positions held by American Jews in the previous Democratic and present Republican administrations.

As a people, can we conscientiously pray that the old year end with its curses? What more can the American Jewish community aspire to?

Let us now look at the other side of the coin.

Recent statistical studies have shown that the American Jewish birth rate is no more than 1.5 percent per year, far below the American standard. Jews are not producing large families, much less than the 2.1 children per family needed for a population to remain stable. We are becoming a minority of oldsters. The median age of the total United States population is thirty, of the Jews thirty-seven. Lack of children means intermarriage and declining voting power.

The scourge of intermarriage has widened. As the late Rabbi Stephen Wise remarked, every case of intermarriage is another stab into the American Jewish heart. Young men and women in rural areas and on out-of-town campuses are prone to interdating and intermarriage. Each one represents not only a loss of one person but also that of a potential family. The increase in intermarriage has prompted some sociologists to bemoan the "vanishing American Jew."

With all the rising synagogues and institutions of learning, Jewish masses of young and old display a sorrowful ignorance of and indifference to basic Jewish values and principles. Jewish homes have lost their reverence and sanctity.

We boast of successful Jewish courses in major colleges, while the majority of our youth spend four or more of their best years physically and spiritually estranged from Jewish life.

We have seen some of our more talented young people

resort to the drug sub-culture with a distinct distaste for our traditional habits of temperance, modesty and discipline. We are shocked to see so many of our young folks in the ranks of the so called New Left, some with open pro-Arabic biases. Some irresponsible evangelists are parading young Jewish boys and girls in their new soul-snatching Jesus movement. The spiritual thirst of these young children is being satisfied with a new poison.

As we approach the new year, the challenge to particular Jewish interest by the intense black revolution can no longer be ignored. As an urban people, we are on the first line of victims, the Jewish landlord, the Jewish storekeeper, the Jewish schoolteacher, the Jewish welfare caseworker are the personification of the hated "white establishment." In the course of the year, additional Jewish properties have been lost, Jewish neighborhoods evacuated, Jewish jobs threatened, Jewish institutions deserted. Moreover, in their blind surge for power, some black demagogues have resorted to crude and blatant anti-Semitism and Jew-baiting.

It is remarkable that in the areas of black and Jewish conflict, the white non-Jewish upper middle-class population remains aloof and unconcerned. These blacks are the people we trained in civil rights. We financed their justified claims to equality and justice. Now they have joined the foreign legion of Al Fatah.

Is it not paradoxical?

On the one hand, American Jews have gained the highest position since the beginning of the Diaspora, and on the other hand, they are threatened with assimilation, prejudice and rebellion.

The prophets of doom review the scene and compare the situation with pre-Hitler Germany. They foresee a tide of anti-Jewish sentiment that may, God forbid, lead to the destruction of our great Jewish society. To follow the maledictions of the extremist Rabbi Meir Kahane, American Jews should pack up and emigrate *en masse* to Israel. Little do these extremists realize the dependence of Israel on a creative American Jewish community. Disregarding the frivolous suggestion of the conservative William Buckley that Israel join the U.S. as the fifty-first state, Israel depends upon American military and economic aid, upon tourism and Jewish American investments.

The story is told of a Jewish girl who was missing from home for a week and then called her mother to tell her she had eloped and married.

Ma: "Can we come see you, dear? Where are you?"

Daughter: "No, we have no place for you to stay. My husband has no job."

Ma: "Come home with your husband, then. We'll take care of both of you."

Daughter: "I can't bring him home. He is not Jewish."

Ma: "That's all right. Don't tell anyone, and no one will know he is not Jewish."

Daughter: "But he is black, Mommy."

Ma: "Bring him home, dear. You know we are a liberal-minded family."

Daughter: "But we have only one bedroom, so where are we going to sleep?"

Ma: "I have it all figured out. You two will sleep in the bedroom, and Papa will sleep on the couch in the living room."

Daughter: "And where will you sleep, Mommy?"

Ma: "Don't worry about me, dear. As soon as you hang up the phone, I am jumping out the window."

Without a strong and influential American Jewish community, the international position of Israel is very precarious.

The solution to our domestic problems of threatening assimilation and social and economic conflict cannot be met by a mass emigration to Israel. Such a movement may endanger both the Jewish communities here and in Israel.

What we need is a united and concerted plan of action to

intensify Jewish education and training. We must reevaluate our goals in American Jewish life in the light of changing conditions. Our federated charities that collect and spend millions to erect hospitals, orphanages, old age homes—some of which cater only to a small percent of Jewish patients—must recognize the greater needs of the community in the schools and colleges. Bnai Brith, American Jewish Congress, Synagogue Councils and Y's should turn their attention to the civil rights of Jewish communities, such as the housing problem in Forest Hills, the contract problems with local boards of education, public aid to private schools and similar challenges.

There is an old traditional custom on Rosh Hashanah eve—to recite the Kiddush over a cup of wine before the festive meal and add the benediction Shehecheyanu. We thank Heaven for our lives, our sustenance that enabled us to reach this day. We make the Hamotzi blessing over the *challah*, dip it into honey and recite, "May the New Year be good and sweet."

Let us face the New Year with thankfulness for the past and confidence for the future.

The Ingathering of the Exiles

Rosh Hashanah
5733 1972

here is an account in I Kings, Chapter 8, of the dedication of the First Temple on Mount Moriah. We read, "And Solomon stood before the altar of God in the presence of all the congregation of Israel and spread forth his hands toward Heaven and said . . . 'If a man sins against his neighbor and he comes and swears before Your altar in this House, then hear You in Heaven . . . When Your people are smitten down before the enemy, when they sin against You, if they turn again to You, and confess Your Name, and pray and make supplication to You in this House, then hear You in Heaven, and forgive the sin of Your people Israel, and bring them back into the land which You gave to their fathers. . . . Moreover, concerning the stranger that is not of Your people Israel, when he shall come from a far country for the sake of Your Name . . . when he shall come and pray toward this House, hear You in Heaven, Your dwelling-place, and do according to all that the stranger calls to You.'"

King Solomon dedicated the Temple three thousand years ago. That Temple was destroyed twenty-five centuries ago, and its successor Temple was destroyed nineteen centuries ago, but Solomon's dedicatory prayer is being fulfilled today before our very eyes. The fulfillment does not take place on the Temple Mount, but within the area in the square below the remnants of the Western part of the outer wall of the Temple Mount. That Wall is never deserted, not by day nor by night. It personifies the *kibbutz galuyot*, the ingathering of the exiles. Men and women, young and old, of all faiths, shade or color, mingle together in reverence and exultation.

As we approached the Kotel in midafternoon, the sound of a plaintive voice emanating from a troubled soul came from the northern corner. A mother and child, hand in hand, pressed their lips in prayer against the moist rocks. A silent young man, a knapsack on his back, lowered his head between the cracks of the faded stones in silent supplication. A *chassidic rebbe* sat at the guard's booth distributing cakes in celebration of a *simchah*. Thousands of people from all over the world join hands and voices in the inauguration of the Sabbath on Friday evenings, and nearly one hundred thousand visit the shrine on Tishah b'Av, commemorating the Destruction of the Temple.

The late Chief Rabbi Kook remarked: "There are humans with hearts of stone, and there are stones with human hearts."

Five times a day the shrill voice of the *muezzin* on the Al Aqsa Mosque shrieks through the hills and vales of the Temple Mount, reverberating over the huge rocks of the Western Wall, as he calls the Moslem faithful to worship Allah.

The bells of the Holy Sepulcher, the cathedrals and chapels encircling the Temple Mount continuously chime and ring all around the Wall.

Nothing interferes with the inspiration of the thousands of pilgrims in whose hearts heaven and earth meet in sacred symphony of chant and prayer fervently expressed in awe and joy as they gaze upon this magnetic Wall.

The *kibbutz galuyot*, dramatized by the multitudes gathered at the Wall, is reflected in the whole miracle embodied in the State of Israel. From Mount Hermon to Eilat, cities, towns, *moshavim* are bursting out of their limits in a spread of sturdy, rising luxury apartment houses, evenly spaced along wide roadways and parks.

Military establishments, huge chemical and industrial plants teeming with steam and power, department stores, supermarkets, hotels and skyscrapers are sprouting all over the country. All along the Mediterranean coast, the Dead Sea coast and the Negev, construction, road building and landscaping goes on incessantly.

In 1948, immediately after the establishment of the State of Israel, there was a popular song which asked:

Where shall I go, where shall I go?

Now, I know where to go. I know where to go!

Indeed, they are coming in by the thousands. They are coming from everywhere—from North Africa, Russia, Romania, Western European countries, as well as the United States. Absorption centers are spread all over the country. And every immigrant is made welcome.

The *kibbutz galuyot,* the hospitable settlement and ingathering of the exiles, seems to be the foremost responsibility of the government and people of Israel. I visited a number of homes of recent Russian, Romanian and American *olim.* They live free in comfortable, airy, well-furnished and adequately supplied apartments. They are given training, assistance and opportunities to assume useful lives as members of their communities. The native population of Israel does not enjoy a portion of the comforts they offer to the new *olim.*

What power draws these thousands to the shores of Israel? Is it simply to enjoy a better life? The Russian Jews arriving in Israel are not the most religious, and American Jews are not escaping persecution or fear of imminent assimilation.

I have talked at length to a number of families in an attempt to identify the exact motives for their leaving careers, houses and friends in exchange for a new life in strange surroundings. I was particularly puzzled by young families from

North and South America subjecting their young children to a new language and foreign habits. Israel is not a refuge, but a haven. As expressed by one American family: "We did not escape *from* a place. We escaped *to* Israel."

I found a whole range of reasons for immigrating to Israel. Some were disillusioned or discontented with their former lives. Some wanted to improve their economic prospects. Many came to escape a *galut* complex, the self-consciousness of a Jew living in the Diaspora. Some were simply moved by the spirit of adventure. And then there were true faithful, people seeking a better atmosphere for religious living.

The basic underlying reason, however, is to feel at home. Only in Israel can a Jew have that unqualified feeling of belonging. It is his land where he can live as he likes as a Jew, where he is accepted because he is a Jew.

As we approach the New Year, Israel faces great problems: The security situation has been much eased. There is no sense of fear anywhere in Israel. Police and security forces are alert to Arab terrorism, but the fear and panic to which we are accustomed in our large cities does not exist in Israel. I had the good fortune of being in Israel two years ago when the Suez cease-fire was accepted, and this summer when the Russian "advisors" were evacuated. Two years ago, many young men and women were seen carrying machine guns and rifles. Last summer, they were promenading in the sun and pushing baby carriages.

The problem now is not so much the hostile Arabs across the border as the more than a million Arabs within the new borders. These Arabs certainly enjoy better living conditions now than they did under Egyptian and Jordanian occupation, but their future and ultimate adjustment presents a challenge to the State of Israel.

There is also fear of civil strife between extremist religious and anti-religious factions. The political system in Israel is constantly threatened by this unresolved strife. Inflation, cheap Arab labor, housing shortages and the adjustment of immigrants are also great problems.

The old religious-national messianic enthusiasm has been formalized into a practical way of life. The sacred Hebrew language is now a living tongue in the classroom, the market, in comics, satire, discotheques and literature as well as in prayer. We are faced with the normalcy of filthy streets, pushy shoppers, stinking *shuks* and sharp business dealers.

But as expressed to me by a former American young mother, "We love it here. We love to be Jews."

In the Haftorah we recited today, Jeremiah bespeaks the *kibbutz galuyot* in the Name of the Lord: "Behold, I will bring them from the north country, and gather them from the extremities of the earth . . . I will cause them to walk by the rivers of waters, in a straight way, wherein they shall not stumble . . . then shall the maiden rejoice in the dance, both young men and old together; for I will turn their mourning into joy, and will comfort them, and make them rejoice from their sorrow."

Let us hope and pray that as we are seeing the fulfillment of the *kibbutz galuyot* as predicted by the prophet Jeremiah, so may we live to see the rejoicing, happiness and peace which he also predicted.

The Yom Kippur Trial

Yom 5733
Kippur 1972

*T*he therapeutic, soul-cleansing tones of Kol Nidre grip the heart of man regardless of how far removed he may be from religious experience. Whether rendered by an orchestra, a solo by a cellist or a humble *baal tefillah*, it never fails to stir the innermost emotions, raising the listener into the spheres of solemnity. A simple congregation of men and women gathered to hear Kol Nidre undergoes a metamorphosis from the mundane to the heavenly, from mortals to angels. A spiritual cleanliness permeates the synagogue. The saintly Rabbi Akiva called out: "How fortunate you are, Israel! Who is it that cleanses you, and before Whom are you cleansed? *Avinu shebashamayim!* It is our Father in Heaven!"

The *chassidic rebbe* Rabbi Levi Yitzchak of Berditchev, who lived in the second half of the eighteenth century, was known as the "Lover of Israel" because he could not countenance any aspersions against the Jewish people. In his mind, there was no bad Jew, and he would defend every Jewish action before God and man. The Berditchever Rebbe was nicknamed "Der Derbaarimdiger," the Compassionate One, because in his pleas he addressed God as "Derbaarimdiger Gott."

He once looked at his Kol Nidre congregation, seated as they were, men, women and children, then he turned and addressed God as follows: "Derbaarimdiger Gott! Jewish law requires us to indulge heavily in eating and drinking on the day before Yom Kippur. It has been a *mitzvah* to eat and drink a whole day. Let us imagine that the non-Jewish peasants in Berditchev would be given a day on which they were told in the Name of God to eat and drink more and more. What would happen on the night after such a day? They would be sick with vomit, nausea, fighting or wallowing in saloons. Now, look at Your people Israel. They had a full day's *mitzvah* of eating and drinking lavishly, and still there is not a single person absent from Kol Nidre. They are all here, solemn, clean, sober." With this statement, the *rebbe* began the chant of Kol Nidre.

The theme for my message tonight is based on another Yom Kippur story about Rabbi Levi Yitzchak of Berditchev. The *rebbe* noticed a tailor standing and arguing during the services rather than reciting the prayers.

"Why don't you pray?" he asked the tailor.

"I have been having a discussion with the Ribono shel Olam," the tailor answered, "and I offered Him a good deal. I told God like this: 'It's true, I confess, that I committed sins this past year. When I get an order to sew up a suit of clothes, they bargain me down to the limit, so that I cannot earn anything. Well, I steal a little material from the pants, from the coat—that's the only way I can earn a livelihood for my family.' That, I told God, was my confessed sin for the past year. But then I reminded God of His sins of last year. 'Look at all the people who have suffered illness and poverty. Men have died, and You have caused so many children to be orphaned. You have widowed innocent women; for life and death are in Your hands.' So I told God, 'I'll make a deal with You. You'll forgive my sins, and I'll forgive Your sins.'"

The Berditchever Rebbe looked at the tailor. "You fool," he

said. "With an argument like that you should have asked forgiveness for the whole community."

You are all familiar with the imagery expressed in the Unesaneh Tokef. We picture God on Yom Kippur as a Great Judge, seated on a throne, presiding over a Heavenly Court. Each of us comes up for trial. There is a file on each person, on his past activities, failures and accomplishments. The Judge examines our records, and issues decrees—who shall live and who shall die . . . Being human, we can only measure the Divine in human terms. Our liturgy has added color to the Heavenly Court. We speak of a *kateigor*, a prosecutor who demands punishment for our sins and transgressions, and a *saneigor*, a defense attorney who pleads our case and claims for us a favorable judgment.

What is our petition to the Supreme Judge? We ask for His greatest gift: Remember us for life! And as the day progresses, we become bolder in our requests and pray for life, blessing, peace and prosperity.

Our soul, part of the Divine, is actually the seat of the Heavenly Court, and the trial takes place in our very conscience. In it takes place the struggle of the *kateigor* and *saneigor*, the prosecutor and defender, personified in the theological divisions of the good and evil instincts in human nature.

Let us for a moment place ourselves on the witness stand with the *kateigor* asking the questions.

"You are requesting life," the *kateigor* says to us, "good life for the New Year. Let's examine your record. Did you respond favorably when you were asked to give help for life? Did you help the poor, the aged, the needy, the sick? For example, U.J.A. appeals assist the lives of thousands. How did you care for these lives? The aged in nursing homes and the unfortunate in hospitals are crying for life. How did you respond to their cries? You are asking for prosperity. In the course of the year, did you consider that your fellow-workers and your employees are also entitled to prosperity?"

Suppose the *kateigor* asks us: "Where have you been all year? We have not seen you since last Yom Kippur. Is it only when we are distributing good life and prosperity that you come to the synagogue? You are expected to be there throughout the year!"

In the introduction to the Kol Nidre, we take out the Torah scrolls and intone the formula of court action in the following words: "With permission of the celestial and congregational courts, we shall worship tonight with the *avaryonim.*" *Avaryonim* are transgressors or traitors. Who were those *avaryonim*? Tradition ascribes the reference to the Marranos, the baptized Jews in fifteenth century Spain and Portugal who took the risk of secretly entering a synagogue on Yom Kippur eve.

Why were these unfortunate people insulted by the congregation and addressed as transgressors, *avaryonim*? Why didn't the congregation demonstrate compassion and understanding for the Marranos?

The answer is that the congregation despised these intruders who lived a life of good Christians throughout the year, retaining their positions, wealth, properties and education, while the congregation maintained synagogue services, education and Jewish responsibilities with utmost difficulty. How could they regard these once-a-year Jews?

The *kateigor* in our own conscience may ask the question, "Where were you all year?"

Originally, Kol Nidre was written entirely in the past tense. It was a Rabbinic formula seeking to annul religious, that is purely religious, rash vows and promises unfulfilled. In the course of the centuries, the ritual was amended to include a hope and resolution for the future. Now we say: "May the period from this Yom Kippur to the coming Yom Kippur be good. With contrite heart, we acknowledge our human frailties and failings and beg forgiveness for transgressions of omission and commission."

To quote the Berditchever Rebbe again: Each *Yom Kippur* he would address God and say, "I know I made promises last year, and the year before, and the year before that, but now I really mean it."

Man's greatness is demonstrated in his humility. To admit to error and acknowledge a mistake is a virtue. A contrite heart is a good heart. Scripture submits to man's frailty and inadequacy by admitting: "There is no one so saintly as to always do good and never sin."

There are the notorious sinners mentioned in Scripture:

Adam was the first man on earth and the first sinner. He was told not to eat from the Tree of Knowledge, but he ate anyway. After he sinned, he ran away and went into hiding. When caught, he was asked, "Did you eat from the forbidden fruit?" But he did not confess and ask forgiveness. He blamed his wife. He was a coward. We are told that he lost Paradise and brought death to posterity.

King Saul was commissioned to destroy Amalek. He won the battle, but spared the life of Agag, the king of Amalek. He also took forbidden booty. When the prophet Samuel admonished him for defying the Will of God, did Saul confess and beg forgiveness? Saul was a great hero. We are told that he stood head and shoulders above all men. But he was not big enough to admit his error. Saul blamed the mob. Saul eventually lost his life and honor.

King David sinned. He fell in love with a married woman. The Rabbis in the Talmud excused David's actions, but King David himself accepted the chastisement of the prophet. He acknowledged his guilt. He confessed and begged God's forgiveness. He showed himself to be humble and big enough to win dynastic royalty for himself and posterity. Like King David, let us seek forgiveness so that we can respond to the call of this Yom Kippur Day.

When Death Counts

Yom 5733
Kippur 1972

At the traditional Yizkor service, we gather *en masse* in synagogues to commune in spirit with our loved ones. We remember with love our parents, grandparents, sisters, brothers. Some unfortunate parents recall the loss of a loving child. The synagogue is filled with a symphony of sacred images and endearing memories which neither time nor death can remove.

There is another Yizkor service in the course of the day. It is recited at the conclusion of the Mussaf in the poem entitled Eileh Ezkerah. In it, we recount the martyrdom of the Ten Sages executed in the Roman suppression of the Jewish rebellion during and after the Destruction of the Temple. The Ten Martyrs included: Rabbi Ishmael, the High Priest; Rabban Simeon ben Gamaliel, the Patriarch; Rabbi Akiva; and other renowned Sages.

This year, it will be the sad privilege of our generation to add to the list of our national martyrs eleven names of young athletes massacred by Arab terrorists four days before Rosh Hashanah in Munich, Germany. These Israeli athletes, who had come to Israel from all the corners of the earth, including the United States and the Soviet Union, were in Munich to participate in the international Olympic games. They were murdered brutally before the eyes of the whole world.

The following story about suffering comes to mind. R. Zushe and R. Elimelech was observing *galut*, voluntary exile, in preparation for *chassidic* leadership. R. Zushe had a reputation as a man of suffering. Once, they stopped at an inn for the night and found that the only place to sleep was on a hard bench. Moreover, there was only room for one person. R. Elimelech volunteered to sleep on the floor under the bench and let his colleague, R. Zushe, sleep on the bench. That night, some soldiers came to the inn, and after getting drunk, they noticed the two sleeping Jews. They pulled R. Zushe off the bench and beat him up.

The next night, R. Elimelech said to R. Zushe, "Last night, you suffered the beating. It is only fair that tonight I should suffer. Let me be the one to sleep on the bench tonight." So R. Elimelech slept on the bench, and R. Zushe slept on the floor. Again the soldiers came, and after drinking, they prepared to beat up the Jews. This time, however, they remarked, "Last night, we beat up the fellow on the bench. Tonight, let's get the fellow under the bench." Once again, R. Zushe was the one to suffer.

"*Oyf tzu shtarben darf men oich haben mazal*," goes the Yiddish expression. "Even for suffering one needs *mazal*."

The story is also told of a cantor who was negotiating a contract with a congregation and insisted that he be paid half his money right after Yom Kippur and the other half right after Passover.

The congregation objected, saying, "What happens if you die after Passover? It's still half a year to the next Rosh Hashanah. We won't have a cantor, and you will have gotten all your money."

The cantor replied, "So if I die, it will be my *mazal*."

Let us consider the suffering of the Jewish people under the Romans. Half the Jewish population of Judea was massacred, imprisoned, enchained or sold into slavery during the rebellion against the Roman occupation. History records their bravery, but only the Ten Sages are eulogized in the Talmud and Midrash. The others did not have the *mazal*.

And how about the *mazal* of our Israeli athletes? The whole world watched breathlessly as German mediators tried to make a deal with the Arab terrorists for the safety of the Israeli athletes. Reluctantly, the leaders of the Olympics even suspended the games during the negotiations for the eleven Jewish lives. And when their dead bodies were discovered, there was an international outcry of horror and expressions of sympathy for Israel.

It is difficult to ascertain the sincerity of the world reaction to the Munich massacre. Four days after the tragedy, the Security Council of the United Nations, with fifteen delegates representing the five great powers and ten leading nations of the world, was ready to condemn Israel for its retaliation, but not the Arab terrorists for their heinous crime. Perhaps the original expression of horror was for the spirit of the Olympiad, which had been marred, and the schedule of games, which had been disturbed.

At any rate, the tragedy of Munich reverberated all over the civilized world. Israel retaliated in force, and the German government offered reparations to the families of the victims.

Eight miles northwest of Munich lies the town of Dachau. Between 1943 and the end of World War II, not eleven, but thousands, no, hundreds of thousands of Jews—men, women and particularly children—were maimed, tortured and burned to death, not by suicidal Arab maniacs but by the elite German *Herenvolk*. The mass murders were scientifically planned in minute detail and carried out. The whole world watched complacently and indifferently as six million—not eleven—were herded together in the most gruesome, cruel and inhuman conditions and sent to the slave camps and extermination in Majdanek, Buchenwald, Bergen-Belsen, Treblinka and Dachau.

There has been a tendency in recent years to deprecate the martyrdom of the six million Jewish victims of Nazi brutality and world indifference to Jewish suffering. Young people, even in Israel, seek to forget this episode of total inhumanity.

Others want to know why the victims did not resist.

Resist whom? A cruel and inhuman world! Resist how? They had no Phantom jets, no tanks, no cannons. All they had was their faith, and with their faith, they resisted. Facing death, they chanted the Ani Maamin, "I believe in the coming of a Messianic period in which our people will find a refuge in a new world."

Only in the Warsaw ghetto was there even the slightest opportunity for resistance, and the heroic struggle of the Warsaw Uprising will go down in the annals of history as the greatest expression of self-sacrifice ever. Thirty thousand starved and emaciated remnants of a half-million expatriated Jews, with sticks and knives as weapons, fought back. They challenged the Nazi war machine and took a terrific toll of the enemy until nearly all of them were crushed or burned to death.

An example of a different kind of heroism is told in a letter from one of a group of ninety-three girls. The letter was written by a girl named Haya Feldman on Rosh Chodesh Elul, 5704. These ninety-three girls, students of a Beth Jacob School in Warsaw at the time of the Nazi occupation, were told they were being removed to a life of prostitution at the mercy of their tyrannical captors. They all committed suicide. The girl, in her letter, describes their preparation and sentiments as they sacrificed themselves on the altar of decency and honor. The poet Hillel Bavli paraphrased the letter as follows:

We cleansed our bodies and we are pure,
We cleansed our spirits and are at peace.
Death does not frighten us,
We shall meet it calmly.

We served God with our life,
We shall know how to hallow His Name in death.
A solemn covenant binds the ninety-three of us:
Together we studied God's Torah,
Together we shall die.
We read Psalms aloud and are comforted,
We confessed our sins,
And our hearts grew strong.
Now we are ready to depart.
Let the unclean ones come to defile us;
We do not fear them!
Before their eyes we shall drink the cup of poison and die,
Innocent and pure, as befits daughters of Jacob,
We shall pray before mother Sarah and say to her:
"We have come,
We met the test of the binding of Isaac,
Come, pray with us for the people of Israel."
Grant mercy, O Father of mercy,
To the people that have known You,
There is no more mercy in mortal man.
Reveal Your love now concealed,
Rescue and redeem Your afflicted people,
Purify and preserve Your world.
The hour of Neilah has come,
Our hearts are quiet.
Our last request to you, our brethren, wherever you are:
Recite the Kaddish for us,
For the ninety-three maidens of Israel.

As we immortalize the eleven victims of Munich, we must not forget the millions of Dachau. The memory of these *kedoshim* must remain a testament to a disgraceful world that sank to a level of cannibalism with regard to our people.

Jewish Indifference: The Enemy Within

Rosh Hashanah 5734 1973

An esoteric passage in the Talmud (Arachin 10b) reports the following celestial dialogue between God and His angels: "The Holy Blessed One was asked by His ministering angels: 'Master of the Universe, why doesn't Israel chant the festival Psalms on Rosh Hashanah and Yom Kippur?' He answered them: 'Is it conceivable that when the King sits on the throne of judgment, the Books of Life and Death open before Him, that Israel should chant hymns of joy?'"

A synagogue attracts a large congregation on Rosh Hashanah and Yom Kippur. There is the natural temptation to make use of this large attendance to expound before you the religious philosophy of the High Holidays, the historical and eschatological significance of *tekiat shofar*, the universal aspects of our cosmogony as richly reflected in the Rosh Hashanah liturgy.

But can we ignore the pressing issues of the day and indulge in the luxury of speculative religious ideas? Can we afford to chant the hymns of joy while the books of our religious life and death are open? To hide the impending problems in a cloak of peaceful pietistic expressions and wishful thinking is to emulate the jubilant promises of the ancient false prophets who preached, *"Shalom, Shalom!* Peace, peace!"—when there is no peace!

Moreover, from the selections of the Torah readings on both days of Rosh Hashanah, we may discern a direction toward a deeper introspection into the welfare of our families, our children, our grandchildren, the families of our friends and neighbors. In the beginning of the New Year, we should examine carefully the problems that challenge the physical, emotional and spiritual welfare of our families.

On the first day of Rosh Hashanah, we read the Scripture portion about Abraham's concern with the behavior of his older son, Ishmael. His mother Hagar, a product of the wild desert, ran away from home with the boy. She later returned, and her son proved to be a bad influence upon his younger brother Isaac.

On the second day of Rosh Hashanah, we read the Scripture portion about Abraham's desire to raise Isaac in the ways of God. We also read about his response to the divine call to sacrifice his beloved son to God.

Let us similarly ask this morning before *tekiat shofar*, which reminds us of the sacrifice of Isaac: How well do we fare with our Isaacs, our Rebeccas, our Ishmaels and our Hagars?

We have already become accustomed to see our youth inspired by the counter-culture. Jewish hippies. Yippies. Some are turned on to the New Left. Others join the blacks in the Third World movement. You find them on campus, off campus, East Village, West Village—that has become normal. But Jews for Jesus? Young Jewish boys and girls in the ranks of the Jesus Freaks, Jesus People? That has not been heard of since the infamous Spanish Inquisition.

We don't know their exact numbers; they may reach into the thousands. But as small in numbers as they may be, they are arrogant, vociferous and challenging. They use campus meetings, radio and television, large public meetings to spread their venomous gospel to other Jewish kids. How ironic! Here in the United States, where Jews enjoy the utmost freedom of religion, where they are fully respected for their religious conduct, in such a tolerant atmosphere, unparalleled in our long history, young Jews would become victims of a Jesus movement! It took the organized Jewish community by surprise—Jews for Jesus!

The Deuteronomic curse of the Tochachah has lashed its scourge upon our generation: "Your sons and your daughters shall be given unto another people, and your eyes shall look and fail with longing for them all day; and there shall be naught in the power of your hand . . . So that you shall be mad for the sight of your eyes which you shall see." (Deuteronomy 28:32-34)

Jews for Jesus—sheer madness! The first reaction to this monstrosity from national Jewish leaders was to blame the recently increased Jesus agitation and concentrated missionary activity. After a decade of ecumenism and Jewish-Christian dialogue, we realized that we are back to the old mission to the Jews. The modern mission is more dramatic, widespread, sponsored by the union of Catholics and Protestants. Under the glamorous title of Key 73, no distinction is made between Christian and Jew. The mission is directed to Christians and Jews alike.

But we know that Christian missionary activity is not new. We have become immune to it in the course of centuries. Christian missions were always active in Jewish communities without success. They were looked upon with disgust and mockery. You cannot stop Christian missions to the Jews. Following the Pauline epistle, Christians must try to salvage the lost Jewish souls. Unfortunately, in their enthusiasm to save our souls, they first destroyed our bodies. Regardless of its intensity, Christian missionary work among Jews has been a failure.

To blame Key 73 or condemn the Broadway musical *Jesus*

Christ Superstar is not the solution to our problem. Let us rather search ourselves for the reason young Jews are more prone today to accept the missionary gospel than they were a generation ago. The missionary is the same, his gospel is the same, his tactics are the same. His Jewish potential victim has changed, however. He has softened. The missionary succeeds where we fail! The missionary fills the spiritual vacuum left by ignorance and indifference to Jewish knowledge, Jewish sentiment and Jewish experience.

Our homes, regrettably, have lost their grip upon the development of the Jewish character of our sons and daughters. The home experience of the Sabbath, the dietary regulations, the *tallit* and *tefillin*, the Sabbath candles, the *tzitzit*, the Modeh Ani in the morning and the Kriat Shema at night no longer serve as safeguards for our children's emotional development. At best, we rely on the local synagogue or temple and its school. At best, we give the child the opportunity of a couple of hours a week during the winter to prepare for the *bar-mitzvah* or *bat-mitzvah* celebration. At thirteen or twelve, all their Jewishness comes to an end. "*Baruch sheptarani!*" the parents declare. "Blessed is the One who absolved me of responsibility!" The parents are rid of responsibility for their child's religious growth, and the child is rid of his Jewishness.

With a childish appreciation of his meager religious studies, without the imprint on his character of the beauty of Jewish life and experience, the child goes through high school, still bewildered by the orgies of his *bar-mitzvah* or *bat-mitzvah* party. In this state of confusion, he proceeds to the college classroom. He is now exposed to the adult influences, good or bad, of the majority culture or counter-culture. He cannot find a soul in the test-tube, and he learns for the first time that the earth may be older than his Hebrew teacher told him. The sensitive boy or girl may take a course in comparative religion or religious literature, taught in the spirit of Western civilization or Christian civilization, and thereby become exposed to Church history and to Christian theology.

Recently, I was visited by a young man, a former pupil of mine. He had serious emotional problems. A college student, he was able to quote St. Augustine and Thomas Aquinas, but he had never learned Maimonides, Yehudah Halevi or the Baal Shem Tov.

Puzzled by confused memories of a *bar-mitzvah* or *bat-mitzvah* party, which may have constituted the entire range of their Jewish experience, such boys and girls become fertile soil for the hungry Christian missionary. The sensitive soul seeks spiritual satisfaction and is easily aroused by the promises of Christian salvation. No matter how lavish a *bar-mitzvah* celebration may be, it cannot counteract the missionary influence of the dominant Christian culture. We cannot dim the glamour of the Christmas tree with the little Chanukah candles, nor the Christmas carols with a childish *dreidel* song. But we can counter Christian influence with a full Jewish home life, with pride and knowledge of our past, of the Jewish martyrdom and heroism of our times and the lofty Messianic hopes for the future. This cannot be accomplished with a couple of hours preparation for a *bar-mitzvah* or *bat-mitzvah*.

The enemy is not the Christian missionary, but our young people's ignorance and indifference.

Let me borrow an example from the popular Passover Haggadah. The four sons are presented in this order: The wise son, the wicked son, the simple son and the ignorant. The old question is that if they had been grouped in the order of their degradation, the wicked son should be the last. The answer is that the wicked is not the worst. It is the *she'eino yodeia lishol*, the ignorant, the indifferent—he is the greatest risk. He can easily be swept away by diabolic forces and influences. It is from this category that our Jesus people come.

Our major defenses against the new missionary activity is *teshuvah*, a return to joyous and meaningful Jewish living—a revamping of our homes and life styles to accommodate more and more Jewish habits, associations and experiences. *Yeshivot* are our strongest fortresses. Undergraduate courses in Jewish history and culture given on various campuses have also been helpful. The old example of the futility of fighting cancer with aspirin when major surgery is required is applicable. Our kids cannot combat the Christian missionary with the memories of the childish lessons in the stories of Adam and Eve. They need Torah, our age-old stronghold, Torah in all its ramifications: practice, knowledge and appreciation.

There is a story going back to the early days of the Nazi terror in Germany. In one community, the Nazis conducted a search for hidden secret weapons in Jewish homes and institutions. A contingent of storm troopers invaded the synagogue in the course of its Sabbath services. They ransacked the building in search for secret weapons.

Failing to find any, one of the invaders pointed to the Aron Hakodesh, the Holy Ark, with elation. "There," he shouted. "There are the secret weapons." He forced open the Ark and beheld the holy Torah scrolls.

Thereupon, the rabbi pointed to the scrolls and exclaimed: "Yes, you are right. This is indeed our secret weapon. With this weapon we have overcome our enemies in the past, and we shall overcome you. It is the most potent instrument in our possession."

Without an army, without a government, without a land, we survived as a people protected by the Torah. Daily, before attesting to our faith in the unity of God and our love for Him, we pray: "O our Father, merciful Father, ever compassionate, have mercy upon us. Instill into our hearts to understand and to discern, to listen, learn and teach, to safeguard, perform and fulfill in love all the words of instruction in Your Torah. Enlighten our eyes in Your Torah, and let our hearts cleave to Your commandments, and unify our hearts to love and revere Your Name, so that we never be put to shame."

The Power of Teshuvah

Yom Kippur 5734 1973

*E*very Sabbath before Mussaf, the cantor chants an old petition emanating from the Babylonian schools: "May He who blessed our fathers, Abraham, Isaac and Jacob, bless this entire holy congregation, together with all other holy congregations—them, their wives, their sons and daughters . . ."

Every Sabbath we bless the holy congregation. At no time does the congregation give a fuller impression of holiness than on Kol Nidre night. Every Friday night is Shabbat, Kol Nidre night is Shabbat Shabbaton—the Sabbath of Sabbaths. Every Friday night is *kodesh*, holy, Kol Nidre night is *kodesh kadashim*, holy of holies.

The plaintive melody of Kol Nidre reverberating through the synagogue envelops us in a solemnity and sanctity that cannot be found on any other religious occasion.

Who cares for the legal significance of the Kol Nidre formula? Who is interested in the difference between the various forms of vows and obligations—*nedarim, issurim, charamot, konamot.* Kol Nidre addresses itself to the heart, not to the mind; to emotion, not to reason; to deep feeling, not to profound understanding.

Attired in *tallit*, we bless our children and gazing at the Torah scrolls with their shining ornaments. our hearts are turned heavenward, toward a Merciful Father who beckons us with open arms, "Come back to Me, My children!"

It is interesting to note that all our Biblical holy days and festivals have served as prototypes for Christian observances. For example, our Passover is their Easter; our Shavuoth is their Pentecost; our Sabbath is their Sunday; our Chanukah is their Christmas; our Rosh Hashanah is their New Year; even our Succoth is emulated on Palm Sunday. We have one holy day on our calendar which Christianity could not accept—that is Yom Kippur, the Day of Atonement. Yom Kippur has remained the unique gift of God to His people. More than that, Yom Kippur is the *greatest* gift of God to His people. On the day before Yom Kippur, anticipating the advent of the Great Day, we are not sad. We rejoice and traditionally indulge in good food, good cheer, friendship and reconciliation. We bless our children and greet our families with firm confidence:

"For on this day shall atonement be made for you to cleanse you; from all your sins shall you be clean before the Lord."

What, indeed, is the basic philosophy of Yom Kippur? Wherein lies its power over the Jewish soul?

The whole versified and poetic liturgy of the Day of Atonement, the whole colorful and impressive ritual of the day, may be synchronized into one single concept—*teshuvah*. The word literally means return. The word for sin is *chet*, stemming from the root which expresses the idea of "missing the mark" or "getting off the road," that is, the proper road of life. In *teshuvah*, we turn back to where we started before we got lost, and we begin anew on the right track. The Jewish doctrine of *teshuvah* has been investigated and studied by moralists and even codifiers in the course of the centuries. Techniques, methods and goals of *teshuvah* have been piously and earnestly formulated in our vast ethical literature.

Fundamentally, *teshuvah* is not penance, self-castigation, self-infliction of punishment. *Teshuvah* is also not a revivalist sudden, mystical experience of conversion. I would define *teshuvah* as an emotional regeneration. It involves an acknowledgment and admission of failure and an enthusiastic resolution for a new beginning.

Judaism concedes that man is small enough to make errors. But he must be big enough to admit his errors—and good enough to correct those errors. Generally, the steps of *teshuvah* are: acknowledgment, confession, resolution and atonement.

God is our Father, our Merciful Father. He is so close to us on Yom Kippur. We repeat again and again:

We are Your people and You are our Lord.

We are Your children and You are our Father.

He is our Lord, our Pastor, our Keeper, our Beloved. We feel every endearing association in His presence. With open arms, He is ready to receive us—if we would only return to Him.

Divine forgiveness is graciously offered to all: "Anyone who desires to cleanse himself receives celestial assistance." (Yoma 38b)

The gates of Heaven are ever ready to receive the *baal teshuvah*, and particularly on Yom Kippur.

A *midrash* on Shir Hashirim dramatizes God's invitation to our return to Him: "My children! Open up your hearts to Me no wider than a pinhole, and I will make for you an opening so wide that whole wagons and chariots could pass through it."

No one may consider himself too young or too old, too righteous or too far gone in the face of *teshuvah*. No matter how repellent one's conduct or corrupt one's character, the doors of return remain open to him.

Moreover, our Sages assure us that: "The position of the true penitent is even higher than that of the one who has always lived a righteous life." Obviously, this is because the *tzaddik*, the righteous person, did not have to struggle all the way back to the proper road.

It is from the aspect of *teshuvah* that Yom Kippur became the exclusive Jewish heritage.

Let me illustrate this with a talmudic passage: "They asked the prophets: 'What is the punishment of the sinner?' Prophecy answered: 'The soul that sins shall die.' (Ezekiel 18:4). They asked the Torah: 'What is the punishment of the sinner?' The Torah answered: 'Let him bring a sacrifice, and he shall be forgiven.' (Leviticus 1:4) They asked the Holy Blessed One: 'What is the punishment of the sinner?' The Holy Blessed One answered: 'Let him repent, and he shall be forgiven.'" (Jer. Makkos 2:6)

The Rabbis did not mean to minimize the teachings of the Torah and the Prophets with regard to sin and sinners. On the other hand, every word and every letter in all of Scripture were sacred to them. They acknowledged God as the Author of life and death and that our destiny is in His hands, as promulgated by the Prophets. They certainly approved the laws in Leviticus regarding the various guilt-offerings in the Temple ritual. But their major emphasis, repeated again and again, was that the nearest way to return to God was to go directly to Him with full heart and conscience.

It is in the concept of *teshuvah* that we separate completely from Christian theology. The sinner in Judaism needs no sacrifice, no death, no intermediary to return to God. The prophet Hosea exclaims: "Return, O Israel, directly unto the Lord your God."

That is the reason there is no Yom Kippur in the Christian theology. It has remained exclusively Jewish. Judaism repudiates the doctrine of predestination in matters of salvation. We look upon the human being as the highest instrument of God's creation. Man has been endowed with a free will in his relation with God: "Every human action is in God's hand, except for man's fear of God."

To stumble and go astray is man's tragic privilege. Yet to return and be reconciled with God is our singular gift, particularly on Yom Kippur.

I recently read a survey that identifies about forty percent of the campus drug addicts as Jewish. Mind you, the Jewish campus population is far below forty percent.

Have you noticed how many psychiatrists have Jewish names? There are also numerous Jewish psychologists, practitioners and therapists. It has become a Jewish business. The majority of the customers are Jewish, and they can relate better to their own kind.

Why have we become so afflicted with psychiatric problems? We suffer from fears, frustrations, guilt-complexes, psychoses, neuroses. These seem to be new Jewish ailments.

Unfortunately, we lost the inherent Jewish therapy for these mental and emotional disturbances. The Jewish therapy has been *teshuvah*, a firm belief that we have been born good, children of a gracious God, in whose merciful care we trust. With wholesome faith in God's redeeming love, we fear no evil. In the closing verse of the popular hymn Adon Olam, we say: "As long as my body and soul are united, I know that God is with me, and I shall have no fear."

The miraculous survival of the Kol Nidre in the Yom Kippur ritual and its position as the opening prayer (if we may call it a prayer) of the Day of Atonement may be better understood from the point of view of our sense of *teshuvah*.

Kol Nidre started as a simple legal formula for the annulment of rashly made personal vows and promises in which no second party had been involved. Early rabbinic authorities condemned the recitation of Kol Nidre as a foolish custom, not suitable for a holy day. Medieval anti-Semitism accused the Jews of perjury and ordered Jewish court litigants to take the humiliating *more Judaica*, a special Jewish oath to overcome the alleged annulments of Kol Nidre. The early councils of Reform Judaism attempted to retain the melody and do away with the awkward Aramaic words. But Kol Nidre overcame all obstacles. It survived them all. In the faithful heart of the humble worshipper, it helped in his efforts to absolve the old transgressions and make a new start. It paved the road to *teshuvah*.

Save the Child!

Yom 5734
Kippur 1973

The Torah reading this morning, the sixteenth chapter in Leviticus, gives us an outline of the ancient Temple ritual for the Day of Atonement—the attire of the High Priest, the offerings for the day, the confession and the purification of the Sanctuary.

The introductory verse, however, is rather peculiar and requires an explanation. We read: "And the Lord spoke to Moses after the death of the two sons of Aaron, when they drew near before the Lord and died."

There is no obvious association between the death of Aaron's sons and the Yom Kippur service, and yet we begin the Torah reading with a reference to "the death of the two sons of Aaron."

The tragedy of Aaron's sons is told in the tenth chapter of Leviticus in only two short verses: "And Nadav and Avihu, the sons of Aaron, took each of them his censer, and put fire therein, and laid incense thereon, and offered strange fire before the Lord, which He had not commanded them. And there came forth a fire from before the Lord, and devoured them, and they died before the Lord."

The nature of the sin of the sons of Aaron is not specified.

"Strange fire" is not a sin punishable by death. Also, it is not clear from the following verses if the young men suffered physical death, that is, cessation of life.

Our sages in the Talmud and Midrash who scrutinized Scripture carefully sought clues in the text to gain a more detailed understanding of this tragic incident. One theory advanced by the Rabbis is that these young priests were guilty of arrogance and unbridled ambition. Entering the Sanctuary for the dedication, Moses and Aaron led the procession, and Nadav and Avihu marched behind them. As they proceeded behind Moses and Aaron, the young men said to each other: "When will these two old men die so that we can take over the leadership in their place?" The Rabbis considered such arrogance a capital offense.

A second explanation put forward is that they entered the Sanctuary in a state of drunkenness. Indeed, the same chapter in Leviticus cautions the priesthood against drunkenness while in service in the Sanctuary.

The young priests are accused by other authorities of uncouth and unbecoming physical and social behavior. In other words, they entered the Sanctuary unwashed and undressed, and they refused to live a normal married life.

It is more than three thousand years since the tragic death of the sons of Aaron in the Sinai desert following the Exodus from Egypt. It is many centuries since our Sages advanced their analyses of the delinquencies of the rebellious young priests of the desert generation gap. Yet as we examine the old Midrashic findings in the light of our current difficulties with rebellious youth, they sound as modern as if they had been submitted by a commission of sociologists today. Indeed, it is a revelation into the centuries!

The sons of Aaron were charged with arrogance and selfish, ambitious careerism. How expressive of our counterculture are their extravagant outbursts and their distrust of the elected leaders of our society! Our moral standards and hallowed values, established institutions of learning and government are deprecated and violated.

The natural desire of youth to effect changes and seek improvement is praiseworthy. Such genuine ambition serves as the spark to advancement, research, adventure, bravery and heroism. But destruction for its own sake, chaos for kicks and the loss of respect for life and property is the shame of our generation, regardless of where the blame falls.

The Rabbis accused the sons of Aaron of entering the Sanctuary in a state of drunkenness, an old escape from duty and responsibility. Instead of a sober-minded, earnest approach to their divine calling, they got drunk. Our drug generation frowns upon the use of alcohol. Our youth requires a more profound escape into fantasy and lightmindedness. They graduated to the misuse of drugs and poisons. Addicted and "stoned," they sink into shelter from the responsibilities which people must assume to maintain a civilized society.

The Rabbis of old charged the sons of Aaron with personal antisocial behavior—uncleanness, nudity, promiscuity. These accusations sound like recent reviews of popular novels and movies. Bedroom scenes and corrupt sexuality have become the central themes of our best-sellers, art and theater. It is not surprising that many young men and women cannot live with their parents. Our homes are too clean for them. The filth and stench of the East Village and the wild orgies of the drug hovels are more desirable.

Although Scripture describes the fatal end of the sons of Aaron with the word "and they died," the Rabbis claim (Shabbos 113a) their souls were burnt out, but not their bodies—dead souls. In modern parlance, we would say they suffered spiritual death even while remaining physically alive—so typical of our drug victims.

In connection with the reading of the portion of the death of Nadav and Avihu on Yom Kippur, our chief Kabbalistic work, the Zohar, states as follows: "Anyone who sheds tears on Yom Kippur while reading the portion of the death of Nadav and Avihu, taking its teachings to heart, will win forgiveness for his own sins and the blessings of long life for his children."

In the Rabbinic understanding of the failure of the sons of Aaron, there is so much reflection on the spiritual decline of our sons and daughters. In taking to heart our own feelings as parents, and in our resolution to effect urgent changes and improvements, we may win forgiveness for ourselves and long life of spiritual well-being for our children.

There is a prevalent custom to light a candle in memory of a deceased parent, spouse or relative before Yizkor. As we pray for the elevation of the souls of our departed parents and loved ones, let us similarly pray for the preservation of the souls of our children.

There is an old superstition not to allow young people who have living parents to recite Kaddish, the prayer for the dead. The fear is that the child's saying the Kaddish may bring the parents' death closer.

You probably heard the story of the young father who engaged a *melamed* to come to his house and teach Hebrew to his son. The father noticed that the *melamed* was teaching the boy the Kaddish.

After some lessons, the father protested to the teacher, "I'm only thirty-two years old. Why are you teaching my boy to say Kaddish?"

And the *melamed* answered, "I realize that you are a young man, but I assure you that by the time your son learns to say the Kaddish correctly, you'll be pretty old."

That may be a joke, but it is not very funny. The awkward recitation of the Kaddish at gravesides, repeating the words prompted by a rabbi, frequently turns a severely mourned loss into a comedy.

There is an old custom to ask young people blessed with living parents to leave the synagogue during the recitation of

Yizkor. We practice this custom in our synagogue. The old reason given was the fear of an *ayin hara*—the evil eye may strike the parents of a non-reciter of Yizkor present. Recently, I heard a more reasonable explanation. It is feared that these young people, taking no part in the service, will converse and disturb those who wish to recite Yizkor.

Frequently, when I think of this custom of sending out the young people from the synagogue, I am inclined to protest that Yizkor should be the occasion when young people are brought into the synagogue. They should be present to see and learn how Jewish sons and daughters traditionally honor the memories of their parents. Are all of us sure our children will go to the synagogue to remember us after we are gone? Have all of us taught our children to recite the simple formula of Hazkarat Neshamot?

A dramatic scene in the Yiddish Art Theater a number of years ago comes to mind. Maurice Schwartz played the role of an immigrant Jew who slaved at his sewing machine day and night with a single ambition—to make his son Yankele a successful lawyer. The father worked and grew old, while Yankele was sent to law school. The father saved every penny to open an office for Yankele. His son graduated from law school, married into a rich family, and his wife calls him Jacques. As the years roll by, Jacques finds no time to visit his aging parents. In response to calls from his parents, his wife and secretary promise their son will call them as soon as he gets a chance.

In the scene I recall, the father is nearing death in a hospital bed. He is pleading for days for his son to come, but Jacques is still busy. Finally, Jacques arrives at the bedside.

The dying old man beckons him to sit nearby and says: "Yankele, my son, I have tried very hard to make a successful man out of you, and I have not failed. You are a prominent lawyer. You don't have any more time to come to see your father. But I failed to teach you that you are a Jew with Jewish responsibilities. My time has come to part with this life, and I want to die like a Jew. When a Jew dies, his son is required to recite the Kaddish. Sit down, Yankele, close to me, and let me teach you the Kaddish. Repeat after me, Yankele. *Yitgadal vey-itkadash shemei rabba*." Father and son repeat the words as the old man fades and expires.

As we recite Yizkor for the sacred memories of our beloved, praying, "Yizkor Elokim, remember, O Lord, the souls of our dearly beloved who have gone on to their eternal home," let us hear the call of Heaven to us: "Remember, parents, the living souls of your sons and daughters, of your grandchildren. Guard them and save them for the sake and merits of your forebears, whose names have been transferred to them."

May the promise of the Zohar come true that, for our contrite hearts and penitent spirits, we may gain forgiveness for ourselves and long life for our children and grandchildren.

The Dangers of Deflation

Rosh Hashanah 5736 1975

*I*n my annual preparation for the High Holidays sermons, I experience a certain discomfort. The general tone of High Holidays preaching is designed to stir the congregation to self-examination in our relationships with God and man, to acknowledge our shortcomings as individual men and women and as members of society.

Basically, the goal of our entire observance is *teshuvah*, repentance; that is, we turn away from evil ways and start on a fresh, new road. As we say: "Let the old year and its curses end, and may the new year and its blessings begin."

A person cannot be called upon to do *teshuvah* without being told of his *aveirot*, the transgressions which he must desert with a contrite heart and resolve never to repeat them. The successful High Holidays preacher is, therefore, the one who can dig deeply into human frailties and dramatize man's failings in the light of our religious and social responsibilities.

It is not my nature to find fault with people generally. And it is particularly difficult to find fault with a congregation of good men and women who have come to worship together, to express good wishes to their friends and neighbors; it is embarrassing for me to tell such a congregation how wicked they have been all year and how they have to improve their way of life.

I heard the story of a *chassidic rebbe* who permitted an itinerant preacher to make a collection in his *shtiebel* between Minchah and Maariv. Before the collection, the preacher made the customary speech exhorting the people for their lack of *kavanah* in prayer, concentration, not responding properly with Amen in prayer, not devoting enough time to Torah study, and so forth.

As the preacher spoke, the *rebbe* suddenly silenced him with a shout: "Because you need a couple of rubles, you have to make criminals of all of us?"

But there is another aspect of the Yamim Noraim, the High Holidays, whose importance fills the pages of our liturgy, yet is frequently ignored by High Holidays preachers. Rosh Hashanah is the celebration of the creation of the world and the formation of the first man—indeed, the anniversary of our civilization. According to rabbinic chronology, the creation began on the 25th of Elul, so that man was created on the first of Tishrei.

Each of the tri-cycle of prayers—Malchiot, Zichronot and Shofrot—begins with the exclamation: "On this day the world was called into being. On this day all the creatures of the universe stand in judgment before You."

The universal theme of our High Holidays liturgy has inspired a non-Jewish preacher to suggest that Rosh Hashanah and Yom Kippur be observed by the whole world as a period of prayer and dedication to the principles of justice, equality and peace.

Let us stop and think for a moment. How do man and his world look today on his birthday in the year 1975?

Economic difficulties are not confined to our country. Inflation, the continuous rise in the cost of living in the face of industrial recessions, has assumed international proportions. There is world-wide fear of economic disaster. However, not only inflation threatens to destroy our society but deflation as well. Not deflation of the dollar but deflation of our sense of right and wrong, deflation of our morals, deflation of our respect for authority, deflation of our regard for life and property, deflation of our good judgment.

The United Nations, the international hope for peace and justice, has become the international arena for political blackmail and diplomatic hypocrisy. Who can forget the ridiculous reception and applause with which Yasir Arafat, the chieftain of international banditry, was welcomed by the General Assembly, while he brandished his gun and threatened to continue his program of murder and terror? "With praises of God in their mouth, and a double-edged sword in their hand." (Psalms 149:6)

The political situation at home gives a dramatic picture (to employ a Christian theological term) of the Fall of Man in our day. For months and months, radio, television and the newspapers ran daily stories about the Watergate scandal, portraying the President of the United States, the Vice President, their most respected counselors and members of their cabinet as thieves, criminals and perjurers. In the end, however, each of them is becoming a national hero, lecturing at college campuses and getting high fees for television interviews.

We live in fear under the shadow of nuclear annihilation. Our cities have become filthy slums in which bands of youthful criminals lurk day and night to prey on honest citizens, taking their property and even their lives. Our double-locked homes have become virtual prisons for the night. (After checking my own four locks, I still look up to my *mezuzah* for protection.)

The recent investigations into the nursing home scandals revealed the horrible conditions into which we banish our helpless aged fathers and mothers. To our shame and disgrace, we have witnessed unscrupulous men, who enjoy high standing in some religious and political circles, plunder millions of dollars from government agencies, taking advantage of our failure to care personally for our aged parents and grandparents. Enriching themselves, merciless merchants in human misery have turned the nursing homes into human waste baskets.

We frequently hear pious complaints that the gangster shows and police programs on television are potentially injurious to the moral development of our children. In fact, the coverage of the international hypocrisy of a United Nations General Assembly session, the revelations of bribery, injustice and dirty trickery in the Watergate hearings, the criminality and inhumanity of the nursing home operators—all graphically displayed on our home screens—make the television gangster stories seem like child's play.

The national religious motto of our people, which has become part of our little children's morning prayer, reads: "The Torah that Moses commanded us is the inheritance of the congregation of Jacob." The 613 *mitzvot* in the Torah are designed to make us exclusively a priestly kingdom and holy nation. The fulfillment of the Torah is our exclusive responsibility. But God is the Creator of the universe, the Father of all mankind. In giving the Torah to Israel alone, could He have forsaken the rest of mankind to perdition and chaos?

No, it is not so. After the Flood destroyed the totally corrupt primeval civilization, Noah and his family emerged from the Ark to begin the development of a new society. We read in Genesis (9:1-7) that the Lord blessed Noah and his family and charged them with a list of regulations which have been summarized by our Sages as the Seven Noachide Commandments. They constitute the minimum requirements for an orderly society. Since the Middle Ages, Jewish theologians have considered the tenets of Christianity and Islam as not inconsistent with the Noachide commandments.

These seven commandments are enumerated by the Rabbis as: the establishment of courts of justice; the prohibition against blasphemy; the prohibition against idolatry; the prohibition against incest; the prohibition against bloodshed; the prohibition against robbery; the prohibition against eating a limb torn from a living animal.

If we were to present a condensed form of seven regulations by which our international society is governed, it would enumerate as follows: glorify perjury; practice ruthless blasphemy; accept idolatry; popularize adultery; permit genocide; justify robbery; promote gross inhumanity.

Let me take you back to one of the early episodes in the story of Creation as recorded in the book of Genesis. God created Adam. Adam was lonely, and God gave him Eve. God placed the two of them in Paradise to enjoy the blessings of life. They had only a single restriction—not to eat from the fruits of one tree in the whole Garden of Eden. In comes the serpent—or what do we call him? Satan, the devil—and challenges the little lady to eat from the forbidden fruit. She likes it, and gently offers some to her husband, who enjoys it also. And now, we read in Scripture (Genesis 3:7-9): "And the eyes of both of them were opened, and they knew they were naked; and they sewed fig-leaves together and made themselves girdles. And they heard the sound of the Lord God walking in the Garden in the direction of the day; and the man and his wife hid from the presence of the Lord God among the trees of the Garden. And the Lord God called to the man, and said to him: 'Where are you?'"

Martin Buber tells the story about Rabbi Schneur Zalman of Liade, the founder of the Lubavitcher dynasty, who was imprisoned in St. Petersburg after being denounced to the Russian government by the *mitnagdim* for his *chassidic* principles. While he was awaiting trial, the chief of the gendarmes entered the cell. The majestic and serene face of the rabbi, so deep in meditation, suggested to the chief a thoughtful person. What manner of man had he before him? He began to converse with his prisoner and brought up a number of questions which had occurred to him while reading the Bible.

Finally, he asked: "How are we to understand that God, who knows and sees all, asked Adam, 'Where are you?' Didn't God know where Adam was hiding?"

"Of course God knew," the rabbi answered, "but did Adam know?"

The question of "Where are you?" is directed to Adam in every age and every generation. God calls on every man to stop and think, "Where am I in this world?"

On this 5736th birthday of Adam, mankind in personification must hear the voice of God asking: "Where are you?" How far have we sunk into the abyss of fear, corruption, sin, intrigue and insecurity? How far can we go before another Deluge devours us all?

Adam, when discovered hiding, blamed the serpent; he blamed the woman; he blamed God for giving him the woman; he blamed everybody but himself.

On Rosh Hashanah, we customarily pray for good health, prosperity and longevity for ourselves and our families. We pray for our people in our land, in Israel, in other lands. And at no time more than now has our personal welfare and the destiny of our people been more dependent upon the return of man's sanity, justice and mercy.

Where to Find God

Yom 5736
Kippur 1975

Man is never as big as when he stoops to help a child. Man is never as wise as when he admits his lack of knowledge. Man is never as virtuous as when he acknowledges his shortcomings and admits his failings.

"For on this day He atones for you to cleanse you from all your sins. You shall be clean before the Lord." This is the theme of Yom Kippur: Confession—Regret—Forgiveness.

The haunting melody of Kol Nidre, repeated three times, enchants and envelops us. Its magical metamorphic power elevates its listeners to celestial spheres.

Unlike other religions, Judaism does not claim cataclysmic conversions to its faith by supernatural visions or revelations.

There are occasions when we are struck by sanctity and serenity to feel the presence of God. When Jacob awoke from his dream of the ladder reaching to the gates of Heaven, he exclaimed: "Surely, the Lord is present in this place."

The plaintive tunes of Kol Nidre associated with the sight of the Sifrei Torah in the arms of the rabbi and the elders of the congregation serve as the key to the opening of the inner Jewish hearts.

Kol Nidre begins with the introduction calling upon the celestial and congregational courts for permission to worship in the company of the *avaryonim*, the transgressors. In the early Medieval period, the reference was to allow those placed under the *cherem*, excommunication, to join the congregation for Kol Nidre. During the Spanish Inquisition, the reference was directed to the crypto-Jews, known as Marranos, who clandestinely came to synagogues to hear Kol Nidre.

In our days, we think of the many Jews who don't attend the synagogue throughout the year but come on Yom Kippur. We think of those who have severed all ties with the Jewish community and yet are drawn to the synagogues on Yom Kippur. We think of those who no longer observe the Sabbath and festivals, those who neglect the dietary laws but are here on Yom Kippur.

What magic power draws them to the synagogue today more than any other day? Throughout the year they cannot control their appetites from forbidden foods, but on Yom Kippur they fast and abstain from food and water for twenty-five hours.

The answer comes from our doctrine of *chet* and *teshuvah*. We generally translate these concepts as "sin" and "penitence." Both sin and penitence bring to our minds their Christian connotation of man's natural degradation and fall. In Judaism, however, there is no "original sin" from which man must extricate himself. Man is born good and is good by nature. Rather, the word *chet* means "error." There is a correct course of life—the way directed by the Torah—but by error we get off the right course and lose our way. *Teshuvah* means return. We correct our error and go back on the right course. Yom Kippur has been designated as the day for *teshuvah*.

The prophet (Isaiah 55:6) calls upon us: "Seek God while He may be found, call upon Him while He is near." Our Sages ask: "When is God to be found? On Rosh Hashanah. When is God near? On Yom Kippur."

Is it only on Rosh Hashanah that God may be found? Is there, indeed, any time or place that God may not be found? And is it only on Yom Kippur that God is near?

The prophet (Isaiah 6:3) tells us:

The whole world is full of His glory.

We recall the words in Psalm 139:

Whither shall I go from Your spirit
Or whither shall I flee from Your presence?
If I ascend up into heaven, You are there.
If I take the wings of the morning
And dwell in the uttermost parts of the sea,
Even there Your hand shall lead me
And Your right hand shall hold me.

Do you recall the touching song ascribed to Rabbi Levi Yitzchak of Berditchev, *Ah Dudele*?

Where shall I find you?
And where is it possible not to find you?
Mizrach du, maariv du,
Zaphon du, darom du.
You are above and below,
You are east, west, north and south.

How then can we designate one day to seek and find God to be near to us?

The story is told of the *chassidic rebbe* who asked his followers: "Where is God to be found?"

"Everywhere," was the answer.

"Wrong," said the *rebbe*. "God is to be found where you open the door and let Him in."

Indeed, God is everywhere, but we run away from Him. Jonah wanted to flee physically: "And Jonah rose to flee to Tarshish from the presence of God." By defying His

Commandments, we run away from God. In disobeying His will, we build an Iron Curtain between ourselves and our Father in Heaven.

On Yom Kippur, however, we open our hearts and let God enter. And we feel His nearness.

We recite: "We are Your children and You are our Father, We are Your sheep, and You our shepherd."

There is but one more difficulty to be adjusted in our Yom Kippur approach.

If we want to come closer to God by proper Jewish living, it would be natural for us to make a list of resolutions, vows and promises, to swear and adjure. In contrast, we begin with the long chant of Kol Nidre in which we call upon the Beth Din to absolve us from all previous religious commitments and declare null and void such commitments that we may assume in the course of the coming year.

The explanation of this anomaly is to be found in the rabbinic dictum: "Transgressions involving man and his God only are forgiven on Yom Kippur. But transgressions involving man and man are not forgiven on Yom Kippur until the aggrieved person is mollified."

There is a story of Reb Meir'l of Premyszlan who delayed the Kol Nidre until each person begged forgiveness from the other and agreed to conciliate his business litigation.

As we annul the rash promises and vows of piety in our obligations to our God alone, it is our duty on Yom Kippur to assume obligations and promise their fulfillment in our obligations to the family, the synagogue and Jewish needs abroad.

Then we will hear the voice of God saying clearly: "I pardon them as you have asked."

Judaism: A Religion for the Living

Yom Kippur 5738 1977

We usually look upon the chanting of Kol Nidre as the keynote to the Yom Kippur service. We sense in its words and plaintive melody the introduction to the solemnity of the day and its ritual. But Kol Nidre is, in fact, not the opening the Yom Kippur service. We begin the solemn day with removing of the Torah scrolls from the Ark and bringing them to the congregation that they may touch and kiss the Torah and exclaim aloud: "A light will shine for the righteous, and to the upright of heart there will be joy." (Psalms 97:11)

We repeat the verse numerous times, as if this would be the keynote to the Yom Kippur day. Why did we select this verse to introduce the holiest day of the year?

We introduce this promise of light and joy to the righteous just before Kol Nidre in acknowledgment of the tension-charged atmosphere in the congregation as we rush to the synagogue to usher in the Day of Atonement. We realize it is the last of the Ten Days of Penitence; our last chance to gain a final verdict of forgiveness. The chanting of Kol Nidre in itself brings forth memories of martyrdom and sacrifice, of Marranos and forced baptism, of suffering and persecution.

To counteract this somber state of mind and put us back on the path of true faith, hope and confidence in the efficacy of Yom Kippur, we display the Torah, the instrument of our way of life, and acknowledge in exclamation: "The Torah is a light to the righteous, and a joy to the upright in heart." We drown our sorrow, anxiety and depression in its light and vanquish the difficulties of our daily lives.

As I look upon this large congregation of men and women who have come on this holy day to find comfort in the synagogue for the loss of beloved parents, a spouse, a child, a brother or sister, I wish tradition had introduced a repetition of last night's ceremony and that we would open the Yizkor service with this same promising Psalm. The Torah and Jewish religious living, we should declare, is a shining light to the righteous and a source of joy and contentment to the upright at heart.

It is not only to be employed as a means of comfort for the mourner, the bereft, the suffering, the depressed and unfortunate. Judaism is designed to be a law of good living, not only a therapeutic antidote for the oppressed and a salvation for those suffering from the effects of death.

Some eight hundred years ago, the famous Jewish codifier and theologian Maimonides, then a consultant physician to the sultan in Cairo, was asked to clarify his belief in life after death, Olam Haba and in the doctrine of the resurrection of the dead. In a lengthy epistle, Maimonides reaffirms his belief in *techiat hameitim* as a cardinal principle in Judaism. He goes on to explain why the Torah does not specifically mention the doctrine of the resurrection of the dead. Indeed, the Rabbis in the Talmud found many allusions in Scripture to a life after death, but no direct reference.

The Torah, explains Maimonides, was originally given on Mount Sinai to the freed Egyptian slaves. The children of Israel had been contaminated with the ancient Egyptian cult centered around salvation from death—a religion for the dead. The Egyptians built pyramids to save their kings from the effects of death. Therefore, to turn the Jewish minds away from a religion surrounding death to a religion of good life, all references to a hereafter were deliberately omitted.

Now, let me state assuredly that, like every rabbi, I am happy to see the synagogue filled on Yom Kippur for Yizkor. And I deeply appreciate the lofty sentiments of the many men and women who, if even for a brief half-hour, come into the sanctuary of a temple or synagogue to recall the sacred memories of their beloved in prayer. The synagogue becomes filled with the souls of the numerous men and women whose sacred names we invoke in the recitation of Yizkor. According to our Sages, the duties of the fifth commandment, honoring parents, do not end with the completion of their physical lives. "Honor them during their lifetime," the Sages taught us, "and continue to honor them when they are only spiritually alive." In this sense, the recitation of Yizkor constitutes the fulfillment of the honor due to a father and mother.

It is most painful, however, that the *mitzvah* of the respect for the dead has become the sole expression of religion for a large number of Jews. To them, the Torah is no longer a beacon of light for righteous living, but a means to respect the memories of their deceased relatives. In the place of the Sabbath, festivals, family purity and dietary regulations they have substituted Shiva, Kaddish, Yahrzeit and Yizkor. The cemetery has replaced the synagogue.

Let me in no way deprecate the hallowed custom of a mourner reciting Kaddish in memory of a deceased parent. The custom has been sanctified by its usage for centuries since early talmudic days. The public recitation of the Kaddish has served as a powerful instrument to unite Jews in daily prayer, and gives the mourner an opportunity to dedicate a portion of his daily life to the memory of the beloved parent.

But there is another word in our religious terminology which stems from the same root as Kaddish. The word is

Kiddush. Kaddish and Kiddush relate to sanctification. In the Kaddish, the mourner sanctifies the Name of the Lord, justifies God's manifestation in the conduct of the universe and finds comfort in the coming kingdom of the Lord over the whole world. In the Kiddush, recited over a cup of wine at the inauguration of the Sabbath, we discover a new life, a life of joy, serenity and holiness. How I pity the Jew who does not have the weekly rejuvenation, the rest, the liveliness and loveliness of the Sabbath. To quote a contemporary orator, Shmaryahu Levine: "More than the Jew did for the Sabbath, the Sabbath has been doing for the Jew."

From early childhood, I have been fascinated by the story associated with the life and death of the legendary Graf Valentin Potocki, a young Polish count who lived in the beginning of the eighteenth century. One Friday, the count and his friends went hunting in the thick forest that he owned. As he and his young frivolous friends were going about their hunting, a heavy snowfall drove them out of the forest, and they decided to lodge in a nearby inn owned by the count. The innkeeper was a Jew to whom the count entrusted the saloon and the monopoly for the sale of whisky to the local Polish peasantry.

As soon as the count and his group arrived, they started ordering around the innkeeper and his family for their service.

With the derogatory name "Moshke" given to Jewish concessionaires, Potocki kept on ordering continuously: "Moshke, more vodka! Moshke, more food!"

Fearing the loss of his position, the innkeeper obediently supplied their demands. In a drunken stupor, the young nobleman summoned the Jewish innkeeper, and with whip in hand, he ordered him to dance for his guests the way Jews dance on their holidays. Like a little obedient dog, the tortured innkeeper danced to the delighted flicks of the count's whip.

As it was Friday—Erev Shabbat—the innkeeper and his family suddenly disappeared as night fell. The count kept on calling for him for vodka and food, but the innkeeper was not around. The count burst into the door of the innkeeper's living room and was literally paralyzed by what he saw.

With a cup of wine in his hand, standing in front of Sabbath candles over a white tablecloth, in clean dignified attire, surrounded by the shining faces of his wife and children, the innkeeper was reciting the Sabbath Kiddush.

Stupefied, the young count retreated from the door and left the inn, challenged by the question on which he continuously pondered: What power in Judaism could change that dog of a Jew into a virtual angel?

The end of the story is not a very happy one. The count left for Paris where he studied and converted to Judaism. He lived in Vilna as a practicing Jew, and when discovered, he was burned at the stake. His ashes were gathered by Jews who buried them, and put up the monument reading: "Graf Potocki—Ger Tzedek—A Righteous Convert." My purpose in repeating this legend to you is to emphasize the magic power of the recitation of the Kiddush on the eve of the Sabbath.

Let us take another example of our devotion to the rituals associated with death—the Yahrzeit light. We keep charts and pay for synagogue reminders to make sure that on the anniversary of the death we should not miss the kindling of the Yahrzeit light. It is, indeed, a meritorious custom. Light is the symbol of life. "The human soul is the light of the divine," says Scripture. (Proverbs 20:27)

How about the light of the Sabbath candles so frequently neglected? These lights of life illuminate our homes and transform our families from the secular to the holy, make our tables altars and our meals hallowed offerings to a loving God. If mothers would only realize their angelic image impressed upon children watching their mother cover her face before the Sabbath lights.

Let me read some verses I once learned by heart from a poem by Philip M. Raskin:

From memory's spring flows a vision tonight,
My mother is kindling and blessing the light;
The light of Queen Sabbath, the heavenly flame,
That one day in seven quells hunger and shame,
My mother is praying and screening her face,
Too bashful to gaze at the Sabbath light's grace.
She murmurs devoutly, "O Almighty, be blessed,
For sending Your angel of joy and of rest,
And may as the candles of Sabbath divine
The eyes of my son in Your Torah ever shine."
Of childhood, fair childhood, the years are long fled;
Youth's candles are quenched, and my mother is dead.
And yet every Friday, when twilight arrives,
The face of my mother within me revives;
A prayer on her lips, "O Almighty, be blessed,
For sending us Sabbath, the angel of rest."
And some hidden feeling I cannot control
A Sabbath light kindles deep, deep in my soul.

Let me take another example of this phenomenon: The month of Elul, the month before Rosh Hashanah, has been traditionally devoted to visits to the graves of our beloved. In America, the custom prevails also to arrange for the unveiling of new monuments during this month. Since it is my duty to join families at these unveiling ceremonies, I marvel at the throngs of people—young and old—that mass around the cemeteries at this season. If all these people who visit the cemeteries at the holiday season would attend the synagogue, we could never accommodate them.

Indeed, visiting the graves of our beloved is a beautiful custom. It reunites the Jewish families in the golden chain of parents, children and grandchildren. It is an occasion for sincere prayer and meditation. For centuries, our people have visited the holy tomb of Mother Rachel in Bethlehem and the Cave of the Patriarchs in Hebron.

The author of the *Hatikvah*, Isaac Imber, had another stanza in our national anthem. It reads:

As long as the tears drip from our eyes as drops of rain,
And a good many of our people visit the sacred graves,
Our ancient hope is not lost
The hope to return to the City of David.

Yes, visiting the cemeteries we also find ourselves gathered in holy places—the Yiddish word for a cemetery is *das heilige ort*, the holy place.

But why so many at the cemeteries and so few in the synagogues? And why when we do come in large groups to the synagogue is it on occasions of mourning, sorrow and need of comfort?

I was told the story of a gentleman who rarely attended synagogue services. One time, he approached the rabbi and asked him to recite prayers for the recovery of a seriously sick child. He offered a substantial donation for the prayers. The rabbi was seeing this man for the first time in his synagogue. He asked the man in what business he was engaged, and the man told him that he owned real estate.

"Do you carry insurance on your properties?" asked the rabbi.

"Of course," answered the man.

"And when do you get your insurance, after the fire has already started?"

A passage in Pirkei d'Rabbi Eliezer relates that when Solomon built the Holy Temple he made two gates through which people could enter—the gate for bridegrooms, also known as the gate of joy, and the gate for mourners and the oppressed. When the High Priest arrived every morning and found the gate of joy open and crowded, he recited psalms of thankfulness and praise. If he found the gate of mourners open and crowded, and the gate of joy closed, he prostrated himself and wept.

Let us resolve to increase our attendance at the synagogue, the contemporary gate of joy.

In the words of the Psalmist: "Let us worship the Lord with rejoicing, and come before Him with song." (Psalms 100:2)

To Live as a Jew, Not to Die as a Jew

Rosh Hashanah 5741 1981

The Torah reading for the second day of Rosh Hashanah (Genesis 22) constitutes one of the most familiar parts of Biblical literature. The story of the binding of Isaac by his father Abraham to offer him as a sacrifice to God is included in our daily Prayer Book and is recited every morning in the synagogue or at home. We repeat the account of this supreme test in which the aged father was told to sacrifice his only beloved son for whom he had prayed all his life. We follow Abraham and Isaac to Mount Moriah with breathtaking compassion and watch the young boy bound to the wood on the stone altar. We see him waiting for the sharp knife in the old man's raised hand to come down and sever his throat.

Then the voice of the angel stops Abraham, shouting, "Do not touch the boy! You, Abraham, have passed the test, for I know now that you are a God-fearing man."

Following the daily recitation of the Akedah in the morning, we add a short prayer borrowed from the Rosh Hashanah Machzor: "Master of the World! May it be Your will, O God our Lord and Lord of our fathers, to remember in our favor the covenant of our fathers. Even as our father Abraham held back his compassion from his only son and desired to slay him in order to do Your will, so may Your mercy hold back Your anger from us; let Your compassion prevail over Your acts of retaliation. Be lenient with us, O God our Lord, and deal with us kindly and mercifully."

The *shofar*, the ram's horn which we sound on Rosh Hashanah, is the instrument that symbolizes the ram Abraham substituted for his son on the altar. And on this Day of Judgment, when we pray for our lives and welfare, we bring forth before the Supreme Judge the merits of our forefathers and particularly the unfailing faith of Abraham.

The Akedah, as this episode is known in the arts and literature, has in the course of the heroic history of our people become the symbol of Jewish martyrdom and self-sacrifice. Indeed, in the Biblical narrative of the Akedah, Isaac did not die for his faith. But Isaac's children, generation after generation, actually did give their lives "for the sanctification of God's Name."

We recall the test of faith administered to Hannah and her seven sons during the Maccabean period. Her husband had already perished in the persecution, and now the widow and her seven sons were threatened with death unless they renounced their faith in the God of Israel. The mother urged her sons to give up their lives but not their faith, and she watched them being led away, one after another, to the gallows with Shema Yisrael on their lips. When the youngest son was removed from the mother, the Book of Maccabees records her farewell: "Go, my son, to our father Abraham and tell him that he only offered to sacrifice one son to God, but I actually did sacrifice all my seven sons on the altar of our faith."

Visitors to Israel are taken on a tour to the Dead Sea and lifted on a cable car to the fortress of Masada, south of Arad. They view and admire the archeological remains of that formidable stronghold on the mountain fortress built by King Herod of Judea. Little do we realize that up there 966 men, women and children held off the Roman invasion for three years. When the fall was imminent, they committed suicide, offering their lives for their God and country, rather than be sold into Roman slavery. The heroes of Masada certainly did more for their faith than Abraham and Isaac.

When we draw closer to our own times, we think of the victims of the Holocaust, the thousands of Abrahams, Isaacs, Sarahs, Rebeccas, Rachels and Leahs who were mercilessly sacrificed on the altars of Auschwitz, Buchenwald, Majdanek, Bergen-Belsen. We have become accustomed to talk about these *kedoshim* with rubber-stamped terminology: victims, survivors, Holocaust, six million. We forget that these cold words refer to human beings—good men, loving women, dear and tender children—not a gruesome statistic of six million.

Some fifteen years ago, I read an editorial in the *New York Times* entitled "One Little Boy." The editorial followed the publication in Germany of a book of actual drawings made in concentration camps by Jewish children. The editorial began as follows:

> *Why still search for Nazis twenty years after World War II?*
>
> *Why does bitterness still burn as a hot coal in the hearts of millions throughout the world?*
>
> *Why can so many decent human beings not find in their hearts the capacity to forgive and forget?*
>
> *A story in this newspaper yesterday suggests one of the reasons. There has just been published in Germany a book entitled* For Theirs Was the Hell. *It is a documented account of the fate which befell some of the 1.2 million Jewish children under sixteen years of age in Hitler's concentration camps. A few sentences from the story are enough:*
>
> *"Then the guard ordered the children to fold their clothes neatly and march into the gas chamber and*

crematorium. One little boy, less than two years old,
was too little to climb the steps. So the guard took the
child in his arms and carried him into the chamber.
*   "There is the reason—one little boy."*

This little boy, this little Isaac, was actually sacrificed, and
no angel came to save him. In the sounds of the *shofar* we hear
the death throes of this little boy and the cries of the one million two hundred thousand other boys and girls who died *al*
Kiddush Hashem.

However, with the emphasis in our liturgy and informal
prayers on the martyrdom and self-sacrifice of the Akedah, we
are missing the major lesson the story of the binding of Isaac
aims to teach us. Human sacrifice was a common practice in
ancient society. The continuous condemnation of human sacrifice in the Torah and the Prophets indicates that this primitive cruelty was not easily eradicated from ancient Israel and
Judea. Abraham does not appear at all shocked when he is
told to bring his son Isaac to Mount Moriah and deliver him
as a burnt offering.

Father and son walked together without protest.
Abraham was shocked when he was stopped from sacrificing
his son to God. And that was the major lesson of the test, to
teach Abraham, and through Abraham the rest of civilization,
that God finds delight not in the destruction of human life but
in the saving of human life. To quote the Sages in the Talmud,
"The *mitzvot* are given to Israel that they may live by them and
not that they die by them." To paraphrase the dictum of the
Sages, let me say that our responsibility is not to die as Jews.
It is primarily to live as Jews. The challenge to Abraham was
to raise Isaac to live in his faith, not to die in his faith.

Alas, we live in a time when many of our sons and
daughters are sacrificed not on the altar of faith, but on the
altar of faithlessness. The Moloch of our time is assimilation—
shemad—and the vehicle to assimilation is no longer baptism

but intermarriage. We lose more through intermarriage than are replenished by births. There is no family that has not suffered the spiritual death of a son or daughter through intermarriage. American Jews were saved from Hitler's Final Solution of the "Jewish problem" during the Holocaust in Europe, but we have developed a technique of destroying ourselves through intermarriage.

I am not here to blame parents or families for the apostasy of their children. On the other hand, my sympathy and compassion goes out to every father and mother who is subjected to the loss of a son or daughter through intermarriage. I know many fathers and mothers would have preferred not to have lived to see their sons and daughters desert and insult their people, their kin, their God, their destiny as Jews.

I recall the curse in Deuteronomy (28:32): "Your sons and daughters will be given unto another people, and your eyes will look on, and fail with longing all day, and there shall be naught in the power of your hands." Even parents who consider it more prudent to cooperate, who go with their *meshumad* to church and dance at his spiritual destruction, they too evoke our deepest sense of pity. They may seek comfort in the distant hope that the marriage will not last too long, or that their child promised that he had been born a Jew and would die a Jew. Unfortunately, he or she will no longer live as a Jew.

Children blame parents, and parents blame children. Parents are confounded by the dilemma, claiming that they had given their children a Jewish religious consciousness; and children accuse their non-observant parents of sheer hypocrisy in objecting to intermarriage.

Can we stem the tide of our Jewish national suicide? It is threatening the future of the largest and most important Jewish community in the world.

Until recently, assimilation through intermarriage did not constitute a grave Jewish problem. We were afraid of pogroms, forced baptism, expulsion, but not intermarriage.

Jews were separated from their non-Jewish neighbors in dress, language, behavior, culture, diet, education, industry and religion. The American melting pot is gradually melting away all the areas of separation. We dress like our neighbors, speak alike, love and hate alike, work together and enjoy similar delights in food, culture and art—and that bridge of separation has narrowed into insignificance. Our huge *bar-mitzvah* parties, expensive Jewish funerals and impressive temple structures are not strong enough to prevent our children from assimilation.

It is remarkable that in the Soviet Union, where Jews do not celebrate expensive *bar-mitzvah* parties, bury their dead in simple funerals and do not construct any temples or synagogues, the rate of intermarriage is much lower than in the United States. The reasons are very clear. Even the Russian peasant is reluctant to marry Jews and suffer discrimination. The Jewish social and cultural position in the United States, however, is high enough to attract non-Jewish romance, so that we are witnessing daily our sons and daughters spiritually burned alive on the altar of assimilation.

Rabbis are continuously monopolized by this problem, not so much by the national challenge as by individual families in their congregations and communities. It is regrettable that when the problem is brought to the rabbi, the situation is already beyond help.

A number of years ago my wife and I were walking along Rechov Harav Kook in Jerusalem on a Sabbath afternoon. We entered a Sephardic synagogue. At the head of a long table sat a young rabbi lecturing to a gathering of men.

In the course of his lecture, he asked the hypothetical question: "When is it time to start teaching a child Jewish ethics?" He answered the question: "Nine months before its birth."

The answer implied that a child's Jewishness must be properly planned well before its birth. We cannot raise our

children without Jewishness and then expect them to give up
their romantic lives for it.

Let me share with you an interesting personal experience.
My children left their one-and-a-half-year-old infant with us
for two weeks. He was not able to speak fully and had mas-
tered only those words limited to family, toys and food. To
entertain him, we picked up a little picture book to read to
him. The title of the picture book was *The Sabbath*. It had pic-
tures of children in a synagogue, a man in a *tallit* reading the
Torah, the open Ark with the decorated scrolls. As we turned
the pages, there was a picture of a Sabbath table with two candles and a lady standing in front of the candles with her hands
covering her face.

At the sight of the picture, he pointed and shouted:
"Mommy, Mommy!" We were both moved to tears, realizing
how the baby had been impressed by the sight of his mother
in front of the Sabbath candles.

The week after this incident, it was my sad duty to attend
mourners' services in two homes in our community. To con-
form with an old tradition of lighting candles for public worship, I asked for two single Sabbath candles. In one home, to
my embarrassment, I was asked to wait until someone would
go to the store to buy them. In the other home, tenants were
sent out to the neighbors in the apartment house to find
Sabbath candles.

The remarkable and astonishing association between
these two incidents is that in both these families a son had
intermarried. I am not here to blame the mothers for causing
the intermarriage of their sons by neglecting to bless the
Sabbath candles. I just want to point out that in a free and
democratic society such as ours we can only save our children
from assimilation by raising them with an intensive Jewish
consciousness in the home, in school and on the street.
Intensive Jewish living must include strict observance of
dietary regulations, strict observance of the Sabbath and

holidays with all the joys and restrictions, a *yeshivah* training where available from early nursery school even through college, finding residence in the most densely populated Jewish neighborhood procurable, and encouraging children to achieve the highest secular academic training in their capacities. We are reaching a stage where a Jewish boy or girl without a master's degree is a drop-out.

I know this is not an easy program. Parents may have to give up their comfort, good jobs, homes, ease, friends, vacations. But in the long run, these are a small price to pay to avoid being invited to the baptism and confirmation of our grandchildren. Abraham was ready to see his son dead to serve his God, but he was taught through the Akedah that God was not interested in seeing Isaac die a Jew. God wants you to live and enjoy the life of a Jew.

Who Are the Avaryonim?

Yom 5744
Kippur 1983

The sources of our liturgy, the prayers we recite daily, Sabbaths and holidays, are limited. They emanate primarily from the Holy Scriptures—the Five Books of Moses, the Prophets, the Psalms. There are some prayers credited to the teachers in the Talmud—the Tannaim and Amoraim.

The *piyutim* we recite and chant, the acrostic and alphabetic poetry—adorations, laws, elegies added to the liturgy of the High Holidays and festivals—come from the Middle Ages and vary in their usage from country to country. We can recognize the authorship and origin of these medieval additions from their literary style, the cleverly concealed names of the authors or their content. Kol Nidre seems to have eluded all efforts to identify its place of origin, time of dissemination and original purpose. So far no one has established with certainty where and when its usage began and at what point it became the keynote to our Yom Kippur services.

With all the obscurity of its past, its archaic and technical Aramaic language, Kol Nidre has conquered the heart of every Jew and established deep roots in our religious awareness. Its melody has surpassed the confines of the synagogue and assumed a high position in the musical heritage of the world. I believe that next to the music of the *Hatikvah*, the Kol Nidre melody would be most easily recognized by people everywhere. And even the analysis of its melody has confounded musicologists. It shows elements of joyous and cheerful trends, as well as the undertones of tragedy and the search for release from the chains of imprisonment.

In recent years, there has been a popular tendency to associate the origin of Kol Nidre with the sufferings from the Spanish Inquisition. But the Inquisition was not introduced in Spain until 1480, and we find derogatory references to Kol Nidre from Babylonian Academies from as early as the eighth century. Rav Amram Gaon referred to it as a "foreign custom" and a "stupid custom." The prestigious school of Sura rejected it completely. The Geonim of Pumpeditha were more lenient.

In twelfth-century France, rabbinic law introduced changes in the text to include not the absolution of the previous year's vows, but a declaration of advance annulment of any rash promises and vows made in the coming year. This change has been retained in our present text. The Sephardic version still retains the old reading of the absolution of the vows of the previous year. Sephardic communities, however, do not chant Kol Nidre as we do. It is recited silently by each worshipper individually.

Regardless of the time and origin of Kol Nidre, the prayer—if we can call it a prayer—assumed its importance and sanctity as a result of its message for and impact on the Marranos in Spain in the fifteenth century before the Expulsion and the Jewish victims of the Inquisition in Spain, Portugal and other Mediterranean lands in the following centuries.

Let us spend a few minutes tonight in reviewing this tragic chapter in the history of our martyrdom. Who were these Marranos, and why did they cherish the message of Kol Nidre?

At first, the Inquisition's concern was mainly with Jews who had returned to Judaism after having been converted to Christianity, or who had assisted in such a return. In 1278, Rabbi Isaac Males of Toulouse was burned at the stake by the Inquisition for having taken back into the fold a Jew who had been a convert to Christianity. A new situation arose as the result of the forced mass conversions in the fourteenth century, particularly in Spain in 1391 and after. In those years, when mobs forced their way into the Jewish quarters and offered the Jews the choice of baptism or death, thousands were forced to embrace Christianity to save their lives. These forced converts, known as the New Christians, were in many instances still loyal to their ancient faith. Though outwardly conforming to Christian life, they secretly practiced as many of the customs and ceremonies of Judaism as possible. This practice could not remain secret for very long. When a number of these Marranos gained positions of eminence, there was resentment and envy which produced the growing demand for a special Inquisition to deal with these secret Jews.

The Inquisition made use of the most barbarous procedures. A list was issued identifying the various practices that would stamp a Marrano as a secretly practicing Jew, such as wearing a clean shirt on the Sabbath, eating bitter herbs on Passover or fasting on Yom Kippur. Arrests were made on the basis of denunciation by anonymous informers and blackmailers. Defense counsel was not permitted. Torture compelled confession. Punishments varied from heavy fines to death at the stake. Those condemned to death were burned alive at the stake—the Church must not shed blood.

Have you ever visited the Touro Synagogue in Newport, Rhode Island? It was dedicated in 1763 and is the oldest Jewish house of worship in America. It is still a magnificent structure, and a guide will show you a neatly covered opening in the center of the *bimah* which leads to a long underground passageway to the end of the next block and a secret exit in a cemetery. Spanish synagogues since the era of the Inquisition were all built with secret escape routes for Marranos fearing raids by the Inquisition.

As Yom Kippur approached, many Marranos could not resist the temptation to return to their people and synagogues for atonement, confidently hoping that the recitation of Kol Nidre would also absolve them from their vows to the Church. They would arrive through secret alleys and subterranean passages, cover their heads to avoid identification and somehow feel a reconciliation with Judaism through Kol Nidre.

The congregation did not take favorable notice of these estranged visitors. There was no hospitality shown to them. We still practice the unwelcome reception before Kol Nidre where the rabbi holding the Torah scroll and the elders standing nearby recite: "With the authority of the Heavenly Court and the congregational Court, we declare it permissible to pray together with the transgressors."

This introduction did not originate with the Inquisition either. It was included in the thirteenth century by Rabbi Meir ben Baruch of Rothenberg to permit transgressors who had been excommunicated to worship with the congregation. Later on, the reference was directed inadvertently to the Marranos with their covered heads in the rear of the synagogue. Nowadays, we still repeat the same formula to permit ourselves to pray with the *avaryonim*.

I was wondering, is it not arrogant and presumptuous on our part to call by the name *avaryonim* those persecuted Jews, forced to baptize and willing to stake their lives to be in a synagogue at least once a year?

These people, whom we call *avaryonim*, were forced to renounce their Judaism publicly and, at the risk of their lives and property, observed the *mitzvot* secretly. Compared with us, they were saints! We are fortunate to live in a place and time where our faith and its observance are respected, and we readily ignore and neglect our religious duties for our comfort and appetites. If we have the audacity to call them *avaryonim*, how will we rate in the light of future generations?

Following the conclusion of Kol Nidre, we chanted the Shehecheyanu blessing and thanked God who allowed us to live, sustained us and let us reach this Day of Atonement. May we resolve to be worthy of these blessings and take advantage of our privileges to live useful, meaningful and intensive Jewish lives.

Kaddish and Yizkor

Yom Kippur 5744 1983

Years ago, when a stranger or an infrequent worshipper walked into the synagogue, particularly a young man, and stood in the rear, he was immediately dubbed a "Kaddish zogger," one who comes to the synagogue only to recite Kaddish for a departed relative. Synagogues in business sections, serving office or factory workers who recited Kaddish morning and evening, were dubbed "Kaddish factories." Some of these business synagogues also catered to men and women who wanted to recite Yizkor on festivals during business hours. Men and women would wait on line for the privilege of walking into the synagogue for five or ten minutes to recite those few lines of Yizkor in memory of a parent or relative. We used to call those synagogues "Yizkor factories."

Rabbis and religious teachers would ridicule the "Kaddish zoggers" and "Yizkor zoggers" in private, because these men and women would not find time or desire for a full expression of Jewish life and prayer; instead, they satisfied their Jewish obligations with homage to the dead. Little did we realize the profound religious and sentimental power of Kaddish and Yizkor in the preservation of American Judaism.

Kaddish and Yizkor have proved to be the strongest links in the chain of our tradition to hold our people tied together, even such as have been fully assimilated. It cannot be denied that, today, the word Kaddish has more direct emotional appeal for the Jew than the word Shema. The word Yizkor conveys more to him than the words Shemoneh Esrei, although no one with an understanding of our prayers would compare their religious values.

Louis Rabinowitz, former Chief Rabbi of Johannesburg, in a paper on the Kaddish observes that nine hundred and nine-ty-nine Jews out of a thousand will tell you with certainty that Kaddish is the prayer recited by mourners, especially chil-dren, during the year following the death of their parents and on the anniversary of that death, known as the Yahrzeit. The aspect of the Kaddish as the mourner's prayer has so com-pletely overshadowed all the others that a popular name in Yiddish for one's son is *"mein kaddishel."* And yet it is the only aspect of the Kaddish not mentioned in the Talmud.

Some thirty years ago, there lived in our neighborhood a gentleman who had been born in the Old City of Jerusalem. He spoke a beautiful Israeli Yiddish. He was a radical, did not give his son any religious education, and the only occasion he came to the synagogue was to tease me with his irreligious remarks.

One Sunday morning, I recall meeting him at Ratner's on the corner. He held a big dog, and as I looked at both of them, he remarked in Yiddish: *"Dos is mein Kaddish.* (This is my Kaddish.)"

My retort was to him: "You are leaving for yourself a bet-ter Kaddish than your father did."

To go back to Rabbi Rabinowitz's paper on the Kaddish, he remarks that the Kaddish is liturgically justified on two occasions only. It was originally instituted to be recited in the House of Study after the completion of the daily lesson in the form of the Kaddish d'Rabbanan—the Scholar's Kaddish. It also finds its place in the service in the form of "Half Kaddish" and "Full Kaddish," depending upon the section of the service.

As such, the contents of the Kaddish are self-understood. It consists of a glorification of God and the Messianic hope of his future reign in the world. It is a prayer of great antiquity and is undoubtedly reflected in what is called in the Christian religion, the Lord's Prayer: "Our Father who art in Heaven, Hallowed be Thy name, Thy Kingdom come, Thine will be done." This is to all intents and purposes a literal translation of the first verse of the Kaddish.

It is when we consider the association of this prayer with the dead that the problem arises. You can search through each verse in the Kaddish but you will find no reference to death or the hereafter. The only association between the Kaddish and the orphan comes from a late legend in which Rabbi Akiba taught a child the Kaddish and a ghost came to tell the Rabbi that it had gained salvation.

The Kaddish has become hallowed by the people's sighs and tears that it has absorbed in the course of centuries. It shows the power of the heart over the intellect, of emotion over logic.

The recitation of Yizkor and Hazkarat Neshamot also crept into the synagogue service through the back door, so to speak. When it was first introduced in the Babylonian Academies around the year 1000, the Geonim took exception to a custom that would mar the festivals with the sad memories of departed relatives and parents. However, the people did not listen to their rabbis; they continued praying for the souls of departed loved ones and donating to charities in their memories. All the learned protests proved ineffective. In such matters, the heart overpowers the mind, and emotion is stronger than the intellect. The Jew found in the recital of Yizkor the bridge to join heaven and earth.

In Yizkor, the magic formula following the pledge for

tzedakah ends with: "*Utzror bitzror hachaim*. And may God bind the souls of our departed in the bundle of life." That phrase is usually interpreted to refer to the spiritual source of life, the mystical gathering of souls to which we relegate the *neshamot* of our beloved. I would like to extend the meaning of this petition that God may bind the souls of our beloved to our souls. We constitute the *tzror hachaim*, the bundle of life. Through our lives and our good deeds we extend the lives of our parents, not just physically but also spiritually. It is from this point that we may rationalize our Yizkor emotions, with the confidence that it brings peace and solace to the souls of the dead as well as comfort to the worshipper.

A Time to Take Stock

Rosh 5745
Hashanah 1984

The Hebrew name for the holiday we observe today is not Shanah Chadashah, the New Year, but Rosh Hashanah, the Beginning of the Year. And it does not occur on the first day of the first Jewish calendar month, but on the first day of the seventh month, which is Tishrei. We adopted the colloquial translation of Rosh Hashanah to New Year to coordinate with universal celebrations of New Year days.

In Scripture, the festival is not called even once by the name of Rosh Hashanah. The Torah refers to the day as Yom Teruah, a day of sounding the *shofar*, and as Yom Zichron Teruah, a day of remembering the sounding of the *shofar*. As a New Year, the Torah prescribes no celebration at all. Indeed, Rosh Hashanah is widely discussed and developed in the Mishnah and the Talmud. But for that matter, the first of Tishrei is not the only Rosh Hashanah in Talmudic tradition. There are four New Year days on the Talmudic calendar— there is the civic New Year, the agricultural New Year, the religious New Year, and the popular 15th of Shevat, also a Rosh Hashanah for trees.

Our normal observance of Rosh Hashanah is a solemn yet

joyous festival. We abstain from work, beautify our homes, prepare sumptuous meals and greet each other with our best wishes. Many go on vacation to resorts and hotels.

Jewish tradition ascribes the anniversary of the creation of the world to this day, and as such, it is also the anniversary of the birth of man—the pinnacle of creation. Man stands in judgment on each universal birthday. His record of the previous year is examined by the Heavenly Court, and his destiny is determined upon that record.

In contrite prayer and supplication, we gather in places of worship and hear the cantor intone: "On Rosh Hashanah, it is inscribed, and on Yom Kippur, it is sealed. Who will live, and who will die. Who will prosper, and who will be impoverished."

Following our solemn prayers, we go home to enjoy the holiday. It is Yom Tov, a day of festivity!

To go back to my original theme: in the Torah, the festival is known as Yom Teruah, a day of the sounding of the *shofar*— and this we surely do. In the course of the day, we sound one hundred blasts of different dimensions.

The *shofar*, the horn of an animal, preferably that of a ram, constitutes one of the oldest musical instruments in history. Its use is mentioned numerous times throughout Biblical literature. Different sounds and combination of sounds announced corresponding occasions. There were sounds of joy and sounds of sorrow, sounds of alarm and sounds of festivity, military sounds of marching and camping, of attack and retreat. The Torah does not specify any reason for sounding the *shofar* on Rosh Hashanah. Indeed, it is the beginning of the new month, and the *shofar* was sounded to proclaim each new month. That day, however, is known as Rosh Chodesh, the beginning of the month, not as Yom Teruah.

Did you ever ask yourself, what is the purpose of this exercise?

The rabbis in the Talmud asked the question. It goes like this: "Why do we sound the *shofar*?"

The answer: "God commanded, and we sound it."

The question is fortified with: "Why do we make so many sounds?"

And the answer is not so clear: "In order to confuse Satan."

This final answer is even more confusing. Some understand the statement to refer to the Satanic demons that made the lives of medieval society miserable. There is a historic political understanding of the Satan in the blowing of the *shofar*. The reference is to the fear of the Roman occupation authorities to whom the *shofar* blasts indicated rebellion.

In any case, the lack of a clear reason in the Torah enriched our literature with many ingenious moralistic and historical motives for the sounding of the *shofar* suggested by saintly teachers throughout the years. The tenth century sage of Sura, Rabbeinu Saadiah Gaon, formulated ten themes for the sounding of the *shofar* on Rosh Hashanah.

Let us offer some of these themes in brief sentences:

- ~ The *shofar* announces the anniversary of creation and proclaims the sovereignty of the Creator.
- ~ It recalls the revelation on Mount Sinai to which our people pledged, "We will do and obey."
- ~ The sounds recall the battle cries of the martyrs at the destruction of the Temple in Jerusalem.
- ~ It brings to memory the sacrifice of Isaac and the self-sacrifice of Isaac's children ever since.
- ~ It inspires and rekindles our hopes and determination for the restoration of Israel.

One of the reasons given by the Gaon, the one I recommend for your meditation, is that the *shofar* announces on Rosh Hashanah the onset of the Ten Days of Repentance, ten days designed for good deeds and repentance culminating with the Day of Atonement. We generally understand the concept of *teshuvah* in the theological terms of repentance, penitence, penance in conjunction with sin, perdition, Hell—these are Christian theological doctrines that have no connection with our gracious divine gifts of *teshuvah.*

Let me illustrate this thought with an old parable from the sermons of the Dubno Maggid, the famed eighteenth century preacher who was reportedly also the mentor of the Gaon of Vilna. He compared these Ten Days of Repentance, beginning with Rosh Hashanah, to the story of a merchant of crockery and glassware who had packed and prepared his wares for a journey to the fair.

Before the journey, the owner loaded the merchandise on the wagon carefully and cautioned the driver to drive slowly to protect the delicate glassware from breakage. It was quite a distance to the fairgrounds, and the driver was careless, allowing his horses to gallop over potholes. The wagon was shaking noisily, and the merchant feared for the safety of his glassware.

The driver pulled into a number of stopovers to buy whisky and water the horses. At each stopover, the merchant begged the driver to allow him to examine the merchandise and assess the damage caused by the hazardous journey. But the driver had no time to spare. He was in a hurry to get there before dark. The merchant was helpless.

Just before they reached the last stop, the merchant grabbed hold of the driver and declared, "You are not leaving until I check my merchandise. I must see what's broken, what I can repair. I need to know what stock I have left for the fair!"

The preacher used this parable to illustrate the oncoming Ten Days of Repentance. The *yetzer hara,* the evil inclination, our spiritual and emotional driver, keeps on driving us relentlessly over hazardous roads, risky paths, shady experiences. And so it rides, month after month—Nissan, Iyar, Sivan, Tammuz—we don't have the time to stop and check for gains, losses, breakage, neglect. When we reach the Ten Days of Repentance, on Rosh Hashanah, we stop the momentum of the *yetzer hara* and look over our neglected stock, take some inventory and examine what we bring to the Day of Atonement.

Our modern lives have become so complex, so obsessed, so challenging. Advanced technology adds to the complexities, drives, goals, failures and achievements. We cannot stop for a moment! Problems! Personal problems, family problems, education for our children, best colleges, paying bills, repairing the house, vacations, mortgages, doctors, operations, pills, drugs, dinners, theater, insurance, banquets, and more and more.

We don't stop for a moment to ponder on the moralistic question: "*Mah chovasi baolam?* What am I living for?" Running and driving like an animal! We jump from place to place, from day to day, from position to position—just like a bird in a cage, with no escape.

Before the sounding of the *shofar*, the *baal tekiah* recites the benediction: Blessed are You, O God our Lord, King of the Universe, who has sanctified us with his *mitzvot* and ordered us to hear the sound of the *shofar*.

Mind you, the *mitzvah* is not to sound the *shofar*, but to hear and understand the call of the *shofar*.

For nearly eight centuries, preachers have recommended the message of the *shofar* as expounded by the great Maimonides: "Awake, sleepers, from your slumber, and rouse yourselves from your lethargy. Scrutinize your deeds and return in *teshuvah*. Remember your Creator, you who forget eternal truth in the trifles of the hour, who stray all year after vain illusions which can neither profit nor deliver. Look well into your souls and mend your ways and your actions; let each one of you forsake his evil path and his unworthy purpose, and return to God, so that He may have mercy upon you."

The Path to Repentance

Yom 5745
Kippur 1984

Let me start with a question: Did you celebrate today? Did you enjoy good meals today? That is, sumptuous food, good liquor, well-prepared holiday meals? If you did, then I have good tidings for you. It is accounted to your religious credit as if you had fasted today. It sounds incredible, but it is true.

Our Sages taught: "Whoever enjoys good and plentiful food on the day before Yom Kippur and fasts on the day of Yom Kippur is credited with having fasted two days." How can the consumption of much delicious food in a penitential season be compared with total abstention from food and liquids? It is certainly easier to fill up a whole day with sizzling hot *kreplach* (the traditional Erev Yom Kippur delicacy) and wine than to fast for twenty-five hours. Why is overeating one day as meritorious as fasting on the next?

One explanation is that it demonstrates the concern and love of God, our compassionate Father, for the good health of His children in view of the upcoming fast day. God, therefore, orders us to eat more on the previous day so that we may more easily sustain the fast. That sounds reasonable.

A more profound explanation is offered by the codifier R.

Joseph Caro in his commentary on the Tur. He illustrates the *mitzvah* of overindulgence on Erev Yom Kippur with an analogy of a person who has just been tried on serious criminal charges and is awaiting the final verdict. Naturally, on the day before judgment is handed down, he will be anxious, worried, dejected—especially if he may lose his life, his property, his health, his family. Could such a person be expected to feast on the day before the issue of the verdict? Now, continues the illustration, suppose the indicted and tried person receives a written promise from the judge that if he stands up in court, confesses his crimes, expresses regret and sincerely pledges to go straight, he will receive a complete pardon from the judge. Will he be able to celebrate? It depends. If he has faith in the judge's promise and honestly intends to make amends, he will have a ball on the day before judgment; he will eat and drink and be happy. But if he lacks faith in the judge's promise and fears the evil verdict facing him, he will spend the preceding day in fear, pain and uncertainty.

Similarly, explains R. Joseph Caro, the Torah promises us: "On this day shall atonement be made for you to cleanse you, from all your sins shall you be clean before God." A person who believes in the Torah and confidently expects to be totally forgiven on Yom Kippur has good reason to enjoy himself the day before Yom Kippur. But a person who has no faith in the promises of the Torah, and still fears the consequences of his actions on the day of judgment, cannot in good conscience celebrate the day beforehand. Hence, the Rabbis' claim that those who eat, drink and rejoice Erev Yom Kippur demonstrate similar faith in the Torah as those who fast on Yom Kippur.

Following the Second Vatican Council in 1965, called together on the initiative of Pope John XXIII, in which Cardinal Bea's declaration absolved Jews from the collective guilt of the Crucifixion, many ecumenical movements among Catholic clergy and laity sought dialogues with Jews and

Jewish institutions. The Brothers in a local parochial high school invited me two years in succession to assist them in a model *seder* before Passover. For a while, some Brothers attended my weekly Bible class in the synagogue. A local church elementary school asked permission to bring their older classes into our sanctuary to receive my explanations of the sacred objects in the use of prayer.

I recall one occasion when I was leading a group of boys and girls through the synagogue and showing them a *tallit*, *tefillin*, a *mezuzah*, a *shofar*, a Siddur, a Havdalah candle, Kiddush cup, answering questions and offering explanations. A sensitive little girl of about eleven or twelve stood close to me and absorbed all the objects with keen interest. She wanted to touch everything and became involved in it.

As we were leaving the main synagogue and going into the lobby, the little girl held my hand, then turned her eyes up to me with an innocent question: "Rabbi, do you believe in the Holy Mother?"

"No," I said. "I don't."

Her eyes filled with tears as she added, "O, Rabbi, how will you be saved?"

Poor child! She is the victim of the doctrine of original sin, in which people are doomed at birth and cannot extricate themselves without baptism, implying death on the Cross and rebirth in the Resurrection. And that is exactly what Yom Kippur is repudiating!

We begin with the premise that man is not born with the burden of Original Sin. In the words of the Talmud, our pledge to accept the Torah on Mount Sinai absolved the sin of Eve and the Serpent. We deny the Pauline doctrines of predestination with regard to our proper conduct and behavior. We say with Rabbi Akiva that man is fortunate to have been born in the image of God, and granted the intellect to discern between right and wrong, between good and evil.

Moreover, we are particularly fortunate to have been the

recipients of the Torah, that precious instrument that is the guide to good life and happiness in this world and in the world to come. However, we have to recognize and acknowledge human frailty, error and misjudgment. No one is so righteous that he always does good and never errs. Our merciful Father in Heaven, in compassion for His children, taught us: Because of his human errors, man does not forfeit his right to life and happiness. All he has to do is correct his way, turn back, start over again and stay on the right track.

Yom Kippur is the day of *teshuvah*, of man's return—it is the greatest gift of God to mankind. Regardless of how low a man may fall spiritually, socially, emotionally, he can always rise again and stand erect. We don't have to die in sin and be reformed again. A *baal teshuvah* is not a "newborn" Jew in the same sense as we understand a "born again" Christian. A *baal teshuvah* is adjusting his way of life.

In *teshuvah*, lip service is not enough. Repeating "Al Chet" and beating the breast a whole day and a whole night is like sounding a fire alarm without putting out the fire. The alarm by itself will not extinguish the conflagration.

Maimonides offers a practical formula for *teshuvah*:

The first step is the acknowledgment of the error—the sin. That is the most difficult part. We are all so self-righteous. Who is ready to admit that he wronged his family, his community, his God? We would call that a guilt-complex. Our habit is to blame others for our failings. Therefore, the first step is to face our error head on and admit it.

Next comes full remorse and regret for the commission of transgressions and failures of the past. We must realize that these errors have removed us from our inner selves, that the failures have distanced us from a loving God and a purpose in life. The misguided road brought on confusion and lack of direction. With intense regret for the past, we come to the crucial aspect of *teshuvah*—sincere commitment for the future, determination and resolve to get back to the right way of life, to be guided by a sense of morality, decency, love and the tenets of Torah.

We need no intermediary to come close to our Father in Heaven with a contrite heart and confession. No system of penance, flagellation or suffering is necessary. The prophet Hosea proclaims: "Return, O Israel, unto God your Lord." The usual translation of the word *ad* as "unto" betrays the real meaning of the prophecy. "Unto" is the translation of the word *el*. By employing the word *ad*, the prophet emphasizes the closeness and nearness to God of those who return to Him in truth. Just one turn toward Him, and you are on the right path.

I would like to recommend a good first project for *teshuvah*. I was inspired to it by an article in the New York *Times* by Natalie Gittelson, executive editor of *McCall's*. The article is entitled "American Jews Rediscover Orthodoxy." It is primarily a study of *baalei teshuvah*, men and women who had been estranged from Orthodox Jewish living and have "returned" fully to religious life. Miss Gittelson had interviewed a number of *baalei teshuvah* in every walk of life—an investment banker, a Nobel laureate, a law professor, a lawyer, an actor, a screenwriter. As I read the interesting study, I noticed that each of the *baalei teshuvah* expressed the delight in the rediscovery of the Sabbath. It is not a day of prohibitions, absolutions and denials; it is a day of pleasure, of rest, spiritual rejuvenation, reunion with God and family.

The author quotes one gentleman who said: "I don't know how I lived without the Sabbath." A Zionist publicist of the early part of this century, Shmaryahu Levine, is credited with the remark that "more than Israel did for the Shabbat, the Shabbat did for Israel."

A return to Sabbath observance is a good start for *teshuvah*.

O Lord, we know there is no man so righteous that he can be sinless in Your sight. But on this Day of Atonement, we resolve to strive for righteousness more zealously. Strengthen us in our resolve, and help us overcome the many temptations that would lure us from the right path. On this sacred night, may our prayers rise before Your throne of mercy. Forgive our sins, and absolve us from wrongdoing. Inscribe us for a year of life, health and peace, and help us rise toward greater accomplishment.

$\mathscr{L}$ife after $\mathscr{D}$eath

Y o m 5745
K i p p u r 1984

*I*n the mid-1940s, a rabbi-psychologist in Boston, Joshua Loth Liebman, published a remarkable book under the title *Peace of Mind*, which became a best-seller for a number of years. In one section, the rabbi discusses the confusing position of the clergyman when called to a house where a death had occurred.

The clergyman finds the bereft family in tears, thanking the retiring nurse for the devoted and tender care she gave their loved one. If the doctor is still there, they express their appreciation to him for all he did and tried to do to keep the patient alive and comfortable. The doctor leaves with expressions of sorrow and is told by the family that he surely did whatever humanly possible to save the life of their beloved.

Then the family faces the clergyman. He is the one who claims to speak the word of God. He is the one who promises life, good health and happiness to all that live a righteous and blameless life. In the faces of the mourners, the clergyman reads an unspoken but deafening question: "Why did this happen to us? Why did he or she suffer so much? What did we do so wrong to deserve such agony?"

The clergyman has no answers. He knows that "the Lord

giveth, and the Lord taketh away," and yet "the Name of Lord must be blessed."

Of all the sermons I have to prepare and deliver in the course of the year, I find the Yizkor sermon most challenging. Preaching on Sabbaths and festivals, I address a congregation gathered to pray and be inspired by the rituals as well as the Scripture reading and liturgy. The sermon accentuates the sanctity of the occasion by delving into the background of the festival and its significance to our way of life.

At Yizkor, we face a different congregation. Men and women, young and old, are gathered for a distinct purpose. They seek natural comfort in invoking the memory of loved ones and, particularly, to demonstrate their hope and conviction that their loved ones are still alive. These bereft people need the assurance and confidence from the rabbi that the lost spouse of many years, the father, mother, loving child, sister, brother is still alive, and that we come closer to each other in the still and sanctified serenity of the synagogue as we invoke their names and memories.

And here comes the dilemma! How can one explain our belief in Olam Haba, the world to come, in a life after death, to modern, thinking, sophisticated people? Even the belief in an invisible God is a more rational concept and easier to accept than the belief in an afterlife or the immortality of the soul. It is purely a matter of faith. We certainly cannot prove it in a test-tube or by mathematical formulae. There is no historical evidence for the existence of "the next world." No one has yet returned from the dead and told us what to anticipate there. The belief in Olam Haba is surely nothing more than sheer faith. To quote a saintly teacher of our century, the Chafetz Chaim, for those who have faith there are no questions, and for those who have no faith there are no answers.

Yet the belief in a life after death is one of the cardinal doctrines in Judaism, expounded in Talmudic literature and affirmed by our religious philosophers and codifiers.

Although the belief in a hereafter is not explicitly developed in the Holy Scriptures, it is implicit in many references throughout Biblical literature. For example, the statement in Koheleth: "And the dust returns to the earth as it was and the spirit returns unto God who gave it." Also, the Psalmist appeals to God: "Do not abandon my soul to Sheol." Maimonides included the doctrine of the resurrection of the dead as one of the thirteen principles of our faith. And Rabbi Akiva stated anyone who denies the Biblical authority of the principle of the immortality of the soul has renounced his share in the world to come.

Normative Judaism regards death as the release of the soul from its imprisonment in the body to continue a spiritual existence. Indeed, we have no speculative literature on the kind of existence the soul assumes after the release from the body. A third century rabbi remarked that "one hour of bliss in the world-to-come is better than all the life in this world." But he also maintained that "better is one hour of *teshuvah* and good deeds in this world than the entire world-to-come." The obvious difference is that in this world all the joys are physical: good food, delightful surroundings, fine clothes, spacious homes. In the world-to-come, the pleasures are only spiritual, as poetically expressed in the Talmud: "The righteous sit with their crowns (of their achievements) on their heads and enjoy the splendor of the Divine Presence."

Our souls have to be trained and conditioned in this world to appreciate and find pleasure in the spiritual joys of the hereafter. A person who has cultivated an appreciation of the arts will find enjoyment in a visit to an art gallery. Only the ear that has been attuned to good music will enjoy a musical concert, an opera. The disinterested person will be bored. Similarly, the spiritually cultured soul will enjoy its rewards in the presence of the Divine glory in the world-to-come.

However, there is still another form of immortality that is more easily understood than the spiritual existence in the hereafter. I believe that it is for this form of immortality that we pray in the Yizkor formula for our beloved: "And bind their souls in the bundle of life." That bundle of life is usually understood to refer to the universal spiritual divine container of soul material. No, I believe that the reference is to us, the bundle of life into which the memory of our beloved have been deeply imbedded.

The immortal souls of our beloved have remained implanted in our hearts, in our minds, in our actions, in our very lives. We the living constitute the continuity of the lives of our parents. As we recall the sweet memories of the love of a spouse, a child, parent, brother or sister, a tenderly loving grandparent, they remain tied eternally to our lives and cherished in our hearts. By setting up our loved ones as our constant mentors and advisors, by acting in harmony with their ways of life and wishes, we actually let them guide us from the grave as they did while on earth. They are no longer dead; and they continue to live in our lives and in our constant communion with their souls.

Father of mercy, in whose hands are the souls of the living and the dead, may Your consolation cheer us as we remember our beloved and honored kinfolk, our beloved parents who have gone to their eternal rest. They are the crown of our heads and glory. Their desire was to train us in the good and righteous way, to teach us Your statutes and commandments and to instruct us to do justice and to love mercy. We beseech You, O Lord, grant us strength to be faithful to their charge while the breath of life is within us. And may their souls repose in the land of the eternally living, beholding Your glory and delighting in Your splendor.

Fundamentalism Overspills into the Jewish Social Structure

Rosh Hashanah 5746 1985

*T*he topic I have selected for my message today is "Fundamentalism Overspills into the Jewish Social Structure." Fundamentalism in its narrow definition refers to Church doctrine and conduct in the literal interpretation of the Bible and its teachings. Fundamentalism in this sense engaged in the saving of souls from eternal perdition, and expressed itself in piety, scrupulous observance of the Sabbath laws, tithing and abstaining from such social activities as smoking, drinking, gambling. Fundamentalist churches are found in a number of Protestant denominations varying in degrees of observance and beliefs.

In its broader sense, fundamentalism guards religious doctrine from liberal interpretation of Scripture and deviation from the literal understanding of the Holy Writ. Liberal interpretation of Scripture is heretical. Critical, literary or historical study of the Bible is prohibited, and even the miraculous events in the Exodus from Egypt or the narratives of Creation are to be accepted as absolute truth and factual. Fundamentalists in this category do not limit their beliefs to personal conduct. It is their duty as guardians of the true faith to make sure that no heresy be transmitted through public education or social and cultural institutions of government.

Not many of you are old enough to recall the Scopes Trial of 1925. John Thomas Scopes, a high school science teacher in Dayton, Tennessee, was arrested for teaching the evolutionary theory of Charles Darwin in his *Origin of the Species*. The evolution of man from earlier species contradicted the Bible story of creation wherein man was formed by God from the dust of the earth.

Two national giants of the bar were involved in the case—William Jennings Bryant, the tribune of conservative America, and Clarence Darrow, the defender of twentieth century liberalism. After a long debate, Scopes was found guilty and fined one hundred dollars. He never returned to his classroom and also did not pay the fine due to some technicality in the trial.

A strong resurgence of religious fundamentalism is overwhelming American social and political life today. Through radio and television, skilled fundamentalist preachers reach millions of men and women, dramatically injecting fear of perdition for violating the strict word of the Gospel. They collect millions of dollars and establish formidable churches and institutions as testaments to their success. These evangelical fundamentalists no longer limit their preaching to personal piety. Their issues are national—abortion, school prayers, homosexuality, feminism, pornography and, of course, foreign policy. We have become very familiar with the oratory of the Rev. Jerry Falwell, whose Moral Majority movement claimed credit for Ronald Reagan's victory in both elections. It is ironic that the new fundamentalists are intensely pro-Israel, since the expected Second Coming of their Messiah is mystically associated with the return of Israel to its homeland.

Fundamentalism is no longer limited to Christians. In Islam it manifests itself in its ugliest militancy. The reactionary government in Iran, the religious wars and genocide in Lebanon, the assassination of President Sadat of Egypt, all these stem from the same understanding—or misunderstanding— of the teachings of the Koran.

The purpose of this lengthy introduction is that you may better understand the influence and impact of this dominant atmosphere upon Jewish society. There is an old Yiddish adage, which means, freely translated, "As the Christians do, so Jews do." We are familiar with what is usually referred to as the three major divisions in American Jewish religious practice: Orthodox, Conservative and Reform. The effect of these divisions has been only congregational and nominal. The divisions may have been very important to Jewish theologians; in actual practice, they were only organizations that signified affiliation and sometimes social status. Changes in affiliations from one to another were frequent. In smaller communities, some families would affiliate with all three divisions and contribute to the seminaries of each one separately. Members of Reform married Orthodox, the Orthodox married Conservative. Officiating Rabbis made no distinction—they were all Jews. Also, in Jewish civic, philanthropic and fraternal life, the divisions had no effect.

In this last year, we have noticed a trend of fanatical fundamentalism threatening the unity of our people. The fanaticism is not limited to the Orthodox; it is equally propounded by the Conservative and Reform.

Let me offer you some examples.

For many years the Jewish community of New York City gathered to observe Yom Hashoah in Temple Emanuel on Fifth Avenue. Last year, this community service was moved to Madison Square Garden ostensibly to accommodate the large crowd, but in fact, the move was made because of pressure from Orthodox groups who objected to entering a Reform temple. At the same Yom Hashoah service, the Kineret Youth Choir of Yonkers, a long-time participant in the ceremony, was not invited to sing because it is a mixed choir of Jewish boys and girls. This, too, offended some Orthodox participants who wanted the boys and girls to sing in separate choirs.

The aggravating circumstances point to the severity of the fundamentalist mentality of the Orthodox. Even in the observance of the sacred memorial to the martyrs of the Holocaust, they persevered in the strict observance of the religious principles as directed by their leaders.

Here is another example bordering on *chilul Hashem*: Early this month, we read the sensational story of a visit by a delegation of the U.J.A. Federation to the city of Cracow in Poland. No more than about two hundred elderly Jews have survived from the sixty thousand Jews that prospered there before World War II. When asked what the American delegation could do for the vanishing community, an elderly lady, Raza Jakubowitz, suggested that they send them a *bar-mitzvah* celebration, because since the German invasion forty-six years ago, there had been no *bar-mitzvah* in Cracow.

Subsequently, Barry and Marjorie Strom of Stamford, Connecticut, were persuaded to allow their son, Eric, to celebrate his *bar-mitzvah* at the Rama Synagogue on the Sabbath of September 7. The Stroms are associated with the Reconstructionist movement, which is the radical wing of the Conservative Synagogue, and the rabbi is a lady named Emily Korzenick. The U.J.A.-Federation that planned and presumably financed the project apparently did not realize the incongruity of the celebration of a Reconstructionist *bar-mitzvah* presided over by a gowned female rabbi in the ancient Rama Synagogue, named after the sixteenth-century codifier of Orthodox Judaism. The *bar-mitzvah* was to be for the pleasure and satisfaction of Jewish people to whom such a scene would seem ridiculous.

The whole business could have passed unnoticed, were it not for the publicity it attracted: television cameras, reporters and photographers gathered in advance for the scoop. American Orthodox fundamentalists intervened. An Orthodox rabbi and cantor arrived from New York far in advance, transferred the service to another synagogue in Cracow, got rid of the television cameras and photographers, and poor Emily Korzenick who had prepared the boy for the service had to follow the recitation from a seat in the balcony with the other elderly ladies.

But it is not only the Orthodox who have been exhibiting militant fundamentalism. In the course of the last year, Reform Judaism, in defiant repudiation of the age-old *halachah* that only the offspring of a Jewish mother can be considered a born Jew, adopted the patrilineal descent for native Jewishness, driving an insoluble wedge between themselves and the rest of the Jewish community. Is it not remarkable that although the early Reformers of the nineteenth century rejected the belief in the resurrection of the dead, the hope for the coming of the Messiah and circumcision as a brutal primitive relic, and even considered substituting Sunday for the Sabbath, they did not dare touch the unity of the Jewish people? American fundamentalists, however, are practically separating themselves completely by accepting patrilineal descent.

This year also witnessed a violent rift in the Conservative movement. I live with the universal clamor to bring women into equal position with men in religious life. Reform and Reconstructionist institutions are ordaining more women as rabbis and cantors than they were a decade ago. The Conservative movement, seeking to capture the larger participation of women at regular congregational services and educational institutions, moved slowly in the process. First, some congregations began to count their women to the ten required for a *minyan*. Smaller congregations that had difficulty in assembling ten men, in particular, found the counting of women for the *minyan* very beneficial.

Some congregations went a step further and began to emulate the Reform by calling women for Kriat Hatorah. Not all congregations followed this innovation. These changes were ostensibly within the confines of Halachah. For a number of years, leaders of the movement attempted to urge the Seminary to accept females as candidates for ordination. Here they stumbled. The opposition came from prominent rabbis and particularly from the learned teachers at the Seminary. The opposition was based primarily on the question of Halachah. This last year, the proponents of the change won out, leaving a number of prominent Conservative rabbis and faculty members in strong opposition as Traditional Conservatives.

In each case, we detect the trend toward radical fundamentalism in defiance of opposition, disregarding the dire consequences. In a few years, Orthodox and Conservative will no longer be able to accept the authentic Jewishness of the Reform movement without investigating parental origin.

Is the proverbial Jewish unity about to disintegrate? Jewish national leaders, social and religious, are disturbed. Do we need a Pharaoh, Haman or Hitler to declare us a unified entity? In the eyes of our enemies, we are all Jews!

You may have noticed that a major theme in the Rosh Hashanah ritual is the prayer for the unity of mankind in the service of God. We pray: "Now, therefore, O God our Lord, impose Your awe upon all Your works, and Your dread upon all that You have created, that all works may fear You, that they may all form a single bond to do Your will with a perfect heart."

We repeat the old prayer: "All the inhabitants of the world shall know and acknowledge that to You every knee must bend, every tongue must swear . . . they shall give honor to Your glorious Name."

A story is told about a *chassidic rebbe* who was asked why we pray on Rosh Hashanah for universal peace and unity rather than Jewish peace and unity. With talmudic ingenuity, the *rebbe* answered, "Our Sages taught us that a person who prays for his friend's welfare, while he himself is in need of the same help, will be answered first."

In the light of our examination of the tragic fundamentalist rivalries and fanatical conflicts threatening the peaceful relationships of religions, races and nationalities, let us pray for universal sanity. Let us pray that bigotry, hatred and divisiveness will be banished, so that it may reflect favorably on our people in a world of peace and security.

Our Spiritual Inheritance

Yom 5747
Kippur 1986

*I*n Tractate Taanit in the Talmud, there is a moot question: "Why do we go out to the cemeteries?" Rabbi Levi ben Chamah and Rabbi Chanina differ in their answers: One said: "It is to signify that we regard ourselves before You as mortals." The other said: "We go to cemeteries so that the dead may invoke mercy for us."

I believe the driving force that brings hundreds of people to temples and synagogues to recite Yizkor comes from sentimental and emotional directives. On the one hand, we come to reopen tender wounds, some old, some fresh. We recall our parents, our spouses, brothers, sisters, and in some painful cases, we recall children, whom we have loved and lost.

Some of us recall whole families lost in the Holocaust. Indeed, we share their pain. We shed a tear, utter a sigh and seek comfort in the petition: Remember, O Lord, the soul of my beloved departed father, mother, husband, wife, sister, brother, child. God be their possession in their peaceful resting places.

Yizkor is also a very positive religious exercise. It helps us get in touch with reality, our own mortality. We often speak of "terminal diseases." But the illness is definitely not terminal. Life is terminal. Life must come to an end for all of us, some sooner, some later; no one leaves this world alive.

So the recitation of Yizkor brings forth mixed emotion. Just as we remember the pain, the suffering, and in some cases also the suddenness of death, we also think of the sweetness and beauty of life—the sharing, the love, the smile, the touch, the warmth. Yizkor becomes a nostalgic instrument with which we seek to capture the past and infuse it into our present lives.

I would like to take this opportunity to join the campaign of recent months to alert the public about the alarming increase in teen-age suicides.

Several years ago, I was called by a Bronx funeral chapel to officiate at a funeral service. The only information we got from the chapel was the name of the deceased. I may have told the congregation about this sad experience. It implanted itself so deeply on my memory that the whole tragedy cannot escape my mind.

When I came to the chapel, I proceeded to the family visitation room where the coffin is usually open in an alcove in the room, and the family is gathered all around.

I walked in, looked at the people and said aloud: "I am the rabbi. To whom can I talk?"

A youngish woman slid off a table and said: "Talk to me."

"Are you the daughter?" I asked.

"No," she said, "I am the mother."

Instinctively I turned around to the open coffin and there lay a beautiful young girl, full of charm, youthfully dressed up. I turned to the mother: "What happened?"

"Suicide," she said.

Right next to me stood a young boy, about eighteen or nineteen. He looked lost and forlorn.

"Who is he?" I asked.

"That's her boyfriend," the mother answered.

Subsequently, I found out that a sister of the girl, two years older, had committed suicide the year before. Their father had died at the age of thirty-seven. The mother tried to give them a home and provide for their normal needs, but she lost both her children.

There is an interesting story of a suicide by Y. L. Peretz, the great artist who depicted so colorfully the life of Eastern European Jewry in the nineteenth century. This story is called: "Four Generations—Four Wills." The changing values of the four generations is reflected in the will the head of each generation leaves to his successor. I have several points in each of the four wills to read to you.

"When Reb Eliezer Chaikels departed from this world, the following note was found under his pillow:

> *It is my will that my children continue as partners in my lumber business. After my death, they are to make a gate for the Jewish cemetery and repair the roof of the synagogue. My unmarried son Binyamin is to inherit my books; my other sons and sons-in-law got their books when they married. My spouse is to have her own quarters in the house; let her take in a poor orphan, so as not to be lonely. She is to share as an equal partner with the other heirs.*

Reb Binyamin, son of Reb Eliezer Chaikels, left a more detailed and elaborate will. Some important points were:

> *As to my wealth, I have no will with regard to its disposal. I am confident that the members of my family will either live in peace and harmony or else they will divide up in accordance with right and justice, and nobody will in any way try to take advantage of another. I ask of my household, namely of my wife, my sons and sons-in-law, that they deduct the tithe for charity. I beg my children to continue the custom of deducting each year before the Jewish New Year one-tenth of the profit of the preceding twelve months for the benefit of the poor. I beg them most urgently to study every day at least one portion of the Gemara. On the anniversary of my death, let the men study Torah all day and women distribute charity—privately, without public display.*

When Reb Binyamin's son, Moritz Benditsohn died, this document was found written in Polish:

> *I bequeath ten thousand as a trust fund, the interest of which is to be distributed each year among the poor. I bequeath ten thousand for a bed in the new hospital, on condition that the bed be named for me. Contributions are to be sent to all Hebrew schools; the teachers and students are to follow my bier. A sum of money is to be set aside as a trust fund for the specific purpose of keeping my grave and tombstone in perfect shape.*

When Moritz's son died, they found the following note:

> *I, Moritz Benditsohn's son, leave this world in neither happiness nor sadness but because of emptiness. I cannot live any longer, because I have nothing more to do on earth. I am fit for nothing, because I have lived my life. I have consumed and used up everything that I needed. I inherited a fortune and it grew and increased without my effort. It grew until it outgrew me. Everything was done for me, everything was bought for me. I die because I am barren, physically and spiritually. I have long been lifeless, long been without the zest of living. Now I have become completely disgusted with everything. The arsenic is on the table, the last drink to make me drunk, the drink from which I shall never emerge sober. Shall I leave word behind about my wealth? What for? My wealth was my misfortune. Is there anyone I want to thank? No, I paid every day for everything. Yes, I even paid for this last drink.*

The tragic lesson of this story is that the spiritual values of the earlier generations were not transmitted to the fourth generation.

Suicide has overtaken homicide as the second largest killer of youths between the ages of fifteen and twenty-four in America. Six thousand teenage suicides occurred last year.

Suicide now claims the lives of more young men and women than cancer. Why?

Are our children so ignorant of death that they don't appreciate its meaning and finality? What pain, guilt and fear is driving these confused young people to inflict such severe punishment on themselves? From what are they escaping?

We hear blame directed at drug and alcohol abuse, family breakups, increased personal freedom and the complex social demands on adolescents. But I am thinking of Jewish teen-age suicides, where these causes are rarely applicable.

Jewish parents, who are first and second generation Americans, who have risen to their social and economic positions the hard way, are constantly giving their children the many things they were denied in their own youth: education, comfortable homes, sports, travel, automobiles, luxuries and opportunities.

From early infancy, we buy our children the toys we could not have, the clothing we could not afford, the schools we could not attend, the friends we could not afford, the neighborhood in which we could not live. These are the values we have set as our ideals for our children. We did not have these things, because our parents could not give them to us. Therefore, we try to give these values to our children.

But while we aim to enrich our children with what our parents could not give us, we are ignoring the noble values our parents did give us: honesty, integrity, self-sacrifice, love of home, devotion to God, sharing, giving, being grateful for the blessings of life, home, family.

As we are about to remember our loved ones, let us rededicate ourselves to the noble values of Jewish living which gave us the strength and stamina to withstand all difficulties. Let us rededicate ourselves to the pillars of healthy Jewish living; the home, the synagogue, the school, charity, prayer and confidence in a just and merciful God.

Reflections on the Akedah

Rosh Hashanah 5748 1987

The reading of Scripture on this day—Chapter 22 in Genesis—constitutes one of the most frequently quoted portions of the Torah. It has become a part of our daily Prayer Book. Every morning, we recite the story of the Akedah, the binding of Isaac for a sacrifice, and introduce it with an invocation culled from the Rosh Hashanah Machzor:

"Our Lord, the Lord of our fathers, remember us favorably, and visit us with mercy and salvation from the eternal high heavens. Remember in our favor, O God our Lord, the love of our ancestors Abraham, Isaac and Israel, Your servants. Remember the covenant, the kindness and the oath You swore to our father Abraham on Mount Moriah, and the binding of Isaac his son on the altar."

Following the daily reading of the Akedah, we recite a stirring petition, also taken from the Rosh Hashanah Machzor, in which we pray for God's withholding His anger from us as our father Abraham withheld his compassion from his son in obedience to God's will.

"May it be Your will, God our Lord, the Lord of our fathers, to remember in our favor the covenant of our fathers.

Even as Abraham our father held back his compassion from his only son and desired to slay him in order to do Your will, so may Your mercy hold back Your anger from us and deal with us kindly and mercifully."

What exactly happened on that fateful day whose anniversary we celebrate on Rosh Hashanah? The story is given in nineteen short verses and never again referred to in all of Scripture. Let us look at the text:

"And it came to pass after these things that the Lord put Abraham to the test, and said to him: 'Abraham!' And he answered: 'Here I am!' Then He said: "Take your son, your only son, Isaac, whom you love, and go to the land of Moriah and offer him there as a burnt offering on one of the mountains that I will tell you.' So Abraham rose early in the morning, saddled his ass and took with him his two servants and his son Isaac. He cut wood for the burnt-offering and started for the place about which God had told him. On the third day, Abraham looked up and saw the place from a distance. Then Abraham said to his servants: 'You stay with the ass, while I and the boy go yonder. We will worship and come back to you.' So Abraham took the wood for the burnt offering and laid it on his son Isaac, while he took in his hand the fire and the knife, and the two of them went off together. Then Isaac spoke to Abraham his father and said: 'My father.' And he answered: 'Here I am, my son.' And he said: 'Here are the fire and the wood, but where is the lamb for a burnt offering?' Abraham answered: 'The Lord will provide Himself with the lamb for a burnt offering, my son.' So the two of them went on together. They came to the place of which God had told him, and Abraham built the altar there, arranged the wood, bound his son Isaac and laid him on the altar on top of the wood. Then Abraham put out his hand and took the knife to slay his son. But the angel of God called to him from the heavens: 'Abraham, Abraham,' and he answered: 'Here I am.' He said: 'Do not lay your hand on the boy, and do nothing to him, for

I know now that you revere the Lord, seeing that you have not refused Me your son, your only son.' Then Abraham looked up and saw behind him a ram caught in the thicket by its horns, so Abraham went and took the ram, and offered it as a burnt offering instead of his son."

From the prayers associated with the biblical story, it is obvious that it was considered a test of the faith and trust of Abraham in the word of God, and to what extent he would go in the fulfillment of God's will. In the earlier chapters in Genesis, we read of Abraham's yearning for offspring, and his joy that he and his wife Sarah were blessed with a son in their advanced age.

From our point of view today, the demand upon Abraham appears cruel, inhuman and irrational. In the society of Abraham's time, the sacrifice of firstborn children was normal and proper. The valley of Hinom in Jerusalem was known by its demanding deity, Moloch, whose diet was young children offered up into his furnace so that he would reward the parents with divine grace. The international word Gehenna, signifying Hell, emanates from that area. Abraham's readiness to comply with God's request for the sacrifice of his only and beloved son should not shock us. When Abraham subdued his love and compassion for his child and bound him to the wood on the altar, offering his child's life in obedience to God's will, he did what was acceptable of a faithful person of his time.

The real lesson of the test came with the divine interference in the act of faith, when the angelic voice came loud and clear: "Don't put your hand on that boy." The spiritual God of the universe, the God of mercy and justice abhors human sacrifice. He desires the offering of man's will—the spirit, not the body.

Midrashic legend has it that Abraham pleaded, "Let me at least shed some of his blood in the service of God." And the divine voice continued emphatically, "Do not do anything to him." If you must shed blood in the way of service to God, open your eyes, Abraham. There is a ram whose horns are entangled in the nearby branches. Let the ram be a substitute for your son.

Over the course of the centuries, our people have substituted the offering of the firstborn with the ceremony of *pidyon haben*. The parents make a party and pledge to raise the child to excel in Torah, marry and indulge in performance of good deeds.

There is another dimension in the story of the Akedah which seems to have eluded our attention. The center of activities in our appreciation of the story is Abraham. Where does the son Isaac shine into the episode?

Isaac, according to all chronologies, was no longer a timid little baby carried in the arms of his father. We see Isaac as a mature young man designated by the Hebrew word *naar*, a teenager or above. He is carrying the wood and the fire and questioning his father, "Where is the animal for the sacrifice?" From the question, it seems clear that he suspected he had been selected for the sacrifice. He had apparently realized it from the start of the journey, and as we are told twice, they both walked together with the same determination— Abraham to offer his son as a sacrifice to his faith and Isaac to give his life in obedience to the faith of his father. Isaac could have resisted or protested. He was old enough to run away, hide, escape. But he did not.

The position of Isaac represents the younger generation in our own times in the light of a phenomenal resurgence of interest in traditional religious values and education among today's Jewish youth. On college campuses, in synagogues, in *yeshivot* throughout the country, and even more so in Israel, young men and women whose parents have long deserted orthodox Jewish living are returning to traditional habits and observance in great numbers and with great intensity.

For a while, it appeared like a passing manifestation of the widespread fundamentalist movements in Christian and

Moslem societies. We thought it was a reaction to the drug cult, and the "do your thing" and long hair sub-culture of the late Sixties and Seventies. It would pass with time, we thought. It looks, however, that the trend is spreading, increasing and steadying.

Do you recall the Haftorah recited yesterday from the Book of Samuel? It ends with Hannah fulfilling her promise by bringing her son Samuel to the Tabernacle at Shilo to minister under Eli, the aged high priest.

In the next chapter, we read that the youth of that chaotic period was corrupt—even the sons of Eli. Young Samuel, however, hears the divine call and warns the priest. The old man tells him, "Go back to sleep. You'll get over it." Samuel hears the call again and again. He is restless and cannot sleep. He realizes it is a divine call, the voice of prophecy.

Jewish youth today is awakening to the sound of the *shofar*. They are responding to the divine call with earnestness, solemnity and conviction.

Isn't it interesting that there were more instruments in the process of the Akedah than the ram's horn? There was the ram, the altar, the knife, the wood, the fire. Yet we recall the Akedah only with the ram's horn.

The *shofar* is more than a reminder of danger, distress, self-sacrifice. The *shofar* rings the epiphany at Sinai, triumph in the battles for freedom, hope and the advent of the Messianic Age. As we are about to sound the *shofar*, let us pray: "For You hear the call of the *shofar* and give heed to its summons. Praised be You, O God, who hears Your people Israel as they call to You with the sound of the *shofar*."

No Fault Judaism

Yom 5748
Kippur 1987

The sounds of Kol Nidre—whether recited by an ordinary *baal tefillah* or chanted by a trained cantor and harmonizing choir—elevate the congregation into an angelic assembly. The melody infuses Heavenly chimes of plaintive longing for the divine into the portals of the synagogue. It inspires self-immersion into the purity of holiness far from the mundane and soiled atmosphere of our daily pursuits. Rejecting food, drinks, normal physical pleasures, we gaze upon the scrolls of the Torah wrapped in white and hear the Heavenly choir whispering: "*Salachti.* I have forgiven."

That is, indeed, the keynote to the Yom Kippur message. The process, however is more complex. Immediately following the Maariv service, the atmosphere changes. We begin the recital of the long catalogue of confessions and beat upon our breasts incessantly, admitting to an endless variety of sins— domestic, personal, social, religious. The lists of iniquities are arranged alphabetically, and there are two sins for each letter of the alphabet. The confessions are not offered at just one time, they are repeated again and again over the course of the day and evening. How guilty can one person be?

Fortunately, the confessions are made in the first-person

plural, not the first-person singular. "We have sinned." "We are guilty." The plural formulation removes the onus from the individual confessor. It also carries the sense of collective responsibility; no one can claim innocence while crime is rampant and uncontrolled.

We are told that during the existence of the Temple in Jerusalem, the High Priest recited the confession on behalf of the whole people of Israel and begged forgiveness for everyone. In his petition, the Kohen Gadol said: "I beseech You, O God, forgive the sins, iniquities and transgressions which Your people, the House of Israel, have committed before You." Our present long lists of "Al Chet" are of post-Temple origin. The petition of the High Priest is based on the characteristics of mercy attributed to God in the Torah: "Forgiving iniquity, transgressions and sin."

I would like to spend with you a moment in examining these three classes of sin for which the High Priest begged forgiveness.

First came the *chata'im*, the least culpable sins, which are committed unwittingly. A person who committed a *chet* was unaware he was sinning, either through ignorance of the situation or through ignorance of the law. Though there was no deliberate intent to sin, ignorance does not completely absolve a person from responsibility.

Avonot are iniquities. The person committing them is completely aware of the situation and the law. He knows that what he is doing is contrary to the law, but the temptation is too strong. Desire or greed overcomes his better sense, and he surrenders to his inclination. Such a sinner must certainly pray for forgiveness, since he should have practiced self-discipline and self-control.

Pesha'im are transgressions committed deliberately in defiance of the will of God. Temptation is not involved, just sheer rebellion against the law. Certainly, when such a sinner becomes conscious of his error, of his attitude, he must seek God's merciful forgiveness.

Now, I would like to introduce a fourth class of sin, more grievous than the three classes for which the High Priest confessed. It is the sin of the entire repudiation of the concept of sin for which our society is guilty. The terms sin and guilt are taboo—they may cause depression, neuroses, complexes, fears or hallucinations. We moderns do not mention sin. We speak of vices, crimes, faults and failings of human nature, but not sin. Even the validity of the concept of sin is often questioned. It is considered the invention of theologians, like the idea of Satan, a superstitious relic of antiquity. In fact, the repudiation of the concept of sin is a repudiation of man's faith in a just social order.

A recent best seller by a University of Chicago philosophy professor, *The Closing of the American Mind*, presents the scathing charge that America has lost sight of the moral truths that give meaning to our lives. I have not read the book as yet. I am waiting for the paperback edition. However, the Editorial Review in the Reader's Digest sounds like a litany from the Yom Kippur Machzor. Professor Bloom claims that "the eternal conflict between good and evil" has been replaced with "I'm okay, you're okay." In the past, most students coming into the university could be counted on to know the Bible and the Psalms. "The Bible was the common culture, one that united the simple and the sophisticated, rich and poor, young and old."

The author reflects on his own background: "My grandparents were ignorant people by our standards. But their home was spiritually rich, because all things done in it found their origin in the Bible's commandments. Their simple faith and practices linked them to the great thinkers who dealt with the same material." Today, he charges, "neither the Bible nor anything else forms a spiritual, intellectual fount." Blaming our rating of proper conduct by "relative values," he concludes that "America today has no-fault automobile accidents, no-fault divorces and is moving toward no-fault choices."

As we approach the Day of Atonement, we ponder on

these charges as reflected in our confessions. Then we hear the voice of the prophet: "Return, O Israel, to the God your Lord." Our merciful Father in Heaven gave us on this day a chance to turn right. Human frailties are acknowledged. Just as no one is perfect, there is no one so righteous to do good always and never err. Nor is anyone so bad that he cannot honestly and truthfully change for the good.

Maimonides in his masterwork, *Mishneh Torah*, formulates three major steps in the process of *teshuvah*:

First, recognition and confession of wrongdoing. This is the primary step. It is not enough to recognize sin; it must be admitted. Admission is perhaps the most difficult step in repentance. Once the admission is made, the rest is easier.

Second, regret at having done the evil. This assures rejection of the sin.

Third, a commitment not to repeat the wrongdoing.

This is crucial to the integrity of *teshuvah*. Repentance is not a momentary recoil but a basic turning to a new way of life and behavior.

I wish to conclude with a prayer published in the Machzor of the late Rabbi Benzion Boksor:

"Master of the Universe, You have given us this day for the renunciation of sin. Humbly we stand in Your presence, overwhelmed by the awareness of our failures. We cannot recite them all because they are too many, but we know we have often been rude and inconsiderate, rebellious and impatient. We spoke when we should have been silent, and we were silent when we should have spoken. We often failed to use our strength in Your service and in the service of our fellow man. We shrank from duty when in our heart of hearts we knew where duty pointed.

"On this sacred night, may our prayers rise before Your throne of mercy. Forgive our sins, and absolve us from wrongdoing. Inscribe us for a year of life, health and peace, and help us rise toward greater perfection before You."

Holiness or Sanctity

Yom Kippur 5748 1987

For my sermon this morning, I have selected a familiar theme—*kedushah*, holiness or sanctity. A number of times in the course of our Yom Kippur liturgy, we plead: "Forgive the holy people, on this holy day, O holy Lord."

We acknowledge the holiness of God as the source of the *kedushah* which appears in the world. The holiness transforms time. The Sabbath day is holy. The festivals are holy. Yom Kippur is even more holy.

Holiness also transforms people. The Jewish people are considered holy because they stood at the foot of the holy Mount Sinai to receive the Torah. God declared them "a kingdom of priests and a holy people."

What are the elements that constitute holiness in man, in place, in time?

Jewish religious ideology singles out two distinct types of *kedushah*. There is *kedushat haguf*, intrinsic holiness, a holiness due to the holy object itself, an inseparable part of its essence and nature. God is holy, so are His angels. Life and its functions are holy.

Then comes *kedushat damim*, derived or acquired sanctity,

a quality which the thing regarded as holy possesses by virtue of the fact that such a quality has been conferred upon it by means of consecration.

For example, it is not the composition of the soil that makes a cemetery holy ground. The mineral content of the dirt is no different from that of any other piece of earth. It is the fact that the remains of human beings, who were greatly beloved, are buried there that invests the land with sanctity. The parchment used in Torah scrolls is nothing more than the skin of animals. What is inscribed on these scrolls makes them holy.

With regard to man and his functions, *kedushah* frequently is not always similar to what we call holiness. For example, we would designate as holy any person who withdraws from the daily pursuits of normal living, such as marriage, work, business, pleasures, and indulges exclusively in prayer, meditation and abstentions. This is not the Jewish concept of holiness. Celibacy is a sin, the violation of the first commandment in Scripture; "Be fruitful and multiply." God created only one human being. Then He divided him into male and female, only to reunite them into a unity through the sanctity of marriage. Do you know the Hebrew word for the marriage formula? It is *kiddushin*—sanctification. One spouse declares to the other: "You are sanctified to me." *Kedushah* lifts up the ordinary and commonplace relationship between man and woman to the noble and pure state of holiness. It links mortal man with the eternity of God.

In the Jewish concept, holiness is not found in the cloister, in the monastery, hidden from the challenges of the ups and downs of our daily routine. Asceticism, abstinence, monastic seclusion are absolutely not virtues. The world was made for us to enjoy. The Nazirite in Temple times had to bring a sin offering at the conclusion of his Nazirite vow. He had sinned by abstaining from the total enjoyment of the gifts and blessings of nature.

The fifth commandment in the Decalogue reads: "Remember the Sabbath day to keep it holy," to which our Sages added: "Remember the holiness of the day over a cup of wine." We call this pleasant ritual Kiddush, sanctification of the day. Ancient Romans looked upon the Sabbath observance as a Jewish superstition. They failed to recognize the sanctification of the day beginning with the blessings over the candle lights, the Kiddush over wine, the *zemirot* (Sabbath table songs) during the meal, and Grace after the meal. The Sabbath home becomes a sanctuary, the table a veritable altar and the food an offering to God in which the family participates.

We call the house of prayer a sanctuary, a holy place. Is it not constructed from the same brick and mortar as prisons, brothels, gambling joints and bars? Of course it is. But the building is sanctified by the prayers, dedication and faith infused into it by the worshippers.

In the commandment in Leviticus to build a sanctuary in the desert, God tells Moses: "Let them make for Me a sanctuary, that I may dwell among them." Mark the words "that I may dwell among them." The commentaries take notice that the more logical reading would be: "Let them make Me a sanctuary that I may dwell in it," not among them. The profound lesson is that it is not the beautiful edifice that attracts the Holy One. The worshippers supply the holiness to the building.

Here is another lesson in holiness. Chapter 19 in Leviticus, often called the Book of Holiness, is introduced with the verses: "Speak to the children of Israel, and say to them: 'You shall be holy, for I, God your Lord, am holy.'"

The Talmud questions: How can mortal man imitate the holiness of God, who is a spiritual Being?

The Rabbis answer that man cannot imitate God's infinite majesty or His eternity. But he can strive towards a purity that is divine by keeping aloof from everything loathsome and defiling. Man can imitate God's merciful qualities. To quote the Talmud: "Be like God. As He is merciful and gracious, so be you merciful and gracious." He heals the sick, frees the captives, does good even to His enemies. These merciful qualities are real links between God and man, and man is never nearer the divine than in his compassionate moments.

Now, I wish to go to another form of holiness in our liturgy—the recitation of Kaddish and Yizkor. Yizkor is a short memorial petition preceding a pledge we usually make to a local synagogue in memory of our loved ones. The prayer that is normally associated with our reverence for the dead is the Kaddish—literally, a prayer of holiness. In essence, it is a statement of faith in an orderly universe in which justice and mercy must reign, and the affirmation of our belief in the Messianic age under the universal Kingdom of Heaven. The association with our reverence to the memory of the departed parent or relative is obscure and mysterious.

In our mind, the holiness ascribed in the Kaddish to Heaven is also extended to our departed beloved whose souls are in Heaven. We must recognize that, by our usage, we have sanctified the Kaddish and Yizkor as the strongest chains in the preservation of Jewish family union and filial adoration.

I once complained to a friendly mortician on the high cost of funeral expenses and chapel services. He justified the costs with the claim that the chapel and funeral are in many situations the last link of some families to their Jewishness. More Jews are familiar with the Kaddish than the Shema and Shemoneh Esrei. The Jewish funeral chapels attract more people each day than temples and synagogues. It may even be the last time some children will recall the Jewish names of their deceased parents or relatives.

I suggest that, as we are about to recite Yizkor in an atmosphere of holiness, we dedicate ourselves to the sanctity of life, that through our conduct and behavior we may bring honor to the memories of our beloved.

Kaddish or Kiddush

Rosh Hashanah 5749 1988

he High Holiday season does not begin with the first day in the month of Tishrei. The preparation for the solemn season begins a month earlier. In Eastern Europe, when the *chazan* announced Rosh Chodesh Elul in the synagogue, sighs and tears emanated from the saintly men and women who sensed the approach of the Yamim Noraim, the Days of Awe. An earnest atmosphere permeated the Jewish community during this time of reckoning and spiritual accounting. Even youngsters in the *cheder* knew we were preparing for a solemn convocation and avoided rough play, teasing or fighting.

Thirty days before Rosh Hashanah, we begin to sound the *shofar* in the synagogue after the morning services. According to the Sephardic ritual, the *shofar* is sounded both morning and evening. Additional psalms alluding to the earnestness of the season are recited in unison. As the month of Elul progresses and we reach the week before Rosh Hashanah, the penitential period begins.

In recent centuries, there arose in Eastern European Jewish communities the very sentimental custom of visiting the graves of beloved relatives to implore the holy ones interred there to intercede in our behalf during the Days of Awe. Since basic Judaism forbids praying to the dead, the Rabbis were not too happy with this custom and urged the people to direct their prayers to our Father in Heaven, that He be merciful to us for the merits of our pure and holy parents and relatives.

It is phenomenal that of all the beautiful and soul-stirring customs of this month, American Jews have put the greatest emphasis on visiting the cemetery. Although we are scattered all over the States, men and women travel hundreds and thousands of miles to visit the graves of their beloved before Rosh Hashanah. Even such people who do not go to the synagogue to hear the *shofar* make sure that the parental graves are visited before the High Holidays. In fact, the majority of visitors are not very scrupulous in their religious observance. In most cases, they have to hire a professional mourner to recite for them the memorial formula—the "Ma-Lay." The hustle and bustle at the Jewish cemeteries at this time of the year demonstrates the religious fervor associated with visiting the graves of our loved ones.

It is remarkable that in the whole ritual of Rosh Hashanah there is no special prayer for the dead. Outside of the normal daily recitation of the Kaddish and the affirmation of the faith in the resurrection, there is not a single reference to the dead. However, special prayers and petitions for life, the living, good life, happy life, useful life are repeated continuously. The Rosh Hashanah ritual is replete with adoration to life. In the Amidah, we add four insertions imploring for life. As these insertions progress, the quality of life requested is intensified. At first, we begin very simply. Remember us for life. At the end we specify: O Lord, inscribe us and the entire household of Israel in the book of life, peace and honorable sustenance.

Several decades ago, *Look* magazine published a series of articles under the heading of "The Vanishing American Jew." The author asserted that the diminishing birth rate, rapid assimilation and intermarriage were leading American Jewry to extinction.

Look what happened during these decades. *Yeshivot* have sprouted all over the country. Hundreds, no, thousands of children are receiving intensive Jewish education. Jewish religious communities are entrenched and developing in every state. Colleges and universities are offering courses in Jewish history and religion. Whereas forty or fifty years ago a high school diploma was a social release from Sabbath observance and *kashrut*, observant Jewish students now dominate admissions to schools of medicine, law and engineering. Observant Jewish professors walk into their classrooms in prestigious universities. In the city of New York, there is an organization of Orthodox Jewish judges, another of Orthodox Jewish scientists.

"If things are so good," you may ask, "why are they so bad?"

Now, let us repeat the enigma—on the one hand we rejoice in the advancement and spread of Jewish traditional life and culture, but on the other hand, there is a mass desertion of young people who become assimilated into the dominant culture.

Of course, the causes are many, and in a free society, cultural assimilation cannot be avoided. One of the causes that comes to mind is the emphasis we place on ethnic and religious preservation. The Jew lives by the Torah—called Torat Chaim, the law of life. The purpose of the observance of *mitzvot* is to enrich one's life on earth. In the dominant faith, a person is doomed by original sin and destined to perdition unless saved by his faith in the divinity of a Jew who died on the cross nearly 2,000 years ago. For our people, Jewish tradition did not stress the importance of sublime faith nor the importance of eternal salvation. The Torah is a manual of life, not a program for salvation from Hell. Influenced by our neighbors' culture, many American Jews accepted the belief that it is important to die as a Jew, but not to live as a Jew. The cemetery replaced the synagogue, and the funeral chapel replaced the Bet Hamidrash, the House of Study.

Kaddish is sacred, but not the Kiddush sanctifying the Sabbath and festivals. The house where the family lives and strives has been emptied of the customs, ceremonies and symbols of Jewish living. Shiva is scrupulously observed at home, not Shabbat and Yom Tov. The Jewish child associates the Yahrzeit candle with his religion more than the Sabbath candle. In this process, the living golden chain that tied the child to his people was severed and replaced by a cult of the dead.

The recent movement of return to authentic Judaism captivating and inspiring a new generation of American Jews is based on the joy of intensive Jewish living. It is not an intellectual or theological movement. It has become a total way of life, bringing contentment and happiness to the whole family. The Sabbath brings joy and rest; the festivals, with their charm and symbols, are seasonal family goals to achieve. You cannot compare the genuine adjustment, the mental and emotional stability of the boy and girl raised in a home with Jewish observance to the gloom and confusion of the Jewish child brought up in an environment where he must condescend to a little Chanukah bush to replace his fancy for the decorated Christmas tree of his neighbor.

On this second day of Rosh Hashanah, it is proper that we recall the profound lesson from the assigned reading from Scripture—the Kriat Hatorah. It is the dramatic story of the Akedah, the binding of Isaac for a sacrifice. I will briefly outline the climatic events of this episode. Abraham hears the voice of God telling him to offer up his only beloved son as a sacrifice. In unquestioning loyalty to the will of God, he proceeds to carry out this request. The unresisting compliance of Isaac is as admirable as the suppression by Abraham of the natural feelings of a father. The altar is prepared, the wood placed upon it, and Isaac is bound. Abraham takes the knife and raises it over the throat of his son, when he hears the loud angelic voice: "Don't touch that boy!"

We generally take from this story the lesson of Kiddush Hashem—Jewish martyrdom. Our people, in the course of history, offered their lives in defense of their faith more than once. A point I have often raised in this story is that child sacrifice was normal behavior during Abraham's time. Abraham did no more than the ordinary religious parent would do. I believe that a major lesson in the story is God's emphasis to Abraham of the need to live as a Jew rather than to die as a Jew. As the Psalmist proclaims: "The dead praise not the Lord, neither any that go down with silence; but we will bless the Lord from this time forth and forevermore."

Yom Kippur: The Day of Holiness

Yom Kippur 5751 1990

om Kippur is known in the Torah as Yom Hakippurim, the Day of Atonement. Moralists have paraphrased the terms colloquially as the Day of At-One-Ment. The rabbis in the Talmud speak of Yom Kippur as Yoma, "the Day," and the tractate dealing primarily with the laws and regulations of Yom Kippur is known as Mesechet Yoma, the Tractate of the Day. In the liturgy, we refer to it as the Yom Hakadosh, the Holy Day. The holiness is stressed repeatedly in the liturgy and prayers: "*Selach legoy kadosh, beyom kadosh, Hakel Hakadosh. Forgive Your holy people, on this holy day, O holy Lord.*"

Everything surrounding Yom Kippur is embellished in holiness. The Temple service prescribed for the day is *kodesh*. The Torah reads: "Herewith shall Aaron come unto the holiness." He shall put on "garments of *kodesh*," and he shall make atonement for the *kodesh*, for the holy. We translate the word *kodesh* as holy. Tonight I wish to spend a few minutes with you in the concept of *kedushah*, holiness. What is indeed the essence of the state of holiness?

Anthropologists would associate the concept of *kedushah* with the primitive idea of "taboo," a state of mystical conditions making the bearer "untouchable." It would be a person, place or object possessing magical properties that make the object either supernatural or injurious. That is absolutely not *kedushah*. Unlike the religions with which we are familiar, Judaism does not consecrate sacred orders and separatist groups. We have no monks, no saints, no monastic orders. *Kedushah*, holiness, is not the exclusive property of any organization or individual. It is the process by which we lift up the time, the object, the place from the commonplace and ordinary to the pure, the noble, the divine.

Time becomes *kodesh* where it is raised to a higher perspective. The seventh day of the week was raised from being an ordinary twenty-four-hour period to become a holy day. The chapter on creation ends with the words: "And the Lord blessed the seventh day and declared it to be *kodesh*."

In the fourth commandment, we are enjoined, "Remember the Sabbath day to keep it holy." There is nothing that can lift man up from his weekday drudgery more than the Sabbath. Without the Sabbath rest, without regard for its holiness, man becomes little more than a beast of burden. With the *kedushah* of the Sabbath, man is let into a new domain, a new realm of life, where he is given a *neshamah yeteirah*, a purer soul which increases his own holiness.

Space too becomes *kodesh*, holy. The synagogue and the Torah school bind the participants in a bond of holy fraternity. Within their portals, we seek and find inspiration to pray and come nearer to our father in Heaven, the source of *kedushah*, holiness.

A major forum of *kedushah* is *kedushas hachaim*, the holiness of normal daily living. The Torah commands us: "You shall be holy, for I, God your Lord am holy."

Dr. Hertz, in his commentary on the Pentateuch, elaborates on this passage in that "man is not only to worship God, but to imitate Him." Mortal man cannot imitate God's infinite majesty or His eternity, but he can strive toward a purity that is divine. He can imitate God's merciful qualities. The Talmud offers examples of how man may imitate God's holiness: "As He is merciful and gracious, so shall you be merciful and gracious." On the first pages of the Torah, God clothed the naked Adam, and on the last page, He buried the dead Moses. Mercy and kindness link us to God in holiness.

Marriage is called *Kiddushin*, holiness. Jewish marriage is not just a love affair between man and woman in response to the physical instincts, but a sacred bond of fidelity, loyalty and trust. A teacher in the Talmud noted that the Hebrew words for husband and wife are *ish* and *ishah*. The middle letter of *ish* is a *yod*, and the last letter of *ishah* is a *heh*. These two letters—*yod* and *heh*—spell the Biblical name of God, indicating the *kedushah* in the marriage relationship.

The concept of *kedushas hachaim*, the holiness of living, embraces all aspects of life. The dining room is enveloped in *kedushah* if the meal is consecrated with the blessings before and after eating and drinking. The dinner table becomes an altar from which we are privileged to share God's gifts. *Kedushas hachaim* means that every move, every action, every relationship, domestic, industrial, social, be enveloped in *kedushah* if they are based on honesty, mercy, love and unselfishness.

Social and political scientists are alarmed at what's happening to our society. There are daily reports of murder, rape, arson, robberies. Before the Deluge, Scripture describes society as: "The earth was filled with violence." Perhaps the lesson on Yom Kippur is the answer. Our lives have been emptied from the sense of *kedushas hachaim*. The living gave up the society of life.

In one of the *piyutim* before the recitation of the Kaddish, we say: "We hope for the day when the world will be perfected under the dominion of the Almighty and all mankind will learn to revere Your Name; when all the wicked of the earth will be drawn in penitence to You."

Parents Never Die

Yom Kippur 5752 1991

The text of my remarks comes from the Talmud (Taanit 5), which states: "Our Father Jacob has not died . . . Just as his descendants are alive, so too is he alive." What the Rabbis were actually teaching us is that parents do not die. If death means the cessation of life, it is not applicable to parents, since their lives continue through the lives of their children and grandchildren.

In another instance, the Talmud observes that Scripture employs two distinct verbs to indicate the end of life. One word is *shechivah*, meaning resting or sleeping, and the other word is *mitah*, meaning death. Following the usage of the two words throughout Scripture, they realized that when a person leaves a family to follow in his or her footsteps the word employed is *shechivah*, indicating "resting", while his life continues through his or her offspring. However, a person who does not leave a family to follow in his footsteps is considered a *meit*, a lifeless corpse.

I maintain that parents cannot die physically. The physical attributes of the parent become part of the offspring. We resemble our parents whose blood and marrow sustain us in so many aspects. Frequently, we also resemble our parents emotionally, in temperament, in responsiveness, in mentality. When the Talmud concluded that "as long as his offspring is alive, he too is alive," it was not fantasy. The Rabbis were establishing a fact and basing it on Scripture.

I do not like to use personal experiences as an example in teaching others—personal characteristics vary widely. In the last five years of my father's life, he was in a wheelchair, and although he constantly had a caregiver with him, rarely did a day pass that I did not attend to him personally as well.

About ten years ago, I underwent surgery. Since surgery is always risky, on my way to the operating room I was thinking of my father who had been so close to me.

The night before, I dreamed I was bathing my father and holding his fleshy arm. I woke as I was squeezing my own arm. The comforting thought came to me: My arm is verily the extension of my father's arm—he is physically alive!

Let me extend this thought to our custom of reciting Yizkor. We solemnly recall the names of our loved ones, parents, spouses, children, God forbid, brothers and sisters and pray: "*Utzror bitzror hachaim*. And bind up their souls in the bond of life." What is that bond of life that we assign for our parents? Are we referring to the lives of the Patriarchs and Matriarchs? But they are mentioned individually.

I have seen a translation of *bitzror hachaim* as "the bond of eternal life." If that be so, it should read *bitzror chayei olam*. I translate *bitzror hachaim* as "in the lives of children and grandchildren." That is the bundle of life to which we should seek to be bound. However, Yizkor is not the prayer of our physical preservation. That is obvious in the characteristics of our offspring. Yizkor emphasizes, "*Utzror bitzror hachaim et nishmoteihem*. Let their souls, their spirits be bound in the bundle of the living." That is a task we do not always fulfill. To perpetuate their values, their aims and goals in life. To preserve what they considered sacred and devote ourselves to their spiritual legacy—that is the prayer in Yizkor. It is to have their *neshamah* implanted in the bundle of life that Yizkor is directed.

The clergy of all denominations are usually conservative in their attire, their conduct and their thought. As such, they usually extol the past and question novel ideas in thought, in art, in diet and so forth. I do not subscribe to these tendencies. I do not believe that the past was all good, and that everything new is all bad. On the other hand, we live better, we live longer, we enjoy more security and surely better health. That is all physical. When it comes to the *neshamah*, the soul, the values of spirit, we are far behind former generations.

The Rabbis making the comparison of the generations make a rather pathetic conclusion: If the earlier generations were like angels, we are like mortals. If they were like mortals, we are like animals.

Here we are in America, the wealthiest and most influential Jewish community in all of our history. We are only one or two generations from immigration. The majority are college graduates and engaged in government service, education, industry and finance. We are both admired and envied by other ethnic communities.

Are we preserving the spiritual legacy of our forebears? Those poor immigrants came without material wealth but so much enthusiasm and piety. They established institutions of learning and welfare. *Shtieblach* were formed in storefronts, in factories and shops, and were filled with worshippers, students and scholars. Can you recall the Yiddish press of the immigrants in the early part of the century? They were so rich in content—cultural, literacy, religious—products of the Jewish soul, the *neshamah*.

That is indeed our prayer in Yizkor: *Utzror bitzror hachaim et nishmoteihem.* May their souls be bound up in our lives.

Isaac

Rosh Hashanah 5753 1992

*T*he dramatic story we read in the Torah today about the Akedah, the binding of Isaac as a human sacrifice, has become part of our daily prayers. It has had a profound and decisive influence upon the very soul of the Jewish people. The Akedah has given meaning and purpose to the sad story of our peoples' martyrdom throughout the ages. It is the symbol of *kiddush Hashem*, martyrdom for the sake of God.

In the Middle Ages, when fathers slew their children rather than permit them to be forcibly baptized, they consciously or unconsciously set before their eyes the example of Abraham and regarded themselves as followers of the *mitzvah* of *kiddush Hashem*. When Rabbi Akiva's flesh was torn by the executioner, the great teacher cried out Shema Yisrael in his death throes, setting for himself the example of Abraham and Isaac as he attested with his very life his love of God.

The Akedah represents the very pattern of Jewish history. It is an event which has occurred and recurred countless times in the long chronicle of Jewish martyrdom. The Talmud records the sad story of Hannah and her seven sons associated with the Hasmonean period. The cruel emperor decreed that every Jew must bow down before his statue and acknowledge him as god. Among the many Jews who defied his decree were the seven sons of a very pious woman who had brought up her children with an abiding faith in the One God, the God of Israel. Each of her seven children in turn refused to comply with the emperor's decree and was executed.

Before the youngest son was led to his execution, his mother said to him: "Go my son and tell our father Abraham, 'You bound a sacrifice on one altar, but I bound seven sacrifices on seven altars. Furthermore, you Abraham were only put to the test but did not actually slaughter your son, but I offered seven sons as actual sacrifices, slaughtered because of their faith in God.'"

In our own century, six million Isaacs, sacrificed because they were the seed of Abraham, died with Ani Maamin on their lips.

Before we continue, let us repeat the bare outlines of this solemn incident in the lives of our patriarchs. Abraham hears the voice of God telling him to offer up his only beloved son Isaac as a sacrifice. In unquestioning, unswerving loyalty to the will of God, he proceeds to carry out the divine order. The unresisting compliance of Isaac is as admirable as the suppression by Abraham of the natural feelings of a father. The altar is prepared, the wood placed upon it, Isaac is bound and Abraham takes the knife to do God's will. At that very moment, his hand is stopped by a voice from Heaven: "Don't put your hand on the boy! Don't touch him!"

The story ends as Isaac is released and, in his stead, Abraham sacrifices on that same altar a ram that became entangled nearby. In the course of the day's services, we sound the ram's horn as a reminder of our people's unwavering readiness to offer their lives for their faith in God.

I believe that a major lesson in the Torah reading of today is also that God does not want us just to die as Jews. Our Father in Heaven wants us to live as Jews. The Psalmist says:

"I will not die, but I will live to recount the deeds of the Lord." In fact, the theme of life permeates our entire Rosh Hashanah service. In the Shemoneh Esrei, where no additions or omissions are permitted, we add the prayers for life: "Remember us unto life, and inscribe us in the Book of Life, for Your own sake, O living Lord."

We conclude the Shemoneh Esrei with the long prayer for life. "In the book of life, peace and good sustenance may we be remembered and inscribed before You."

Our religious fulfillment is not reached by death, as it is in the dominant religion. We recite the psalm: "The dead praise not the Lord, neither any that go down into silence, but we will praise the God, from this time forth and forevermore."

It is interesting to note how this formula of seeking religious fulfillment in life instead of death has changed in American Jewish lives. So many of us who have given up Jewish life in prayer, diet and marriage are still conscious of their Jewishness in that they want to die Jewish. A Jewish mortician recently remarked to me that he does more for the perpetuation of Jewish consciousness than I do. The cost of Jewish dying is rising from day to day. The same person who resents the minimally higher cost of Jewish living will instead be ready to spend thousands, literally thousands, to die as a Jew. It is also remarkable to see non-Jewish entrepreneurs don little *yarmulkes* and make a fortune on this weakness of our people to die as Jews. If we were to spend as much for meaningful Jewish living as for Jewish dying, synagogues and *yeshivot* would have no financial problems.

There is the story of the elderly gentleman who was on his deathbed in a hospital room, surrounded by his sons. They were discussing the funeral arrangements for their father within earshot of the dying old man. One son suggested they use Campbell's funeral chapel so that his non-Jewish friends would feel comfortable. The others objected because of the high cost at Campbell's. Another suggested a sturdy metal casket, to which others objected. As the sons continued arguing as to who would pay the intolerable costs, the old man opened his eyes and said: "Listen my children, stop fighting about my funeral. The cemetery is not far from here. If you bring me a pair of pants, I'll walk over myself."

It may be a ridiculous story, but it demonstrates dramatically the lesson of the Akedah. God does not want us to die for our Jewishness. He desires that we live a healthy, happy and meaningful Jewish life. The Kaddish indeed expresses our sanctification of God's house. But there is also *kedushah* in the Kiddush by which we inaugurate the Sabbaths and festivals. Our marriages should be based on the *kiddushin* of the wedding ceremony, bringing holiness to our homes, to our places of work and associations.

May the sounds of the *shofar* fill our hearts with a desire and determination to live a full Jewish life dedicated to goodness, mercy, peace and happiness.

Ishmael

Rosh 5753
Hashanah 1992

ccording to tradition, the custom of the public Reading of the Torah on the Sabbath was instituted by Moses. Since the time of Moses, the Torah, the five Books of Moses, also known as the Pentateuch, was not only publicly recited on Sabbaths, it was interpreted, discussed and studied. This custom of Kriat Hatorah brought about the translations, commentaries and sermonic lessons comprising our Biblical literature. The Septuagint, the Greek translation, goes back to the third century before the common era. In fact, all of the Kitvei Hakodesh, the Holy Scriptures, were translated with meticulous care and superior scholarship.

I want to focus your attention on the particular portion assigned for the Reading of today. The choice of the portion read on each Sabbath or holiday is not made by the Reader or the congregation. After generations of varying customs in the divisions for the annual or tri-annual cycle for the completion of the whole Torah, the present division of the Torah into fifty-two *parshiot* or portions, one for each Sabbath of the year has become prevalent. The fifty-two portions also cover the leap year of thirteen months. In a regular year of only twelve months, we double up on some Sabbaths to complete the cycle on the last day of Succoth, Simchat Torah.

The weekly portions, known colloquially as *sidras* or *parshahs*, follow each other consecutively, regardless of the content of the material of that Sabbath. Should there be a calendar change in the ensuing week, an additional scroll is removed from the Ark and the reference to the occasion is recited from the second scroll. For example, on the Sabbath before Purim, the reference to the condemnation of Amalek is read; on the Sabbath preceding Chanukah, we recite from the second Scroll the reference to the dedication of the Tabernacle and the lighting of the Menorah therein.

However, on all Biblical holidays and festivals, whether they occur on the Sabbath or a weekday, we read from the Torah the portion wherein the laws and regulations of that particular holiday are ordained. On Yom Kippur we read the order of the Yom Kippur service as prescribed in the Torah; on Pesach, we read the order of the Passover *seder* as observed in Biblical times; on Shavuot, we read the portion describing the epiphany on Mount Sinai and the Ten Commandments.

The Readings of both days of Rosh Hashanah seem to have no connection whatsoever with the nature and observance of the holiday. The name of Rosh Hashanah is not there, and there are no references to a new year or the special ritual of sounding the *shofar*. The closest association between the Torah Reading and Rosh Hashanah on the first day of the holiday is a later tradition that Isaac was born to Abraham and Sarah, our first Patriarchal family, on Rosh Hashanah in pre-Biblical times. If Rosh Hashanah were to be just a birthday celebration, the services are too solemn. Also, we do not find in Scripture birthday celebrations. Only one birthday celebration is mentioned, and that is the birthday of the Egyptian Pharaoh who elevated Joseph to be his viceroy.

I would venture a new approach to the association between Rosh Hashanah and the Torah Reading of the day. It is not Isaac that stands out in the Torah Reading, but his wild, older half-brother Ishmael, whose birth and early life teach a major lesson on the anniversary of man's creation and civilized society.

In recent months, we saw in the conventions of both political parties, Democratic and Republican, unusual attention given to the ostensible decay and dissolution of the good American family. The unusual attention to the condition of the family came about by accident. It was the result of our vice president's aversion and dislike of a popular television comedy whose heroine acts as a single-parent family. His unfavorable remarks about the comedy were not well accepted by the public, and in reaction to the public ridicule that followed, the national attention was focused on the whole problem of the breakdown of the traditional two-parent American family.

Now, the traditionally healthy, solid American family has become a national, political issue. Obviously, as a political issue, it is only debatable. The changes in the family structure are rooted in the revolutionary economic, social and industrial changes taking place in our current civilization. The wife and mother is no longer anchored to the family structure.

It is interesting that on the first day of Rosh Hashanah, the Torah Reading leads us to a tragedy in the lives of our first Patriarchal family. Abraham and Sarah did not experience a peaceful happy family relationship. They endured migrations, wars, famine, disputes. Their worst problem was Sarah's barrenness. Unable to conceive, Sarah employed an old remedy which we now call Hagarism—that of allowing the husband a concubine, a sort of slave-wife, whose child would be the offspring of the mistress.

Let me read the introductory chapter directly from Scripture. "Now Sarah, Abraham's wife, bore him no children; and she had a handmaiden, an Egyptian, whose name was Hagar. And Sarah said to Abraham, 'Behold now, the Lord had restrained me from bearing children. Go, I pray you, to my maid; it may be that I shall be built up through her.' And Sarah, Abraham's wife, took the Egyptian and gave her to Abraham, her husband, to be his wife. Hagar conceived, and when she realized she had conceived, her mistress became despised in her eyes. And Sarah said to Abraham, 'My anger is at you. I gave my maid to you. Now that she conceived, she despises me.' Abraham answered, 'She is your maid; do with her whatever you wish.' And Sarah dealt harshly with her, and she fled. The Angel of the Lord found Hagar by a fountain of water in the desert and said to her, 'Hagar, where do you come from and where are you going?' She answered, 'I am running away from my mistress Sarah.' And the Angel of the Lord said to her:, 'Return to your mistress and submit to the torture under her hands.' And the angel continued, 'Behold you are with child, and you shall bear a son, and he shall be a wild ass of a man. His hand shall be against every man, and every man's hand against him.'"

The peculiarities in this story are as follows: First, what was the purpose of the angelic tidings to the fugitive mother that her son would be a wild ass of a man, continuously fighting? And then, why go back and be tortured by a jealous mistress when she could be free in the desert?

The best explanation is that the angel warned Hagar of what might happen to her son without the stable family. Ishmael would need a home with a caring father like Abraham to train him properly. Without a caring father and mother like Abraham and Sarah, he would become a wild ass of a man. Without proper supervision and direction, he would not survive.

The family is the nucleus of society, wherein each member, according to age and ability, has privileges, duties and responsibilities. A large number of families form the tribe, the village, the city, the state, and it is in the proper division of responsibilities and privileges that governments are formed.

On the anniversary of creation of man and civilization,

we are reminded of the basic need for an orderly society, the solid, healthy family. We are facing an environment of fear, insecurity, violence, the breakdown of social control. At this moment of prayer, let us concentrate on the prophetic hope: "And he shall turn the heart of the parents to their children, and the heart of the children to their parents. And the hearts of both to their Father in Heaven."

The Yom Kippur Guilt Complex

Yom Kippur 5753 1992

om Kippur, the Day of Atonement, does not begin with the chanting of Kol Nidre. The observance of the holiest day of the year begins a day before, that is Erev Yom Kippur. In the morning service of Erev Yom Kippur, we omit the recitation of Avinu Malkeinu, which we have recited daily, morning and evening, since Rosh Hashanah. We do not recite Tachanun, the daily confessional, and other parts of the service usually omitted on festivals.

Moreover, the Rabbis in the Talmud ordained that "whoever eats and drinks more than usual on the day before Yom Kippur is as meritorious as if he had feasted on the day of Yom Kippur." Is it not peculiar to compare the feasting on sumptuous meals and consumption of liquor with the total abstention from eating and drinking for twenty-five hours?

Rabbi Joseph Caro, the sixteenth century compiler of the Shulchan Aruch, rationalizes the peculiarity with a parable. Suppose a man or woman must stand trial on charges of having committed capital offenses and, if convicted, face the loss of life and property. On the day before the trial, such a person would remain alone in fear and sorrow. He would have no appetite for eating, drinking and partying, but would rather remain isolated in fear of the loss of his life, family and property.

Let us now assume that the litigant received a solemn promise from the judge that if he rises in court and expresses sincere regret for his wrongdoing, and if he promises never to repeat the alleged crimes, the judge would pardon him and set him free. What would this person feel?

It depends on the person's faith in the promise of the judge. If he trusts the judge implicitly and believes the promise of a pardon, he will rejoice the day before the trial and confidently celebrate his forthcoming pardon and freedom. If, however, the accused has no faith in the judge's promise, he will continue to spend the day in fear of losing his life and family.

Similarly, the Torah promises us: "On this day, you will be forgiven all your sins, if you release yourselves before the Lord." If we believe in the Torah and trust in its divine promises, then we are inaugurating the most glorious day of the year, and how can we not rejoice with eating, drinking and feasting?

However, the celebration of the day does not include hilarity and unrestrained partying. It is a day of celebration with sobriety, earnestness and humility. We have confidence in a favorable verdict, but we still have to stand trial.

One of the legends associated with the Berditchever Rebbe is connected with Erev Yom Kippur. The *rebbe* constantly argued with God for not treating the good Jewish people fairly. He once stood at the *bimah* before Kol Nidre and argued with God, saying: "Let us assume that the *muzhiks*, the peasants of Berditchev, were to be given a day on which it would be a *mitzvah*, a good deed, to overeat and overdrink throughout the day. By nightfall, they would all be drunk, vomiting, fighting or sleeping. Compare the scene with those present here in the synagogue—sober, earnest, dressed in white, clean, serene, prayerful. Are we not entitled to Your forgiveness?"

Following this argument, the *rebbe* began the chanting of Kol Nidre.

As the day of Erev Yom Kippur progresses, our festive mood changes. The sun inclines into the western skies, and we proceed to the synagogue for the public worship of Minchah. At the close of the Shemoneh Esrei, we start the long confessions of Al Chet, to make the atmosphere more solemn even before the concluding meal of the day.

At home, we eat a satisfying meal, and then the woman of the house begins the sanctification of the day with the candle-lighting ritual. Covering her face with her hands, not to gaze at the Shechinah that hovers over the brightness of the lights, she intones the old supplication: "O Lord of forgiveness and love, extend Your mercies to me and all the members of my household, among all Your children who will come before You on this Day of Judgment. Guide us to acknowledge our weaknesses, our failures and our sins, that we may be renewed in Your grace. As the lights I have kindled soar ever upward, so may the lights of Your Torah ever raise our lives, our homes and all mankind toward You. O God, remove from us the burden of our guilt and grant us the joy of knowing that we are forgiven. Inscribe us in the book of life, contentment, and peace. Amen."

Following candle-lighting come the blessings of the head of the household upon the children and grandchildren. Placing his hands upon each one, he pronounces the priestly benediction: "May God bless you and keep you; may He cause His presence to shine upon you and be gracious to you; may He turn with favor upon you and give you peace." And then comes the personal prayer: "May our Heavenly Father sustain you, our beloved children, in life and health, and may He put in your hearts to love Him and fear Him, and to pursue the study of the Torah and the fulfillment of His commandments. May He enable us to fulfill and meet the obligations of parenthood, to provide amply for your needs, and to guide you toward good and upright character. May He bless all your undertakings and grant you a long and happy life, together with all the righteous and the entire household of Israel. Amen."

With our hearts full of prayer, we proceed to the synagogue to gaze at the open Ark, the elders holding aloft the holy scrolls, and we listen to the wondrous, plaintive, haunting melody of Kol Nidre. Our religious emotions reach a height which they attain at no other moment of the year. We feel our souls attuned to divine influences. For a few moments, we are purged of all the dross and impurities which clog our souls continuously. Our emotions conquer our reason as the heart conquers the mind.

Don't look at the translation. You will be very disappointed. It is not a prayer. It is more of a public declaration of our failures and irresponsibility. It was instituted in circumstances which do not apply to the present day. Its introduction into the synagogue was resisted by the greatest authorities in Judaism, and has become a common weapon in the bands of renegades and anti-Semites. And still it conquers the heart of every Jew, and the melody has become part and parcel of the musical heritage of the world. Who would not recognize the stirring tunes of Kol Nidre? What indeed is the magic of Kol Nidre?

You may recall the frequently quoted dicta of Hillel, the sage who lived in the first century before the common era: "If I am not for myself, who will be for me? And if I am only for myself, I am a nobody."

A medieval novelist paraphrased the second stanza to say: "And if I am alone by myself, who am I?" That is what I believe occurs at Kol Nidre. I stand alone, all alone, before my conscience, my God. Covered with my *tallit*, my prayer shawl, without color, without camouflage, without the exaggerated image I have built for myself, and I ask myself: "Behold, I am a year older, three hundred and sixty-five days and nights have passed me by since last Kol Nidre. Where did I fail?"

Kol Nidre. What happened to all my resolutions, my promises, my goals, my responsibilities as a human being, a spouse, a son, a daughter, a father, a mother?

Looking back as I stand alone, I realize that *"nidrana lo nidre, ve'esarana lo esarei."* My promises have not been fulfilled, my resolves were neglected, my duties were ignored, my goals, my aims—all failed.

My conscience is disturbed! That is what Kol Nidre does to us. It is the silent confession of our frailties, hypocrisy and failures. We see ourselves in the spiritual and emotional nude.

Whereupon, we hear the Reader announce: *"Venislach."* It is the divine voice coming from our Father of Mercy: "And may atonement be granted to the whole congregation of Israel and to the strangers who live among them, for all have transgressed unwillingly."

And we respond confidently and gratefully: "Blessed are You, O God our Lord, King of the Universe, who has kept us alive, and has sustained us, and privileged us to reach this day."

Remember, O God

Yom Kippur 5753 1992

*V*ery soon, we shall reach the most solemn moment of the most solemn day of the year. We shall interrupt our regular prayers in which we petition our Creator to grant us atonement and an extension of life, and we shall pray for the dead. In the words of King David, we pray for all those who "were beloved and pleasant during their lifetimes and even in their death they are not parted."

We pray that they also be granted atonement and release from suffering in the afterworld. The Rabbis in the Talmud comment on the verse in Deuteronomy: "Forgive your people Israel whom you have redeemed." They explain: "'Forgive your people Israel' refers to a plea for the living. 'Whom you have redeemed' refers to the dead." From this verse, they deduced that the dead also require atonement.

By remembering our dear departed, we bring balm and solace to their souls with the knowledge that they are not forgotten by those they left behind. This brings us all together on Yom Kippur day to pray for the dead.

We pray with our sighs and with our tears. Indeed, tears on Yom Kippur and prayers go together. Our anxieties and tensions are relieved with the shedding of a tear.

An old legend tells of the consternation that struck Adam and Eve at the sight of the first death in biblical history. When Cain murdered his brother Abel, and the bereaved parents beheld their dead son, they were shocked, bewildered and motionless. God in his mercy sent down a tear to soften and moisten their eyes, and the tears from Heaven relieved them.

Yom Kippur is traditionally a day for shedding tears, signifying our sincere resolve to repent and thereby earn God's forgiveness. "Though the gates of prayer may at times be closed to us," says the Zohar, "the gates opened by our tears are never closed." We are told in the Talmud that one who sheds tears over the passing of a pious person is forgiven for all his sins. There is a legendary cup stored in God's treasure-house, and tears shed for the righteous dead are counted and stored in this cup.

The Torah Reading for today began with a reference to the death of the two older sons of Aharon Hakohein. Our Sages assure us that one who weeps over those sudden tragic deaths will be spared tragedy during the coming year, that he will only shed tears of joy.

You are probably all familiar with the psalm chanted before the recitation of Birkat Hamazon, Grace after Meals, in which we read about God bringing the exiles back to Zion. There is a meaningful reference in this psalm to the shedding of tears. It reads: "Those who sow in tears will reap in joy." It teaches us that tears should not be wasted. Tears should be sown in our hearts and minds as one sows seeds in the ground. Then they will germinate and produce joy and satisfaction. Our generation can testify to the truth of this lesson.

For generations, our people wept over the destruction of the Beth Hamikdash, the Temple in Jerusalem, as we read in the Book of Lamentations on Tishah b'Av. Those tears were not wasted. They entered our souls and kept alive our yearning for the return to Zion. The tears made it grow into a consuming passion which finally sprouted in the Zionist movement and now yielded its precious fruit—Jewish sovereignty in the State of Israel. Our oppressed from all over the world are reaping in joy the fruits of our tears.

When we recite Yizkor, let us ascertain that the tears we shed are sown and planted in our hearts. May they refresh and stimulate us as Jews committed to a life of Torah and *mitzvot*. Unfortunately, many of us waste our tears and leave them unproductive. We do not sow them in our hearts and minds. For many, the shedding of tears during Yizkor is purely mechanical, like turning on the tap in the kitchen sink with the water going down the drain.

The Yizkor formula is so simple. We petition our compassionate Heavenly Father to remember our beloved who are no longer among the living for the sake of the charity we donate in their memory. The salient part of the prayer reads: "And bind their souls in the bundle of life." What exactly is that bundle of life?

For a long time, I understood it to be the mystical source from which souls are given to each person at birth. Or else, it may refer to the bond of eternal life. In the course of time, however, I have become convinced that this bundle is a reference to us, the children, the grandchildren, living spouses, sisters, brothers. We constitute the "bundle of life," the bundle of life into which we pray that the souls of our beloved be bound. Just as we are a physical continuation of their physical lives, we pray that we may also be the spiritual continuation of their spiritual lives.

Alas, our prayers are so frequently recited in vain; our tears are so often shed uselessly. Our recitation of Yizkor should result in a resolve to cherish and follow the spiritual legacy of our loved ones, to follow the beautiful qualities of life with which they bequeathed us, their love and devotion to our traditions, our people, our God, the Torah and the synagogue.

Father of mercy, in whose hand are the souls of the living

and the dead, may Your consolation cheer us as we remember our beloved parents and relatives who have gone to their eternal rest. We beseech You, O Lord, to grant us strength to be faithful to their charge while the breath of life is within us. May their souls repose in the land of the living, beholding Your glory and delighting in Your goodness.

When Is Rosh Hashanah?

Rosh Hashanah 5754 1993

hen is Rosh Hashanah? Sounds like a simple question for which nowadays there would be a simple answer. Take a look at any calendar, religious or secular, and you will find the date clearly marked.

A passage in the Midrash tells of a celestial colloquy in which the ministering angels ask God: "When is Rosh Hashanah?" God does not respond by referring His angels to the calendar. In the Midrash, God answers the question of the angels with a question: "You are asking me? Let you and I go down and ask the High Court on earth."

Now, you may ask, doesn't the Torah give us an exact date for Rosh Hashanah as it does for all other Biblical holidays? Yom Kippur is on the tenth day of Tishrei, Passover is on the fifteenth of Nissan, Succoth on the fifteenth of Tishrei, Shavuot on the sixth of Sivan.

It is true that Rosh Hashanah has a clear and definite date in the Torah. We read in Numbers 29: "And in the seventh month, on the first day of the month, you shall have a holy convocation. You shall do no servile work; it shall be a day of sounding the *shofar* unto you."

So we have a definite date—the first day of the seventh

month which we call Tishrei. Then why the angelic question?

Until the establishment of the present astronomical calendar, there was always a problem as to when the new crescent of the moon was sighted to start the new month. The new month had to be hallowed by the highest court in Jerusalem. Since Rosh Hashanah falls on the first day of the new moon, the problem was always to establish exactly and accurately the sighting of the new moon. That is the reason for two days Rosh Hashanah, even in the days of the Temple.

I wish to take the opportunity today to clarify the ancient trouble with the calendar. Our legal calendar, used almost universally, consists of twelve months or three hundred and sixty-five days. Legal and religious holidays based on the calendar occurring in different seasons remain stationary—each festival observance is fixed annually in the same season. Our religious calendar, however, is based on the lunar year and ordinarily consists of twelve months, each having twenty-nine and one half days, for a total of three hundred and fifty-six days.

We run short of the sun year, on which the seasons are based, by about eleven days each year. If we were to observe Passover, for example, on the fifteenth day of the first month, Nissan, each year without fail, within the course of ten years we would lose some one hundred and twenty days off the seasons. Passover would come out in the winter instead of the beginning of spring and Succoth in early summer instead of autumn. But the Torah calls Passover a spring festival and Succoth the harvest festival.

Since time immemorial, our people have intercalated an extra month when necessary to adjust the festivals with their seasons. The extra, or thirteenth, month was a second month of Adar, pushing Passover ahead by one month. The intercalations were sanctioned by the Sanhedrin, the high court in Jerusalem, in the Temple.

By the end of the fifth century, when the Patriarchate in

Jerusalem was dissolved by the Roman authorities, a perfect astronomical and mathematical formula of intercalation was permanently established, whereby a thirteenth month is added to the lunar year five times in a cycle of nineteen years, and the festivals and seasons are harmonized. But until this calendar of Hillel VI, the last patriarch in Judea, although the Rabbis were well versed in astronomy and knew exactly when the crescent of the new moon arose, they still followed the age-old system of hallowing the new month by the testimony of witnesses who sighted the new crescent of the moon and intercalated a thirteenth month by the examination of early spring.

In this connection, a very dramatic story is told of the first Sanhedrin established in Jamnia following the destruction of the Temple in Jerusalem. It took place probably in the early 80's of the first century. The patriarch of the time was the wealthy patrician Rabban Gamaliel II, a noble and respected scion of the Hillel dynasty who conducted his leadership with a vigorous iron hand. One of the highly venerated scholars on the court was Rabbi Joshua, a poor man who made his living as a blacksmith. Rabban Gamaliel, as the head of the assembly, received and accepted the testimony of the sighting of the new moon from allegedly untrustworthy witnesses. Rabbi Joshua and others in the Academy rejected the testimony and chose the following day as the first of the month, so that Yom Kippur would come out a day later than the established date.

To confirm his authority and enforce strict obedience, the patriarch ordered Rabbi Joshua to appear at the Assembly with his staff and his purse on the day he had calculated to be Yom Kippur.

There was concern and anticipation about how Rabbi Joshua would react to the patriarch's order. When the day arrived, Rabbi Joshua, the most honored scholar of his time, walked in holding his staff and his purse. The patriarch humbly left his station at the head of the Assembly, rushed to the entrance and greeted his honorable opponent with the words: "Welcome, my master and my disciple—my master in learning and my pupil in obedience. It is not for my personal honor that I commanded you to obey me but for the preservation of the Patriarchate."

With this background on the transient character of the calendar in the early talmudic period, we can better understand the peculiar discussion between the ministering angels and our Father in Heaven on the question of when Rosh Hashanah would occur. The lesson in that colloquy is that the Heavenly Court judges the destiny of every human being on the day the earthly court designates as Rosh Hashanah.

I would like to extend that lesson to mean that Rosh Hashanah is when we, the people, want it to be, and even more, it is what we want and choose it to be.

In the Torah, the festival is not called by the name Rosh Hashanah, the beginning of the year. It does not even occur in the first month of the year. In the Torah, it is designated as the first day of the seventh month, and named Yom Teruah, a day of sounding the *shofar*. The Rabbis in the Talmud named the festival of the seventh month Rosh Hashanah.

For that matter, the Rabbis named three more dates as Rosh Hashanah. The Mishnah reads: "There are four dates in the year called New Year. One, the first of Nissan is new year in the chronology of royalty and festivals. Two, the first of Elul is New Year for animal tithing. Three, the first of Tishrei is the New Year on the calendar, for Jubilees and Sabbatical restrictions. Four, the fifteenth of Shevat is the New Year for trees."

However, from the earliest portions of the Talmud, it appears that the day was always considered the day of creation and the day of judgment. As we recite in our liturgy, "This is the anniversary of creation; this is the day of the judgment of all creatures." We read in the book of Ezra that when the scribe returned from Babylon in the year 445 B.C.E., he read the Torah to the people in Jerusalem on Rosh Hashanah, and they wept and reacted in mourning. Ezra admonished them for their sad attitude on the holiday. He ordered them to go home and celebrate with good food and rejoicing.

The Torah has only one *mitzvah* for us—to sound the *shofar*. The rest is what the people want to make of it. For some people, Rosh Hashanah is an occasion for family celebration. They travel to hotels, visit friends and enjoy the beginning of a happy New Year. Indeed, they are doing the right thing. Ezra said: "Eat the best and drink the sweetest. It is your Yom Tov and should be observed as such." To this day, the custom calls for bringing symbols of sweetness and culinary delight to the table. We dip the *challah*, over which we made the Hamotzi blessing, in honey to demonstrate our hope for a sweet year.

However, we must not ignore the other side of Rosh Hashanah. It is a Day of Judgment and ushers in the Ten Days of Penitence preceding Yom Kippur, the Day of Atonement. At the end of these ten days, we believe, the Tribunal of Heaven will issue the final verdict of who shall live and who shall die, who shall prosper and who shall be impoverished. However, "repentance, prayer and charity remove evil verdicts."

The Dubner Maggid, the famous eighteenth century preacher whose sermons inspired the whole Jewish world, spoke in parables. He always had an attractive story to illustrate his oratory message. He compared this solemn season to a merchant of glassware preparing to bring his wares to a fair for display and sales. The merchant cautioned the wagon driver to drive slowly and carefully, to avoid bumps on the road for the merchandise was fragile and precious, but the driver drove with reckless abandon. Every once in a while, the driver stopped at a roadside pub to water the horse and buy himself a drink. At each stop, the merchant begged the driver to give him a little time to examine the condition of his wares, to see what may have been broken by the careless driving. The driver refused to wait and continued speeding ahead, unmindful of the merchant's concern. At the last stop before reaching the fair, the merchant grabbed hold of the driver and declared, "You cannot run away any more. I must examine my wares. I must see what I am bringing to the fair—what has been broken, what has been spoiled, what I have to display."

In our pursuit of what we call happiness and fulfillment, we stop at nothing. We rush, we run, we fly. From home to the shop, to the office, to the train. From work we rush home, from the television to the kitchen table, exhausted, we rush to sleep. We have no time, no patience to stop, to examine how far we have gone astray. Are we on the right path? What is our goal?

On Rosh Hashanah, the shrieking blasts of the *shofar* call upon each of us to stop for a moment, to mentally withdraw from the hustle and bustle, from all the pressures and preoccupation, and listen to the *shofar* addressing our souls: Look at yourself, time is fleeting. You live for a higher purpose! What are you doing to fulfill it? Turn your heart and mind to your Father in Heaven, for only in His service will you find peace.

Confessions

Yom 5754
Kippur 1993

onight I would like to discuss the most often repeated yet least understood part of the Yom Kippur liturgy. Ten times in the course of the day, we will rise, beat our breasts and recite the long lists of sins beginning with the words *al chet*. Each time we will count forty-four different sins based on the double Hebrew alphabet plus ten additional classified transgressions.

Are we suffering from a phobia of guilt? Is the Yom Kippur liturgy designed to develop a guilt complex? The first aim of the clinical psychologist is to discover any feelings of guilt on the part of his patient and attempt to relieve him of that feeling and provide him with a clear, clean conscience.

Let us first examine some peculiarities in the Al Chet program. The usual transgressions with which we are familiar are not even mentioned. We do not confess to the desecration of the Sabbaths and festivals. No mention is there at all of the neglect of prayer services. There is no confession of eating non-kosher food—unless it is included in "the sin we have committed by eating and drinking." It would be clearer if it read by overeating and overdrinking—a sin for which many of us are guilty. There are no confessions of such heinous crimes as murder, theft, arson, rape. The author could not conceive of a Jew being guilty of such crimes. Primarily, the sins in the lists are of a moral nature such as we unwittingly commit in our daily lives. We express contrition for callousness, pride, insolence and hatred. We confess to the abuse of our capacities of speech, envy, slander, gossip, deception, bribery and disrespect for parents and teachers.

It is interesting that the confessions are not made in the singular form. The word for a personal confession would be *shechatati*—that I have committed. The verb we employ is the plural *shechatanu*—that we have committed. In other words, I am a member of a culture, a society that is guilty of this unethical and immoral behavior. At the close of each group of transgressions, we pause and pray: "For all these sins, O Lord of forgiveness, forgive us, pardon us, grant us atonement."

A passage in the Jerusalem Talmud discusses the effects of sin and the antidote. The question is put to the Torah: "If one commits a sin, what is the consequence?" The Torah answers: "Let him offer a sacrifice and atone for it." The question is put to the prophets: "What is the consequence of sin?" The prophets answered: "The sinner will die." When the question is put to our Father in Heaven, He answers: "Let the sinner repent, and he will be forgiven."

The two cardinal words are *teshuvah* and *chet*. We translate *chet* as sin, the violation of the divine order. In the dominant religion, the punishment is death, and the sinner is reformed through grace. In normative Judaism, *chet* is a "miss," an error in the proper road of life. Error is human. "There is no one so righteous as to always do good and not err." The right road of life is laid out to us by the Torah. It is human to miss the right road and go astray. The antidote is *teshuvah*, literally, "return." God wants us to turn back and find the right road. In the act of a transgression, the Torah uses the expression, "You have gone astray from the road." Now you have to find the correct way of life and follow it.

In the repetition of Al Chet, we do not run away from guilt. We acknowledge it, but we do not wallow in it. In the process of *teshuvah*, as outlined by Maimonides, we admit our failings, express regret for our iniquities and resolve sincerely to correct them. The Talmud makes the fascinating observation that when an individual repents out of love and eagerness, *teshuvah me'ahavah*, the sins he committed with full awareness and intent can become merits. The individual uses his past experiences to build a new meritorious future.

Rabbi Akiva recognized God's love for His people by proclaiming the filial association, "You are the children of our Father in Heaven." Just as a loving father receives a recalcitrant child with warmth and forgiveness, so too does God welcome us when we approach Him with a contrite heart and love. It is the same Rabbi Akiva who extolled the gift of Yom Kippur in his remark: "How fortunate you are, O Israel! Before whom do you come to be cleansed, and who cleanses you? *Avinu shebashamayim!* It is our Father in Heaven!" Rabbi Akiva died a martyr's death with the love of God on his lips.

Lord of the universe, You have given us this day for the renunciation of sin. Humbly we stand in Your presence, overwhelmed with the awareness of our many failures. We know we have often been rash and inconsiderate, rebellious and impatient. We spoke where we should have been silent, and we were silent when we should have spoken. We often failed to use our strength in Your service and in the service of our fellow man. We shrank from duty when in our hearts we knew where duty pointed.

O Lord, we know that there is no man so righteous that he can be sinless in Your sight. But on this Day of Atonement, we resolve to be more careful in our striving after righteousness. Strengthen us in our resolve and help us overcome the many temptations that lure us from the right path. Inscribe us for a year of life, health and peace, and help us to rise toward greater perfection before You.

The Questionnaire

Yom Kippur 5754 1993

We are told that the custom of reciting Yizkor, that is, saying memorial prayers and mentioning the names of the departed, began after the massacre of the Jewish communities of Western Europe by the Crusades during the Middle Ages. Each community maintained a list of the victims and recalled them in prayer, making pledges to charity in memory of the martyrs. Gradually, the list was extended to include personal family—parents, spouses, sisters, brothers and, God forbid, lost children.

The public recitation of Yizkor began on Yom Kippur, and was later extended to the Three Festivals. The association with Yom Kippur is understandable. In the Torah, the name is Yom Kippurim, literally meaning a Day of Atonements—in the plural. The understanding was atonement for the living and atonement for dead. Also, we read in Deuteronomy: "Forgive Your people Israel that You have redeemed." Midrashically, this verse is interpreted as follows: The phrase "forgive Your people Israel" is a reference to the living; the phrase "that You have redeemed" is a reference to the dead. This indicates that the dead need forgiveness.

The Talmud poses a hypothetical question of behavior.

"What motivates us to go to the cemetery?" Two scholars offer two different opinions.

One says: "We go to the cemetery so that the beloved departed may plead for divine compassion for us."

The other says: "We go to the cemetery to confess that we are mere mortals—like our predecessors."

I believe both reasons are valid. We go to the cemetery to seek reality and humility as well as affinity with the remains of our loved ones. I also believe these are the same motives that fill synagogues and temples for the recital of Yizkor. We seek to unite with the spirits of our loved ones in prayer and we are also facing up to the realization that we too are just mortals, that the time will come when our children will recite Yizkor in our memory.

In this connection, let me present to you a hypothetical questionnaire formulated by Rava, a third century talmudic scholar. Rava believed that this questionnaire is put to every newcomer in the world to come before the High Tribunal of Justice. There are four questions listed.

What is the first question? Let us guess: Did you keep a kosher home? Did you light Sabbath candles? Did you fast on Tishah b'Av?

None of these is asked. The first question is: *"Nasata venatata be'emunah?* Were you faithful?" Were you faithful in your financial dealings? Were you faithful in business? Were you faithful in your friendships? Did you keep faith with your parents, your children, your wife, your husband?

When our parents and grandparents were asked this question, the answer was probably a "Yes." They may have been poor, but they were faithful, honest, hard-working, loyal. Can we say the same for ourselves?

Let us see the second question:

"Kavata itim latorah? Have you set aside a time for Torah living—religious life?" That is, the study and practice of Torah. You were born to be a member of a kingdom of priests

and a holy nation. How did you fulfill that mission? Our parents and grandparents, if they could not attend the synagogue for daily prayer and study, made sure to be there on Sabbaths and holidays. Can we say that for our generation? I know I may not see some of you until next year, if God grants us life.

Let us examine the third question of the Heavenly Tribunal.

"*Asakta befiria verivia?* Did you raise a family?" Marriage and love in Judaism is a prime *mitzvah*. Adam and Eve were told to be fruitful and multiply. In the mind of the Talmud, this question meant: Did you raise a Jewish family? When our parents and grandparents were faced with this question, their answer was a proud "Yes!" Your presence here in our Sanctuary is evidence of their training and upbringing. Are all our children in synagogues today? Are they the future Jewish families?

And one more, the fourth question of Rava: "*Tzipita leyeshua?* Did you look forward and participate in Salvation?" Did you visualize the coming of a better world? Despite persecution, deprivation and discrimination, our people always looked forward to ultimate salvation. Even facing the crematoria, they affirmed their faith in universal salvation, chanting feverishly, "I believe with perfect faith in the coming of Mashiach, who will bring peace, security and happiness."

From the ashes of their martyrdom, salvation came to our heroic people in the State of Israel. Our parents and grandparents worked, fought and built a proud state due to their faith in the salvation of our people. Let us look ahead and ask: Have we imbued our sons and daughters with the hope and determination of the salvation of our eternal people?

Almighty God, Creator and Sustainer of the Universe, You rule Your creatures with infinite wisdom. Each life is precious in Your sight, and You are near to all who call You in the hour of their needs.

We have come to remember our loved ones whom You

have taken from our side. They were to us a constant source of comfort and inspiration. Their passing has left us with sorrowing hearts.

Those we have loved and lost continue to abide with You. They are bound up in the bond of everlasting life, for only the body is mortal and laid to earth, but the spirit is a spark of Your eternal Being, and the hand of death cannot touch it.

Help us, O Lord, to cherish our loved ones in thoughts and in deeds of honor and righteousness. Inspire us to build a bridge of memory and love through which they may continue to be a deep-felt influence in our lives. Amen.

The Ten Days of Teshuvah

Rosh Hashanah 5756 1995

Today, we begin the first of the "Ten Days of Penitence." Aseret Yemei Teshuvah. After the indulgence of ten days in the process of *teshuvah*—that is, the process of returning to God—we reach Yom Kippur, the Day of Atonement. By then, we shall have achieved forgiveness. We will culminate the long penitential period with the blast of the *shofar*, proclaiming our unity with God with the solemn chanting of the Shema.

We are told in the Book of Exodus that on the third day of the week, the sixth day of Sivan, after the Exodus, Moses mounted Mount Sinai alone and received the two Tablets bearing the Ten Commandments. Moses tarried on the mountain forty days, and during his absence from their midst, the Children of Israel, fearing he would not return, lapsed into the then-prevalent calf worship.

When Moses reappeared, he found the people dancing and frolicking around the golden calf. In anger and disappointment, Moses broke the two Tablets, and God in His anger was ready to annihilate the Children of Israel.

Moses prayed for compassion and mercy, and God agreed to forgive the sinful Jewish people and give them a second set of two Tablets inscribed with the Ten Commandments.

It is with the delivery of these second Tablets that our High Holidays season is concerned. Rabbinic tradition gives the first day in Elul as the day of Moses's ascent onto the mountain. To make sure there would be no error, each of the thirty days in Elul and the additional ten days in Tishrei, the last of which would later be designated as Yom Kippur, were publicly counted and added. Moses's reappearance on the fortieth day with the new set of the Tablets marked complete divine forgiveness.

Since then, these forty days, beginning with the first day of Elul, are considered in our ritual life as special days of self-examination, introspection and spiritual retreat designed to bring us nearer in spirit to our Father in Heaven. Prayer, penitence, fasting, Torah study, charity, visiting the graves of our beloved ancestors are some of the methods we employ to encourage spiritual awakening.

It is ironic that this annual national religious retreat comes at the end of a pleasant summer. Weeks of rest, vacations, sunshine, travel, visiting friends and relatives have rejuvenated our outlook on life with an atmosphere of hope, cheer and frivolity. The warmth of the summer is not yet over. The lakes and the rivers still lure us, yet we are stopped cold to consider the sobriety of realities, health, work, responsibilities, indebtedness, loyalties, taxes and so forth.

That is Rosh Hashanah, a turning point in the middle of life, a stop-over for a ten-day introspection. We are facing a new year whose destiny is based on our performance of the previous year. It is not just a new year for our nation, for our people, but a new year for the universe. Unesaneh Tokef, the popular *piyut*, visualizes the judgment of mankind in graphic terms:

"Like the shepherd counts his sheep, so too are we counted, each one individually, by the Eternal Shepherd's rod as final judgment is pronounced upon each one of us." The

Piyutist continues: "Who shall live and who shall die, who in old age and who at an early age."

Here, we stand alone in prayer and examine ourselves. Behold, we tell ourselves, today is the anniversary of creation. I am a specimen of the highest creature of God's handiwork. As a human being, I have been endowed with an intellect to discern between good and evil. I have been given free will to choose what is good, just and useful. Have I lived up to my potential?

My family claims descent from the *chassidic* dynasty of the eighteenth century miracle worker Rabbi Meir'l of Premyszlan. One of the legends repeated in our family in his name is his confessed fear of judgment in the world to come. He remarked that when he would come before the High Tribunal and be asked why he was not as creative in the study of Torah as R. Akiva, he would answer that he lacked the native high intellect of R. Akiva. If he would be asked why he was not as charitable as R. Tarphon, he would answer that he did not have the wealth of R. Tarphon.

What he feared most was to be challenged as to why he was not "a good Meir'l," why he had not fulfilled his own potential.

Within our own limitations, we have the ability to do so much good—and fail. As parents, did we fulfill our obligations in raising our children, or did we conveniently cop out? As children, have we properly carried out our responsibilities to our parents? Husband, wife, neighbor, we have benefited so much from these relationships but contributed so little.

Unfortunately, two main goals drive our social and domestic pursuits—being successful and having a good time. In social life, the question is always, were you successful? In business, politics, entertainment, our aim is success, and nothing must stand in the way of our success. In our personal and domestic relationships, the goal is a good time. No matter what the enterprise, a good time is the highest achievement.

What is a good time? A good meal, a good show, pleasant company—the satisfaction of our appetites.

Moses, our teacher, in one of his last discourses in Deuteronomy cautions us: "Man cannot live on bread alone; only on that which emanates from God's mouth can man live."

Some thirty years ago, I attended a funeral service at Mount Lebanon cemetery. Before reciting the Kaddish, one of the mourners began counting the number of men present to form a *minyan*.

Not to embarrass the gravediggers, whom I believed to be non-Jewish, I remarked in Yiddish: "*Tzeilt nisht die bagreiber; zey zenin nit Yidden.* Don't count the gravediggers; they aren't Jews."

A rough-looking, rugged digger retorted in a loud, gruff voice, "*Ich bin a Yid.* I am a Jew."

He didn't stop working, and when I asked him where he was from, he replied that he had just come from Poland.

Continuing my questioning, I asked, "*Vie leiben Yidden in Poilen?* How do Jews live in Poland?"

"*A katz leibt oich—men leibt,*" he said. "A cat also lives—we live."

During these ten days of penitence, our ritual is replete with prayers for life. Four times in the silent and repeated Shemoneh Esrei, we interrupt and interject prayers for life.

First, we petition simply: "Remember us for life, O King who delights in life; inscribe us in the Book of Life, for Your sake, O living Lord."

In the second interruption, we become more bold and ask for life for all humans: "Who is like You, Merciful Father; in mercy remember all Your creatures for life."

In the third instance, we qualify the kind of life: "Inscribe all the people of the covenant for a good life."

In the last of the petitions, we specify: "May we and all Your people Israel be remembered and inscribed before You in the Book of Life and blessing, peace and prosperity, for a happy life and peace."

Before we begin the *mitzvah* of *tekiat shofar*, let me sound the usual prayer for meaningful life we recite each new month and extend its petition for the full year.

May it be Your will, O God our Lord, Lord of our fathers, to grant us this new year for happiness and blessedness. O grant us long life, a life of peace and well-being, a life of blessing and sustenance, a life of physical health, a life of piety and dread of sin, a life free from shame and disgrace, a life of honor and prosperity. A life marked by our love for Torah and fear of Heaven, a life in which the wishes of our heart shall be fulfilled for happiness. Amen.

The Legacy of Rabbi Judah the Prince

Rosh Hashanah 5755 1996

The last words and testament of Rabbi Judah the Prince, the editor and compiler of the Mishnah, which is the core of the vast Talmud, have been faithfully and dramatically recorded by his loyal disciples. Imagine the great leader on his deathbed, surrounded by doctors, colleagues and disciples in his royal palace. Suddenly, he exclaims from his bed, "I want my children! Bring my children!"

When his children arrive, he gives them the following testament: "First, be careful to give your mother her due respect. Second, let there be lights to illuminate the palace as before. Third, let my table remain open and set in its place. Fourth, let my bed be made and properly spread."

In the Gemara, the part of the Talmud that complements the Mishnah, the Rabbis discuss each point of the legacy, questioning and explaining every request thoroughly. For example: The Rabbis ask: Why was it necessary for Rabbi Judah to caution his children to respect their mother properly when that is the essence of the fifth commandment: "Honor your father and your mother"?

But before I go into an exposition of the last testament of

this great rabbi, let me offer you a short review of his life and influence, which is in itself a model lesson for this holy day. Rabbi Judah the Prince is generally known in the Talmud as simply "Rabbi"—the rabbi *par excellence*. Due to his extreme piety, he is also called Rabbeinu Hakadosh, our saintly master.

In my university studies on the period of the Mishnah, I was very fascinated by the colorful personality of this great Master, and I quote this information from my book *The Doctrine of Election in Tannaitic Literature*, published by Columbia University Press.

Rabbi Judah was born in the year 135 on the day Rabbi Akiva was martyred, and the coincidence is poetically expressed in the understanding of the verse in Ecclesiastes 1:5, "The sun also rises, and the sun goes down." Even before the sun set on the life of Rabbi Akiva, the sun of Rabbi Judah had risen.

Rabbi Judah was compared to Moses, and reflecting the Biblical story of Moses's childhood in the royal palace of Pharaoh, legend embellished the infancy of Rabbi Judah with a similar story. During the persecution of the Jews under the Roman emperor Hadrian, it was decreed that the death penalty be imposed on circumcised Jewish children. Rabbi Judah was entrusted to the care of a non-Jewish royal family and was thus saved from death.

His personality impressed a contemporary as possessing beauty, honor, wealth, age and the blessings of a large family. Although he was fabulously rich, he denied himself the personal pleasures of wealth and used his possessions for the maintenance of needy students and the support of the poor during a severe famine.

One of his favorite prayers has been added to our daily liturgy: "May it be Your will, O God, my Lord, the Lord of my fathers, that You deliver me this day and every day from arrogant men and from arrogance, from a bad man, from a bad companion and from a bad neighbor, and from any mishap or evil hindrance, from a hard judgment or a hard opponent, be it Jew or gentile."

The description of his demise is very touching. The Talmud relates: "On the day Rabbi Judah died, the authorities declared a fast day. They prayed for mercy, and said: 'Whoever will say that Rabbi is dead shall be pierced through with a sword.'

"'Go into the sick room and investigate,' the Rabbis said to Bar Kappara.

"Bar Kappara went in, and finding that Rabbi was dead, he rent his garment and turned the tear around to his back.

"As he came out, he said, 'The angels and the mortals both seized the holy ark [in other words, they struggled for the soul of the master]. The angels overpowered the mortals, and the holy ark was captured.'

"They asked, 'Is he dead?'

"Bar Kappara replied: 'You said it. I did not say it.'"

Now with this background, let us return to my Yizkor lesson on "the Legacy of Judah the Prince."

From the throes of death, he cried: "I need my children!" And when his children arrived, he said to them: "Be careful to give your mother her due respect. Let there be lights to illuminate the palace. Let my table be set. Let my bed be made."

What did the master mean by these requests?

About twenty-five years ago, as many of you may recall, a young assistant district attorney named Andrew Stein started an investigation of the nursing homes who were allegedly milking Medicare and Medicaid of millions while neglecting the necessary care of their elderly charges. One of Stein's primary targets was a Jewish man who had made millions in the nursing home business. He was charged with fraud, neglect and misappropriation. This man was tried and subsequently jailed.

I knew this man from my student days and never considered him a saint. Still, I was shocked by the public's condemnation of the man. He was fulfilling a very needed public service by building and operating these nursing homes. The institution of the nursing homes is, in a sense, a blessing in our changing society. Medical advancement has increased life expectancy by more than twenty years in the last century. To reach the age of eighty, ninety and older is no longer unusual. However, medical science has not been able to preserve the minds, emotions and energy of the new octogenarians. Old parents have become a burden on their grown sons and daughters who are occupied with their own responsibilities as well as their own children and grandchildren. Years ago, when society in general and Jewish society in particular considered it a privilege to care for elderly parents, nursing homes were not a social necessity. Nowadays, how could we manage without these profiteers and vampires who enrich themselves at the expense of the disabled and helpless old men and women?

Some of us remember the so-called "good old days," before the Social Security System was instituted. Old men and women used to beg or sell apples and shoelaces in the marketplaces. I recall as a child that when the cantor chanted in Shema Koleinu, "Lord, do not cast me aside in old age," the congregation responded with sighs and cries, reflecting their fear of the hazards of advanced age and infirmity. Now, we call advanced age the Golden Years. Social Security benefits provide health care and insurance that give stability and self-respect to the elderly.

The nursing home system itself is not to be condemned. It is the misuse of the system by unscrupulous operators, neglectful children and merciless attendants that makes many homes virtual morgues. Oh, may Heaven forgive me. I visit nursing homes often, and I try to comfort the residents. When I leave, I wonder if such a life is worth living.

In the light of these conditions for the aged, we can readily understand the legacy Rabbi Judah the Prince proclaimed with his dying lips, "I want my children!"

Just think! The richest man of his time, the most respected, most honored, most accomplished person of his generation is crying for his children. Old people want only their children. Their lives are perpetuated by the lives of their children.

I recall some voluntary chaplain work I did a number of years ago at the State Mental Hospital. Those poor, helpless people would call me by the names of their children. They substituted me in their disturbed minds for their missing sons. Just as young children need and crave for their parents, so do elderly parents crave for their sons and daughters.

The dying prince continued in his bequests: Let a light continue to shine in its place, let my bed be made and my table set. For centuries, these bequests were interpreted spiritually and allegorically. The light that the Master asked to be maintained perpetually was understood to refer to the light of Torah. The bed was a reference to family purity and privacy. Our experiences are such that these requests have assumed literal meaning and practical purposes.

As long as an elderly couple is together, even feeble and in poor health, the two manage to maintain themselves and their home intact. They assist each other, they secure outside help when necessary, yet remain in control of their own destiny. Once one of them departs for eternal life and the burden of the other falls on busy children, the first victim is the home. The remaining parent is taken to one of the children or to a nursing home. I believe that is what Rabbi Judah cautioned his children. He wanted the house to continue to serve as their mother's sanctuary, that no physical changes result from his demise.

For a number of years now, I have gained a new insight into the most pertinent phase in the Yizkor formula: *Utzror bitzror hachaim*. It is translated as begging God to bind up the souls of our beloved in the bundle of life. I always accepted the usual interpretation that the bundle of life is a reference to the divine source of life to which we relegate the souls of our